While My Country is in Danger

The Life and Letters of
Lieutenant Colonel Richard S. Thompson
Twelfth New Jersey Volunteers

Captain Richard S. Thompson c1862
(*From the Authors' Collection*)

While My Country is in Danger

The Life and Letters of
Lieutenant Colonel Richard S. Thompson
Twelfth New Jersey Volunteers

GERRY HARDER PORISS AND RALPH G. PORISS

Edmonston Publishing, Inc.
Hamilton, New York

ISBN 0-9622393-6-4

Printed in the United States of America on pH neutral paper.

∞

10 9 8 7 6 5 4 3 2 1

Library of Congress Cataloging-in-Publication Data

    Poriss, Gerry Harder, 1927-
    While my country is in danger : the life and letters of Lieutenant Colonel
    Richard S. Thompson, Twelfth New Jersey Volunteers / by Gerry Harder
Poriss and Ralph G. Poriss.
    p. cm.
    Includes bibliographical references (p.) and index.
    ISBN 0-9622393-6-4
    1. Thompson, Richard Swain, 1837-1914. 2. United States. Army. New
    Jersey Infantry Regiment. 12th (1862-1865) 3. United States—History—
Civil War, 1861-1865—Campaigns. 4. New Jersey—History—Civil War,
1861-1865. 5. Soldiers—New Jersey—Biography. I. Poriss, Ralph Gibbs,
1923- . II. Thompson, Richard Swain, 1837-1914 Correspondence. Selec-
tions. III. Title.
    E521.5 12th.P67 1994
    973.7'449—dc20

                                                    94-11305

Dedication

To the memory of the Civil War soldier: not a Northerner or a Southerner or an immigrant or native-born, or black or white, just an American whose courage cannot be surpassed and must not be forgotten.

Table of Contents

List of Illustrations

List of Maps

Foreword

Richard Swain Thompson is the epitome of an individual who grew up in the mid-nineteenth century. Born in 1837 to an upper-middle-class family, he received a splendid early education which eventually led to his going to law school. Before his education could help him develop a full-fledged law practice, turbulent national events changed his life forever.

As with most men of that time period, the coming of the Civil War drew him into an experience that would never be forgotten. Thompson, as did so many of his fellow Northerners, rallied on the national flag to preserve the Union. Caught up with this patriotic fervor, he joined his comrades from New Jersey as they left to fight in the South. Because of his educational background he immediately found himself in the leadership role of Captain, Company K, Twelfth New Jersey Infantry.

Captain Thompson would not "see the elephant" until the war was well under way, his first taste of action being in May 1863, at the Battle of Chancellorsville. His regiment did not perform as well as it could have in this fight; for that matter, the same can be said of General Joseph E. Hooker's entire army. With the Confederate army now confident that they could defeat any threatening force, General Robert E. Lee decided to lead his men on an invasion into enemy territory. Consequently, that summer he marched his army into Pennsylvania where he ran into the Union army at a small town called Gettysburg.

It was here that the Twelfth New Jersey and Captain Thompson would make their distinguished mark in history. Heroically participating in the repulse of General George E. Pickett's famous charge on July 3, Thompson would recall vividly in a letter home his unit's role. This, coupled with an earlier action at the Bliss farm, would more than balance his regiment's poor performance at Chancellorsville.

Unfortunately for history, Captain Thompson was detached from the unit for recruiting duty in late 1863, thus missing newly appointed General U. S. Grant's Overland Campaign. He would not return to active service until the operations around Petersburg were under way in June 1864, rejoining his regiment on the 23rd as a major. Seeing action in the various engagements fought by General Winfield S. Hancock's Second Corps, Thompson was commissioned Lieutenant Colonel of the Twelfth New Jersey in July.

By August Lieutenant Colonel Thompson's military career would shortly be coming to a close. Receiving two painful and life-threatening wounds in the Battle of Reams' Station on the 25th, he did not return to field service for the rest of the war.

His successful post-war life in the civilian world was reinforced by the attributes of his character, no doubt strengthened by his notable military performance. As with many Victorians who fought in the war, their combat experiences would prove to be the apex of their lives. It is indeed regrettable that Lieutenant Colonel Thompson was never able to write his own soldier's memoirs before he died.

He did, though, leave for us extensive snippets of his past in the forms of a letter collection, diaries, a uniform coat, and the very piece of artillery shell which wounded him at Reams' Station—all poignant reminders of the man who fought for what he believed. Thanks to the diligent research and editing by Gerry and Ralph Poriss, we now have a welcome addition to the understanding of our nation's most tragic war.

Chris Calkins
Petersburg National Battlefield, Virginia

Preface

Had Richard Swain Thompson lived a little longer, we believe he would have written his memoirs. Many other former soldiers had done so; his family and friends surely must have encouraged him to work on his story. He left many notes, written on the backs of old envelopes and other scraps of paper, that are copies of entries from his wartime diary. Like most Victorians, he and his family saved memorabilia by the box- and drawer-full. He saved just about every piece of paper or document that came into his possession during the war: his commission, signed by Lincoln; his uniforms; swords; and Grand Army of the Republic medals. At his request, his sisters saved every one of his battlefield letters. The material we bought in the winter of 1988 included the above mentioned letters and excerpts from his diary, notes, military orders, school records, newspaper clippings, photographs, and hand-drawn maps. They filled a cardboard carton and the tin campaign box he carried with him during the war.

At first we planned a pamphlet of just his letters, but as we read and researched his papers and learned more about him, the book of letters became the story of a Civil War soldier. It became the history of his family, his life, his place in the preservation and growth of his country.

This is Colonel Thompson's book—not, to be sure, as he would have written it. We could not begin to give adequate color to the scenes he had etched forever in his mind's eye. Thompson's writing reflects his awareness under combat conditions with acute and clear descriptions. He knew he and his companions in arms were making history.

We tried to avoid intruding ourselves too much into his story. We let him tell it best in his letters to Hannah, his favorite sister. Steadfast Hannah and her husband, Coleman Leaming, a locally prominent doctor, seemed to be the ones to whom he turned most often for support. Hannah, of strong moral fiber, was practical and sentimental at the same time. Thompson counted on her to send him letters, food, and clothing boxes; and he counted on her husband to oversee his financial affairs. It was Hannah who preserved the letters he wrote home; after the war, she gave him the whole lot.

The mail from home did not always find him. He often complained that his family was negligent. He mentioned again and again that he read and reread every letter he did get. Every so often, especially before going on a march or into action, he sent these precious messages back to Hannah for safekeeping.

The rather detailed biographical chapters at the beginning and end of the book, based on information obtained from his letters, newspaper clippings and our research, seemed necessary to establish a more complete picture of the man and his family. However, many questions relating to family relationships in his early life in Cape May and later life in Chicago remain unanswered.

The chapters concerning battles in which he took part are the bulk of the book. They follow this pattern: a short synopsis of the situation followed by a review of the action. We merely "introduce" the engagement and let Thompson tell the rest as he experienced it, using quotes from his diary, notes, and letters. No individual soldier "sees" a war. While he is fighting, he is only aware of himself and the struggle to stay alive. After the action, if he is able, he may record what happened, sometimes adding information supplied by others. So it was with Thompson.

We edited Thompson's letters for clarity, regularizing spelling and punctuation as required. The letters of others were also edited, except as otherwise noted. Excerpts from Thompson's diary are courtesy of John W. Kuhl.

Many Civil War generals wrote their memoirs and many volumes of letters and diaries written by rank and file soldiers have been published, but few mid-level officers have had their stories told. Thompson entered the Army of the Potomac as a Captain and left as a Lieutenant Colonel. As you read, you will see that he took part in engagements that were of pivotal importance to the outcome of the war. He had a praiseworthy military career and a successful post-war life. He became a respected attorney, a loving family man, and a pillar of his community. A brave, intelligent, patriotic, and articulate man, he was honored by his country, community, and peers. Hopefully, this book will do honor to his memory.

Gerry Harder Poriss and Ralph G. Poriss
Williamsburg, Virginia

Introduction

From his first taste of war at Chancellorsville to his wounding at Reams' Station Richard Swain Thompson lived for nearly three years with the sights, sounds, and smells of a terrible conflict. The events of those years moved him to record his actions and impressions in a daily diary and frequent letters to his family.

It was a family with a proud heritage. (See Appendix A.)

Richard Thompson inherited his interest in military and political matters from his forefathers. He had his own strong personality and character, lightened by a sense of humor and charm. His school records show he was intelligent with a special gift for oratory. He was gentlemanly, polished, and not without a sense of self-importance.

Just at the beginning of his career as an attorney the rumors of a "war between the states" were heard everywhere. He responded by joining a militia unit in the city of Philadelphia where he was working in a law office. When the rumors became a fact, he became one of the many thousands of patriotic, idealistic, and romantic young men who were the backbone of the great volunteer army. Citizen soldiers, eager for military glory, flocked to "save the Union." The volunteer system, vitally important to the outcome of the war, was vulnerable to abuse. Officers, usually men with the best education, were most often chosen by their friends or through political connections. But this did not make those chosen good leaders nor protect them from acts of cowardice. Many less-educated, non-military men rose from the ranks to become excellent officers as the war went on. Thompson had all the advantages: education, leadership ability, and ambition.

Through family and political connections he obtained the captaincy of Company K, Twelfth New Jersey Volunteers. He did not intend to remain at that rank. (Indeed, he chafed somewhat when passed over for the position of major in the fall of 1862. However, since he was a Republican and the governor a Democrat, the advancement was vetoed.) He was well aware of his abilities and did not fail to make his superiors aware of them. He did not, however, put his ambition before his duty to his men and they loved and respected him. His concern for his men continued strong as he rose in rank.

His courage under fire was proven by his actions in the Battle of Gettysburg when he led a successful charge against the Bliss barn, with the odds not in his favor. It was proven again in the Battle at Reams' Station, again under the most difficult of conditions. This time, he sustained very serious wounds.

He could thank Providence that his ability to write a very descriptive phrase and his talent as a persuasive speaker were well-known to his superiors. During 1863 and the first part of 1864, his commanding officers detailed him to use these aptitudes to secure the enlistments of badly needed recruits to fill the gaps in the ranks of the Army of the Potomac. During his hiatus from combat his companions in the Twelfth New Jersey fought some of their bloodiest battles. While his military career was not brilliant, it was worthy of praise. He received several commendations, including a letter from President Lincoln and one from his respected commander, General Winfield Scott Hancock. After the war his civilian career in the areas of law and politics brought him prominence and wealth. He and his wife Catherine became respected leaders of Chicago society and enjoyed no little local fame.

Thompson's letters home reflect the drive of his oratorical compulsion. Many of them are narratives that could be used as speeches. They also reflected the changes he underwent as the war progressed. At Chancellorsville he was a green soldier—at Gettysburg, a combat veteran. Perhaps he began to suffer from anxiety or perhaps the months he spent in the recruiting office underscored the reality of the enormous casualties for which he had to find replacements, but he started to question the security of his personal future. His fighting days ended during the Battle of Reams' Station.

In the letters he wrote to his sisters, which they so lovingly preserved, he tells the story of his participation in the conflict with vivid descriptions and patriotic fervor. But near the end of these battle letters one senses an almost routine reaction to the fighting and bloodshed. Despite the pressure of conflict he never lost sight of his place in history.

Acknowledgments

No book can be written by just its authors. We owe an enormous debt of gratitude to Mr. John W. Kuhl, owner of Richard S. Thompson's diary, who shared with us valuable information and several of the photographs that are used in the book. Without his generosity the book could not have been written.

We must acknowledge, with special respect, the work of Mr. Edward B. Longacre, whose definitive book on the history of the Twelfth New Jersey Volunteers, *To Gettysburg and Beyond*, was published while we were still avidly reading Thompson's letters. This volume is a "must" for anyone interested in the Civil War and specifically for those interested in the combat record of a unit of the Union Army. His research was staggering and he gave Colonel Thompson excellent publicity.

The list of people on whom we depended must begin with Chris Calkins, author, historian and park ranger at Petersburg National Battlefield, who helped us in so many ways; Mary Ann Bamberger, Assistant, Special Collections and Librarian, Library of the University of Illinois at Chicago; Michael D. Brown, Reference Department, Regenstein Library of the University of Chicago Library; Elwood W. Christ, author and licensed guide *extraordinaire* at Gettysburg National Military Park whose book on the action at the Bliss barn came out just in time; Emily Clark, Associate Librarian, Chicago Historical Society; Margaret Cook, Curator of Manuscripts and Rare Books Department of the Earl Gregg Swem Library of The College of William and Mary, who organized and supervised an exhibit of Thompson's letters at the library; John R. Davis Jr., Petersburg National Battlefield; Owen and Dolores Doss, part of our Chicago connection; Otis Lee Haislip, Jr., teacher, friend, and computer consultant who gave us the key to the keyboard; Dr. Phyllis Hall, author, friend, and critic, whose patience was unending; Dr. John Haskell and Nancy Marshall of Swem Library who put us on the local map; Dr. "H," our anonymous medical expert; James Keena, balladier, and John Millar, dance master, who broadened our knowledge of Civil War music and dance; Eugene R. McVicker, licensed battlefield guide, Gettysburg National Military Park; Rudy and Edna Ness, who tackled trivia; Joy Piscopo of F. O. Bailey in Portland, Maine—without her, we would have never known; Mrs. Lori C. Stauber, research assistant and the other part of the Chicago connection; Stephen A. Treffman, archivist, the Hyde Park Historical Society; Mrs. Hannah Swain (deceased) and Mrs. Ione Williams of the Cape May County Genealogical and Historical Society Library, whose help has been invaluable; Ralph R. Workman, historian and keeper of the flame of the Twelfth New Jersey Volunteers; and Dave Weakley and Bert Wisner who added last minute information.

In addition, there were many unsung but much appreciated helpers at the Chancellorsville and Wilderness Battlefields; the staffs at the U. S. Army Military Institute in Carlisle, Pennsylvania, and at the National Archives in Washington, DC; the members of the congregation of the Oak Grove Methodist Church; and our hapless relatives and friends on whom we practiced the first drafts of our manuscript. There were also special people to whom we wrote or phoned for information but never met—we owe you much!

We must also thank each other for the patience we each needed in transcribing to the computer all those nearly indecipherable handwritten pages, and for making the many, many corrections and additions to the manuscript.

GHP and RGP

Chapter One

The Thompsons of Cape May

*Before the bright flame of Liberty . . . shall be extinguished . . . I am
ready to sprinkle with my blood . . . its holy altar. . . .*

William E. Potter to RST, May 3, 1861

Cape May Court House, county seat of Cape May County, is only a
few miles inland from the southernmost tip of New Jersey. It was,
and is, a small community. Its citizens have a proud heritage dating
back to the founding of our country. Mainly farmers and fishermen,
they built solid homes and raised law-abiding, God-fearing families.

Richard Swain Thompson was born at Cape May Court House on
December 27, 1837. A belated Christmas present, he was the youngest
child and most welcome only son of Richard and Elizabeth Holmes
Thompson. His father Richard had been married before, his first wife,
Mary H. Pisant, living only two years after their 1819 marriage. Their
son, John P. Thompson, died at the age of three.

In 1823 Richard Thompson, Sr. married Elizabeth Holmes when he
was 28, she 23. Elizabeth was born at Cape May Court House,
February 28, 1800, the seventh and youngest child of Revolutionary
War Major Nathaniel Holmes and Hannah Hand Holmes. The couple
moved into Woodside, the Holmes family homestead.[1] As their family
grew, they added to the original house. Richard and Elizabeth
Thompson already had four daughters when Richard Swain was born
in 1837, the third generation male to bear the name Richard. Mary
Elizabeth, the eldest daughter, was 13 when Richard was born. She
most likely helped care for him when he was a baby but she married
when he was five or six. Her husband, the Reverend Napoleon Bonaparte Tindall (Tyndall),[2] was the first minister of the First Baptist
Church of Cape May Court House. Mary and Richard had a friendly

Contemporary View of Woodside, the Thompson Family Home in Cape May Court House, NJ.

(*Photograph by Ralph G. Poriss*)

if somewhat distant relationship. Shortly after Mary got married, Elizabeth Thompson, their mother, died.

Richard's other sisters, Isabella (Bell), Hannah (Hann) and Emma (Em), helped care for their little brother. Richard formed his closest bonds with the two youngest. He wrote most of his battlefield letters to them. Hannah often addressed her letters to "brother dear" or "dear, dear brother." Such affection developed between Richard and Hannah's husband, Dr. Coleman F. Leaming,[3] that they addressed each other as "brother" in all their correspondence.

That the family had means is evidenced by the several newspaper clippings announcing when they spent holidays at the prestigious Mansion House in the city of Cape May. After the mother's death in 1844, a hired cook and servants took charge of most household responsibilities; Isabella oversaw the ledgers.

As the only son and youngest child, Richard held a special place in the family. His father and sisters may have told him stories of their family's long history. One can imagine young Richard, playing soldier, marching through the halls of Woodside with his dog Jack at his heels.

Photographs taken when Richard Thompson was a young man suggest that he had a fair complexion with fairly deep set eyes—not handsome, but pleasant looking. He was above average height (all Thompson men averaged six feet) and of slender but sturdy build. He described himself as "spare." A newspaper article described him as having a "commanding figure and mellifluous voice."[4]

His education was typical of an upper-middle-class family. We have no record of Richard's earliest education except that he attended district schools. We do know Mary attended Cape May Court House Academy;[5] Richard may have also. At age 13, he entered Treemount Seminary[6] at Norristown, Pennsylvania. Thompson's father wanted his only son to have a gentleman's classical education and be prepared to enter one of the professions. Bills for board and tuition were sent to Thompson's father, but Isabella paid them. (There is one notice in which payment had fallen behind.) Records show that Thompson quit the school on July 1, 1854, spending the summer and September at home.

Because of his position in the state legislature, Thompson's father was acquainted with many New Jersey politicians, most of whom were lawyers. He may have asked some of them to recommend a good school in which Thompson could be prepared for a law career. Senator James M. Scovel,[7] an attorney friend, had a kinsman who was headmaster of a seminary in Bordentown, New Jersey. On September 23rd, the elder Thompson wrote the Reverend Alden Scovel,[8] asking to place his son in Scovel's care. He noted Richard as "between 16 and 17 years" and that he could send him by the latter part of October.

> *Bordentown, N.J.*
> *September 30, 1854*

Dear Sir,

Yours of the 23rd has been duly received and in reply would say that if you should deem it advisable to send me your son Richard, he will be received into my family and treated as one of its members. At present it is my desire to receive in no other way. His accommodations will be plain and simple, entirely after our social order. His studies will be as you may prescribe. He may prepare either for entering college or for any advanced standing in college—for the practical or professional duties of life. Charges per session of 22 weeks, board tuition, washing, etc., with the exception of books, $100. The session will commence the 1st of October. Please call and see me.

> Respectfully & truly yours,
> *A. Scovel*

Richard was enrolled by October of 1854. Isabella apparently saved all the receipts for his board and tuition, including even the notes of debts incurred when Richard borrowed pocket money from the Reverend Mr. Scovel.

Money was not a problem in the Thompson family but his father did not spend it freely. He did not give his son any more than he thought necessary. This lack of spending money made Thompson very appreciative of money and he always kept an eye on his savings and investments, even while he was in the army. Years later, when the dollars piled up, he watched his pennies. For example, even though he could well afford the regular fare, he carried a special "charge" card from a Chicago taxi company, which permitted him to pay monthly.

Because he lived in the headmaster's own quarters, he became friends with the Scovel's son and daughter, Cortland ("Cort") and Catherine, called "Kittie" by her family and friends—but to Richard, she was always "Kate." When they met he was 16 and she was 12. He studied his lessons diligently, but he did not neglect the headmaster's daughter. It was not too long before Richard and Kate became childhood sweethearts. Despite the temptations from flattering and flirtatious young ladies he met while in the army, he remained true to the curly-haired girl who captured his heart when they were so young. Their romance withstood the rigors of long separations and they were finally married in 1865. (Unfortunately, no love letters were found among Thompson's papers.)

A seminary student in those days prepared to enter college to study for a degree in one of the professions, especially law or medicine. Thompson was an excellent student. He graduated as salutatorian of his class on March 31, 1857, giving the address entirely in Latin. Showing his talent for public speaking and dramatics, he took part in a dialogue, playing a character named Surrey. The graduation program also noted he gave a reading as the Irish character, Pat Flanagan.

Somehow, he injured an ankle shortly after graduation which forced him to remain in Bordentown until it healed. He wrote his father, who was ill.

Bordentown, N.J.
June 23, 1857

My Dear Father,

Your kind letter and its contents I received this morning and was sorry to find [that] you are improving so slowly. If you get any worse, you must let me know it. Now, don't think you will keep me from being worried by not writing as that is the very thing above all others that produces such an effect. You will have to excuse all writing and mistakes as it is but a short time before the mail starts and I want to put this letter in.

Does Dr. Wiley[9] understand the management of the jaundice perfectly, or not? If there is any doubt on the subject, had you not better have someone more able to tend the case? But I hope that by the time this letter reaches you, you will be much improved. My ankle is entirely well, but I am still [very] careful of it so as not to injure it over and thereby make it much worse than it was in the first place.

[He went on to personal news and the repairing of his gun.]

From your affectionate and loving son,
Richard

At this time, both Mary and Hannah and their husbands were living in Philadelphia. Apparently the senior Thompson went there for special treatment as he had jaundice, dropsy, and was lame. In

Philadelphia, a Dr. Pancoast,[10] probably a local physician, treated him. Hannah and Mary took turns as nurses. But Hannah, expecting her third child, was often too weary to be of much use. She had sent her two other children, Josephine and Emma, back to Cape May Court House to be cared for by Isabella and Richard, who had now returned home.

As the illness worsened, the father became bedridden. On August 11, 1857, Richard Thompson, Sr. sent his son his last letter. He asked young Richard to send a ham and some terrapins up to Philadelphia so he could have some good turtle soup. Both daughters added personal and family news at the end of the letter, commenting on their father's condition. Hannah expressed her fear of dying in childbirth; significantly, it is the only time in her letters that she called her brother by the diminutive, "Dick." The girls were mistakenly encouraged by their father's appetite. He grew worse and suffered for five more weeks. He must have known he would not recover; in September he returned to Woodside. On September 27, 1857, exactly three months before Richard's 20th birthday, his father died. On the envelope of his father's last letter, the grieving young man wrote, "Father came home to die."[11]

The entire family was affected by the loss, but only Hannah and Thompson were uprooted. With her husband and baby son Edwin, she left Philadelphia and moved to Woodside. Interested in the law, Richard now had to assume the responsibility for continuing his education on his own. Help came from Kate's brother Cortland, now in James Scovel's law office, and a distant relative, attorney Jeremiah Leaming ("Uncle Jerry"). Leaming may have arranged for Thompson to "read for the law" in the office of Asa I. Fish, an attorney practicing in Philadelphia. Fish, originally from New Jersey, had met the elder Thompson in Cape May years before. Thompson took the position.[12]

When in Philadelphia Thompson rented a room at a Mrs. Stewart's or Stuart's at 923 Chestnut Street, despite the fact that his sister Mary lived in the city. But with five children and a husband to house, she probably had no room to board her brother. Whenever any of the family came to the city, they usually stayed at Mrs. Stewart's. Details of his life during the next two years are sketchy, with no specific record of exactly when he left the family home.

He came to the attention of the Cape Island Baptist Aid Society in April of 1858, when he was asked to speak before their group on the 28th. This was one of his first public speaking engagements, and he was well received. His father had been a lifelong and devout Baptist and would have been proud of him.

On the Fourth of July, he wrote and delivered a short speech in honor of the day. His flowery language would be considered amusing today, but his fellow Victorians found his bombast to their liking. The following quotation contains one of the longest sentences ever found in his papers: "While we are now celebrating this, the birthday of our Independence, and exulting over the many blessings we are enjoying, as countrymen of Washington, as citizens of this glorious Republic, throughout whose land Freedom reigns supreme, and the glad sound of Liberty bursting forth in her valleys, echoing from her mountain tops, 'rendering back to heaven a praise harmonious,' let us not forget amid our joy, deeply to feel how great is the responsibility resting upon us: let us remember it is our duty to promote all institutions whose object is the welfare of our common country; let us renew our vow, never ignobly to deviate from the precepts of those, who in that dark hour, framed, and carried out the Declaration of Independence, to which alone every American vows, at this day, all that makes his life a blessing, and his existence honorable."

Shortly thereafter, Thompson experienced a religious awakening that resulted in his baptism during the summer of 1859; sister Emma was baptized at the same time. He was somewhat unsure of his decision, wondering if his new faith would demand a more serious outlook, but in a July 5th letter, Hannah wrote, "You can be a Christian and lighthearted, too."

On August 25th, she again wrote him a long letter, in which she gushed with Victorian sentimentality,

" I think you are as near perfect as a man can be. You want only one thing and that in religion; I cannot love you more than now, but for our dear lamented Father's sake. . . .

"Oh, you can never know the joy it gave me, for words are too weak to express what I feel. It has been my nightly prayer that God would make you *good* and *great*, as good that He would grant you wisdom and understanding, *health* and a *long* and *peaceful* life, to which prayer, dear brother, you can respond *amen*. As you go down into the water, you will feel the eyes of none upon you but your God's, your dear Papa's, and sainted Mother's together with those of our relations in heaven—be assured this heavenly choir will rejoice over you."[13]

On August 30, 1859, a friend of the family, William G. Nixon, sent Thompson a letter of introduction to his brother-in-law, William E. Potter.[14] Richard and "Willie" Potter became close friends. When fall classes opened at Harvard, the two young men left Philadelphia and traveled together to Cambridge, Massachusetts, where they entered Harvard College of Law.

A full Bachelor of Law course took 18 months. The first term began on September 1, 1859, and ended January 18, 1860. The second term began March 1st and ended in July, with Commencement on July 17, 1860, for those who had completed the full 18-month program. Thompson and Potter were members of the "Middle Class," a group of 49 students between the Junior and Senior classes. They shared a room (number 43) in Brattle House[15] for the first two terms; the third term Thompson lived off campus at a Mrs. Hurd's. Because of his family's shipping interests, he may have studied commercial and maritime law.

Life on campus was influenced by the political, religious and cultural mores of the antebellum era. From his and his friends' letters, we know students and faculty alike discussed current politics constantly. The young Republican Party, the slavery question, and states' rights were favorite topics, while thoughts of secession and a civil war entered everyone's mind.

Early in the spring of 1861, while Thompson was again working in Asa Fish's office, he and Potter corresponded. Excerpts from two of Potter's letters give an indication of what was uppermost in their minds.

Bridgeton, N.J.
March 9, 1861

My Dear Friend,

I have now become settled in my new habit of life, and for the past two weeks have been reading very satisfactorily. I miss, however, the sense of independence, which belongs to student life. I am not altogether certain but that it would have been better for me to have returned for another term to Cambridge. Indeed, the scale was so evenly balanced upon the question, that had you returned, I should most certainly have accompanied you.

During the last term, the indisposition which clung to me so long prevented me from studying as I wished. Is it not strange [that] since my return home, I have not had the slightest trace of it? Hon. Jno. T. Nixon[16] has returned from Washington. He seems to know very little that is new concerning [our] national difficulties. For myself, as we have often remarked, I have from the first had not the shadow of a doubt that one of two things must happen.

Either there must be a withdrawal on the part of the Seceding States from th[eir] present position, or there will be a collision between their forces and those of the Government. The Southern Confederacy have now taken to themselves the powers of Government; they have inaugurated a Revolution, or what they term such, and their pride will not suffer them to retract. I may be a false prophet, I hope that it may be so proved, but it is my firm belief that there will be blood shed on this continent within six months. But there is little use in discussing this interminable theme.

On the day of the Inauguration, I attended a party at R. G. Bucks given in honor of the 18th birthday of his daughter Miss Clara, the younger of the two whom you met when in B[ridgeton]. The ladies were in full party dress and looked very pretty. But this is vanity, as you well know.

I shall be happy to hear from you soon.

I remain yours truly,
Wm. E. Potter

Nearly a month after Potter wrote this letter, the first shots of the Civil War were fired. Hostilities between the states opened on April 12, 1861. A deeply affected Potter put his thoughts and feelings on paper.

Bridgeton, N.J.
May 3, 1861

Dear Friend,

It is almost impossible to write letters in these stirring times, as indeed it is to do anything else. I am undergoing continual self-denial in endeavoring to keep out of the volunteer movement. I have anticipated the necessity of a resort to arms since last fall.

The principles for which we are fighting are those to which I have been fondly attached since I have been able to understand governmental affairs. I have youth, health, and strength; and yet I am restrained by a personal consideration mainly, namely, the desire to have a liberal education. I console myself only in this, that as yet there is no absolute necessity for my volunteering. Whenever that necessity ar-

Lieutenant William E. Potter c1862
(From the Authors' Collection)

Dr. Coleman F. Leaming
(Courtesy of the Cape May Court House, NJ Genealogical & Historical Society)

rives, as I told you in Philadelphia, I shall drop all and enter at once into the [service] of my country.

Civilization, humanity, free government, permanent and beneficent institutions, everything which renders life most dear, depend upon the issue of this struggle. Before the bright flame of Liberty, which has burned so steadily within our borders for the past eighty years shall be extinguished by the onward march of slavery, I am ready to sprinkle with my blood its holy altar, in its defense.

Our county is fast becoming organized. We have in Bridgeton alone three Companies. One fully organized, has been drilling six or eight hours daily for the past two weeks; owing to some delay in the election of officers, it did not get away among the first troops from New Jersey, but is now ready and expecting orders at any time. It is as fine a company as I have seen—name, "Cumberland Grays." Besides this we have a German Company many of whom have been in the regular service which drills daily and is fast filling up. We have still another company fast organizing. My brother Col. [David] Potter has been elected Brigadier General of the Cumberland Brigade and will proceed at once to organize the whole militia force of the county. I see that at a meeting at Cape May Court House they have resolved to raise a company in every township in the county. Your county will be much exposed if not well defended.

But to turn from grave to lighter subjects, a friend of mine has made me promise to assist him in the very important ceremony of marriage. What is the proper costume on the occasion? Coat and pants of black, of course. What should the vest, cravat, and gloves be? You know how distasteful these things are to me. Will you be good enough to write me information concerning these points? Also any hints as to the groomsman's duty, any [little] conventionalities which he may be expected to observe, etc. will be agreeable and acceptable. Your experience has probably informed you as to these matters. I would like you to become well acquainted with Westcott in Mr. Myham's office. I think you will find him in every way congenial. He is a cousin of John T. and Wm. G. Nixon, and well acquainted in Bridgeton—a man of the highest character and will probably be distinguished in his profession in the future.

I have my hands full in endeavoring to compress a year's work into the space of about eight weeks or a little more. Will you please write as above asked as soon as possible?

With wishing for your welfare, I am most truly yours,
Wm. E. Potter

These letters illustrate that Potter and Thompson were facing the most important decision of their lives: to continue to follow the plans they had made for their futures or to put aside all personal ambitions and join the army.

Thompson's character, personality, and intelligence so impressed his classmates and teachers that he formed many lasting friendships. He developed a reputation as a public speaker who moved his audience with his powerful voice, presence, and emotion, as well as with his words. He knew that when he became an attorney he would need to call upon that ability to sway a jury. He did not imagine his talent would someday be called upon to persuade men to march off to war.[17]

Notes

1 Woodside is still standing in Cape May Court House, at the corner of Main Street and Romney Place. It has been added to through the years and remodeled, but kept in good repair. Alfred E. Wool, in an article written for the *Cape May County Magazine of History and Genealogy* ("A Tour of Cape May County," Vol. 14, No. 3, 1989, Pp. 185-210), wrote the following commentary on the house: "In my younger days, I always heard that the kitchen of the Morgan Hand House (now the Ritterhof House) at the corner of Route 9 and Romney Place had been the living room of the house of Daniel Hand (1730-1787). I have heard that Nathaniel Holmes, who built the house, married Daniel Hand's daughter."

[2] They had five children. After Reverend Tindall's (Tyndall) death in 1855, she married R. S. Magonagle.

[3] Originally the Lemyng family of England, they were pioneer settlers in Cape May County. Early Leamings were whalers. The Leaming brothers, Coleman and R. S., were born on Sluice Farm at Sluice Creek. Their father had a store at Dennis Creek Landing; later he went into shipbuilding. He built 10 or 12 coasting schooners to sell or use. From this enterprise the family became quite wealthy and moved to Dennisville, N.J. The Leaming and Thompson families were interwoven through Charlotte Leaming, the second wife of Thompson's grandfather. This union produced no children, but her children from her first marriage (who opposed her second marriage) produced the men who eventually married Isabella and Hannah Thompson.

[4] *Bridgeton Chronicle*, Bridgeton, NJ, Saturday, August 10, 1862.

[5] An example of Mary's woolwork dated 1838, when she was 14, is in the John Holmes House, a museum of the Cape May County Historical and Genealogical Society.

[6] A seminary was a boarding school usually founded and run by someone with training in theology as well as general education. Thompson studied algebra, arithmetic, chemistry, geography, grammar, history, Latin, and reading. His bill from April 16th to September 16th, 1851, totaled $78.64 of which $2.10 was for eight textbooks. The rest was for board, tuition, and clothing.

[7] James Matlock Scovel (1833-1904), attorney and politician, was a member of the legislature of New Jersey from 1859 to 1863. He became a leader of the New Jersey War Democrats. However, he addressed several Union League (see Chapter 11, Note 25) rallies and helped organize the League in the state of New Jersey. Since the League was staunchly Republican in membership, this was unusual. He was one of the principal speakers at the convention of the League on April 15, 1863. See Silvestro, C. M. *None but Patriots: The Union League in Civil War and Reconstruction.* Ann Arbor, MI, p. 69. Relative of the Reverend Alden Scovel, he brought Cortland Scovel, the Reverend's son, into his law practice as a partner and became a "friend in high places" to Thompson. When Governor Andrew G. Curtin (1815-1894) of Pennsylvania became panic-stricken by Lee's invasion of his state, he wrote Governor Joel Parker (1816-1888) of New Jersey for assistance. The Independent Company of Camden, one of ten companies of New Jersey Militia, volunteered to help defend their sister state. James Scovel was a captain in one of these companies. The militia remained in Pennsylvania until after Gettysburg, operating mostly in the vicinity around Harrisburg. See Toombs, S. (1888) *New Jersey Troops in the Gettysburg Campaign,* Orange, NJ, p. 87.

[8] The Scovel family originated in England. The name has been spelled Scovell, Scovill, and Scoville. After living in New Jersey for many years (Mrs. Scovel was born there), the Reverend Alden Scovel moved his family to Bloomington, Illinois. See Appendix A.

[9] Surgeon John Wiley was born on August 7, 1815, near Penn's Grove, New Jersey. The son of a farmer, John attended Jefferson Medical College for three years. After graduation in 1837 (the year Thompson was born), he practiced medicine in Cape May Court House. He married Daniela Hand in December of 1845. When the Civil War broke out, Dr. Wiley was 46. His wife was a semi-invalid so he had heavy family obligations. After Bull Run (Manassas) he offered his services and was commissioned Surgeon of the Sixth New Jersey Volunteer Infantry on August 17, 1861. He served with distinction, becoming Surgeon-in-Chief, Third Brigade, Second Division, Third Army Corps. He attended men in 19 engagements, including Gettysburg. He was offered the

post of Division Surgeon but declined due to his wife's health. He mustered out on September 17, 1864. He died December 24, 1891, and is buried in the Baptist Cemetery (Cape May Court House). See Damman, G. E. (1988) *Pictorial Encyclopedia of Civil War Medical Instruments and Equipment*, Vol. 2. Missoula, MT, p. 6.

[10] There may have been two doctors Pancoast practicing in Philadelphia. After the war broke out, Dr. William H. Pancoast served as visiting surgeon at the Master Street Hospital which opened July 1, 1862, at the corner of Sixth and Master Streets. The hospital closed when the large Mower Hospital in Chestnut Hill opened January 17, 1863. A Dr. D. P. Pancoast is listed as being an assistant surgeon at Mower. See Taylor, F. H. (1913) *Philadelphia in the Civil War, 1861-1865*. Philadelphia, p. 228.

[11] Among the properties which Thompson and his sisters inherited were the freight schooner *Isabella Thompson*. The *Isabella* was a source of the family income. Thompson got $55 from one of his shares of the sale of her cargo before she was sold for $75. They also inherited some woodland property (which was divided equally) and the family homestead, Woodside. Dr. Leaming may have been executor of the estate; he sent Thompson money while at Harvard and managed his financial affairs while he was in the army.

[12] An 1845 newspaper clipping listed the names of prominent guests staying at a hotel at Cape Island, as the city of Cape May was then known. The guest list included Charlotte Leaming, Miss Hannah Thompson, Miss Isabella Thompson, Mr. Richard Thompson, Sr., Mr. A. I. Fish of Trenton, New Jersey, and Miss E. M. Fish. Richard was about seven then. Since the Fish's were friends of his father, it was natural that they would be interested in the son. Later, Asa I. Fish had his office on Library Street in Philadelphia. His brother, A.H. Fish, was a doctor in the same city. Both men and their wives were very fond of Thompson. Dr. Fish attended him after he was wounded and it may be that his skills saved Thompson's life.

[13] A devout Baptist, Thompson's father served the church as a deacon for 37 years. For much of that time, he was treasurer of the Board of Trustees. Upon his death, the local newspaper printed long eulogies given by friends and fellow church members. Hannah was elated when Richard and Emma joined the church, but when they became members of the Episcopal Church only a few years later, she was dismayed. In a letter dated January 14, 1863, he called himself "your renegade brother" alluding to the family tradition of belonging to the Baptist Church. The Scovel family's Episcopalian tradition influenced him to study the doctrine of that church. His and his sister's confirmations took place on August 12, 1860, in the parlor of Woodside, surrounded by family and friends. It was the first Episcopal service and confirmation ever held in Cape May County. He remained a member of this denomination until his death. Years later Hannah also became an Episcopalian.

[14] William Elmer Potter was the son of James Boyd Potter and Jane Barron Potter of a socially prominent and politically active family of Bridgeton, New Jersey. William's father was president of Cumberland Bank, and a relative, Dr. Robert E. Potter, with George F. Nixon, was editor and publisher of the *Bridgeton Chronicle.* One of Nixon's sons was married to one of Potter's daughters. Young "Willie" Potter studied law in the Honorable John T. Nixon's office from October of 1857 to September of 1859. (George F. Nixon and John T. Nixon were cousins.) He graduated from Harvard in January of 1861 and went on to Princeton in September of that year. See Toombs, S. *op. cit.,* Pp. 381-384.

[15] In addition to tuition, Thompson had to pay for room, board, furniture, laundry, firewood, and a servant to do chores. This ranged from $120 to $245 per term. He had some money from his inheritance; there were also profits from the shipping interests and he may have saved something from his position in Fish's office to help pay his expenses. See Harvard University Archives. (1859) *A Catalogue of the Officers and Students of Harvard University for the Academic Year 1859-60.* Cambridge, MA, Pp. 56-57, 61-69.

[16] John Thompson Nixon, born August 31, 1820, was the son of Jeremiah S. and Mary Shaw Thompson Nixon. He was a New Jersey Assemblyman, served in Congress from 1858 to 1863, and was a trustee of Princeton University. He died October 10, 1905. See Malone, D. (Ed.) (1934) *Dictionary of American Biography.* Vol. 8. New York, p. 531.

[17] Background material for this chapter came from the archives of the Cape May County Historical and Genealogical Society and Museum, Cape May Court House, New Jersey.

Chapter Two

To Manhood and to War

The most serious enemy . . . is the dust.

RST to Hannah, August 17, 1862

The future Richard planned for himself was profoundly changed by the outbreak of the Civil War. When President Abraham Lincoln called for a volunteer army of 75,000 to put down the southern insurrection on April 15, 1861, the regular Army of the United States consisted of about 17,000 men. This was too few to fight a war, even the short one (three months) predicted by all the experts. On April 18th, Lincoln offered the command of the army to Robert E. Lee of Virginia, considered to be the best of all his generals. Lee declined. The day before, Virginia had joined the Confederacy; Lee could not deny what he felt was his duty to his native state. The first blood of the war flowed on April 19th in Baltimore between members of a Massachusetts infantry unit and civilians with strong Southern sympathies.

Throughout the North men rallied to the President's call. Newspapers, broadsides and patriotic rallies urged men to sign up. In the early months of the war the North had little conception of what war between the states really meant. Many young men enlisted in home guard and militia units, eager to show themselves off in new uniforms and dazzle the ladies. By July, over 200,000 had responded.[1] Captain John Stevenson, married to Thompson's sister Emma, was drilling with the Third Pennsylvania Artillery when the President's proclamation was issued.[2] He may have encouraged Thompson to join a militia, or Thompson may have been caught up in the excitement.

On April 23rd Thompson enlisted in Captain Chapman Biddle's Company I of a Philadelphia militia artillery unit.[3] War talk was everywhere; on the Harvard campus, it was the main topic of conversation. Thompson saved letters from classmates which reflect the war fever of the students. One, T. K. Betton, of Cleveland, Ohio, a Harvard underclassman, wrote on April 28th,

". . . all the students are infected with military aspirations, and not the students only but even the directors of this institution . . . have felt the influence of the contagion. The members of the professional departments have already organized a drill club and have been at work for a week or more learning the formulae of infantry tactics. All the undergraduates who so wish will be formed into a battalion and instructed in the maneuvers of the same. The unity of the government must be maintained and if it is not, where are we? Our nationality and our national honor are both gone forever. The South has brought on the war and . . . must abide the consequences; they mistook the sentiment and loyalty of the North and find that they have to fight against a united people and not against us only but Canada also, if need be, and against the public sentiment of the whole civilized world, excepting themselves. Moreover, things have come to such a pass that Lincoln must prosecute the war . . . and if Lincoln does not do something before the end of this week, anybody who would pitch him into the Potomac and take the leadership into his own hands would be supported in it.

"Let the two sections once fairly get to war. Let them be fairly aroused and one section must certainly submit to the other and you cannot doubt for a moment which will be victorious, and this party victorious will not permit the cause of the contention to continue to exist. In other words, the war will be one of abolition.

"I was willing for the sake of peace to allow slavery to be worn out by the irrepressible conflict, but now that we are in for it let's tear it out root and branch."[4]

Lincoln issued another call for volunteers on May 1st. There were no stringent rules for recruitment. Newspaper articles, broadsides, or posters were written in prose that "fairly dripped red, white, and blue." Posters were put up in conspicuous places in cities and towns in every county, urging young men to volunteer. Since this volunteer army would be raised on a state-sponsored basis, incentives varied. The amount of bounty money depended on the wealth of the community. Recruitment posters for the Twelfth New Jersey, which Thompson eventually joined, promised a month's pay ($13) in advance plus a $25 bonus. Extra pay per month was given to married men or sons of widowed mothers. Upon honorable discharge, the federal government promised an additional bonus of $75 and 160 acres of public land. Bonus money increased as the war went on and recruitment lagged.

The same day that Lincoln's call went out, Thompson wrote a friend from Harvard days, Nelson Taylor. Taylor was, in Thompson's own words, "a warm friend" who had graduated in 1860 at age 39. To Thompson's letter of his desire to serve the Union, Taylor sent this long reply.

New York
May 5, 1861

My Dear Thompson,

Your note of the 1st inst. came to hand in due course, and I was much pleased to hear from you and particularly to know that you are devoting yourself in preparing to render efficient service, if an emergency should demand it, in defending our Union, Constitution, and Laws.

We have indeed fallen upon troublous times, and it has become the stern duty of every law-abiding citizen to contribute his mite in sustaining the government under which he lives, no matter what may have been the cause of its having been imperiled.

I hold that governments are established for the protection of its citizens, *in life, liberty,* and the *enjoyment of their property;* and so long as this protection is adequately afforded by the government and persons are content to live under it, that it is an imperative obligation enforced upon them to sustain the government under which they live with their fortunes, and to the extent of risking their lives if circumstances require it. That our government has amply afforded such protection, no one can deny, and that the stability and perpetuity of its existence is endangered is beyond peradventure, for if once we admit the principle of secession, we may bid farewell to the greatness of our republic and a prosperity unparalleled in the annals of history.

That the Southern people had a right to complain of the interpretation put upon some clauses of our constitution by a majority of the Northern people has been a long-settled opinion with me, but the course they have adopted to obtain redress for their grievances is flagitious and wicked. Nor can they be justified in any one act of their program from the inception of their rebellion to the present time, and they ought and I have no doubt will be punished to the full extent of their offending by the strong arm of the government.

I am doing what I can here to assist the cause in helping to organize regiments and instructing their officers, which two years actual service in the Mexican War tolerably well qualified me for.

I am not connected with any military organization here, but am ready and willing to engage in any enterprise that will have a tendency to speedily restore our republic to its pristine unity and harmony.

I shall be much pleased at all times to hear from you and if you go away in any regiment, be sure to let me know in which one it is.[5]

Sincerely yours,
Nelson Taylor

On April 19th, Captain Chapman Biddle's I Company, to which Thompson still belonged, enlisted as Company A of the First Regiment of Light Artillery of the Philadelphia Home Guards. General Alfred Pleasonton himself entered the company on the rolls; Captain Biddle kept command. For the next ten months Thompson divided his time studying for the Bar exam, drilling with the Light Artillery, working in Fish's law office, and playing chess.[6]

In the meantime, army troops saw occasional action but no serious engagements until July 21st. That day, the first Battle of Bull Run (Manassas) taught the over-confident North that this war would not be easy and would last for much longer than they first supposed.

Finally, in March 1862, Thompson's preparation for admittance to the Bar was over. He took his examination at Philadelphia and as soon as he knew the results, wrote sister Hannah on March 6th, "The Board of Examiners met (7 worthies) and there appeared five poor lambs for the slaughter—among them myself. . . . Well, as for myself, they examined me longer than any of the others, [my] being the last. . . . It lasted three-quarters of an hour and during that time I missed one question by not understanding it and another I told them I did not know. . . . So this morning at 10:00 a.m. I received my certificate. I must confess that although I felt sure, still there is a certain feeling of satisfaction which I had not before my examination."

He was admitted to the Bar at Philadelphia as an attorney and "Counselor at Law." He then served on a Home Guard draft board, but was soon transferred to Camden, New Jersey, to do recruiting. He wrote home.

Camden, N.J.
April 8, 1862

My dear Sister,

I am now here on duty having been transferred from the draft to the recruiting service. Kate [Scovel] will be here on Saturday. Should the draft take place on the 15th inst. as now ordered, I shall then go to the front (my Regiment). Cannot you come up?

Love to all from your affectionate brother,
Richard

In July his one-year term of enlistment in the Home Guard Artillery Company ended. Instead of re-enlisting, Thompson went to Milwaukee and Chicago at the behest of his former headmaster, Reverend Scovel, to assist him in settling a legal matter. On his way home he met the Scovels in Niagara Falls, New York, to report on his success and spend a last holiday with them before joining the Volunteer Army.

While in Niagara Falls, Thompson received the following letter from Potter.[7]

Princeton
July 7, 1862

Dear Friend,

Your letters from Chicago and Milwaukee were duly received. If you still desire to enter the army, as I suppose you do, you had better come home at once. You can obtain your captaincy now, I believe. If you were on the ground, I think we could raise part, if not all, of a good company in our county. How it will be hereafter, I cannot say. There is some talk of certain parties starting a company here. I doubt their doing it. There are good men in the county, which you could get if early in the field. I could probably meet you at Niagara, if I knew when to start. That, however, I do not know. There is nothing else here interesting. If I do not hear from you, and do not volunteer, I shall start on my Boston trip on Monday next. I should wish to see you have a company whether I can go or not. I *will* go, however, unless the objection of my friends make it altogether impracticable. Write me at once.

Do not promise your lieutenant until you see me.

As ever, your true friend,
Wm. E. Potter

The two friends met in Philadelphia and set out to seek commissions in the Union Volunteer Army. State governors usually awarded commissions as officers as a form of political patronage. New Jersey Governor Charles S. Olden (and later Democratic Governor Joel Parker)[8] was no exception. Thompson's father's activities in the state legislature and Potter's connections with the Bridgeton newspaper (*Bridgeton Chronicle*) and several state senators helped both young men secure the positions they wanted.

From Philadelphia they went to Potter's home in Bridgeton. There they joined several notables who spoke at a large rally on July 26th. Back in Philadelphia once more, Thompson wrote a short note home to let his family know the latest news.

Philadelphia
July 29, 1862

My dear Sister and Brother,

I arrived here this morning at 9 o'clock and met Potter who has been waiting [for] me in this city for two days to offer me a position in the company now forming in Bridgeton. He offers 1st lieutenant certain; I think captain—Nixon says captain. Am going to Bridgeton to see about it. Will see you soon and tell you all the particulars.

Em and John are in the city and while writing this a nig [Negro] brought in a note telling me to call on them at the Washington house.

In much haste and with much love to you all,

Your affectionate brother,
Richard

Thompson returned home to Cape May Court House in early August, then enlisted as Captain of Company Y, Cumberland County

Volunteers. He and Potter worked diligently at recruiting others.[9] On August 2nd, they spoke at a rally at Cedarville. Thompson kept his family informed.

Bridgeton, N.J.
August 3, 1862

My dear Sister Hann and Brother,

I have gone into the military life and am to be Captain of the company now being raised in the counties of Cumberland and Cape May. I have had this promise in a way that insures me the position. Daniel Dare will be 1st Lieutenant and W. E. Potter, 2nd Lieutenant; Colonel [to be] Robert Johnson of Salem. Last Thursday eve without any previous notice I was called upon to address a mass meeting in Midville. This I did and have thereby got myself into business. Last night I addressed the citizens of Fairfield Township in company with Nixon and Potter and we made a good thing in the way of volunteers. Hon. J. T. Nixon, Elna Potter and the rest of the good people [have] been quite insistent upon my remaining in Cumberland County until the last of this week to help stump the county! I am to come down into Cape May for the same purpose and want you to tell all men who can say anything at a public meeting to hold themselves in readiness. I sent bills [handbills or recruitment notices] by the stage. I want you to let it be known that there will be soon mass meetings in the county and who are the officers of the company. Tell Rev. Mr. Scrinden and hold him engaged to help me in this good work. Try and wake up the people.

I will be with you either on Tuesday or Friday of this week.

Pardon this letter's faults as it is written on a Sunday morning in a country tavern barroom where the smell of stale things and the abundance of flies is beyond imagination.

Much love to you all from your affectionate brother,
Richard

On the 6th, the young men addressed two rallies. One was in the afternoon at a beach party at Pierce's Point, Cape May; the other in the evening at Cape May Court House. Two days later, another mass meeting at Dividing Creek in Cumberland County starred Thompson.

By August 11th, the work of recruiting was finished. They had signed up a full company of men in 12 days.

The men Thompson and Potter recruited came from all walks of life. They listened to the flowery and impassioned speeches, then nearly stampeded to sign up. Some were motivated by patriotism, others by the glory and adventure, and others by the bounty money. Potter's family hosted a noontime dinner for the new company at the Davis Hotel in Bridgeton. Afterward, Captain R. S. Thompson addressed his new command. During the recruitment campaign, Thompson wrote Hannah.

Bridgeton, N.J.
August 10, 1862

My dear Brother and Sister,

Our Company now numbers 85 and some 30 are coming in on Monday, but we are limited to 101 and will have to refuse many. I shall so arrange as to give the Cape May boys a chance should they come. Tell Frank he will have a chance in another company that will be started here immediately, and Mr. Nixon told me last evening that he (Frank) should have a chance for a lieutenancy. We have in our meeting done the work for this second company, and if we had authority to raise a hundred more men, could do it in a week.

We are now taking our pick of the men, refused eight yesterday. Friday we had a mass meeting at Dividing Creek and after the meeting had a big supper—terrapins, oysters, and spring ducks. This evening we are invited to attend Rev. Mr. Hubbard's church. Tuesday Nixon, Potter's brother and others are going to give the Company a big dinner at this hotel, and then there will be addresses by Hon. J. T. Nixon, Rev. Mr. Hubbard, and Mr. Paul I. Jones after which we take the cars for Woodbury, taking into camp a full company.

Mr. Nixon will write either you or Frank about this second company, and I trust it will be able to succeed.

Love to all. Kiss the children.

In haste from your affectionate brother,
Richard

On August 12th, the new captain took his company on their first rail journey together. They went to Camp Stockton, near Woodbury,

New Jersey.[10] There, Company Y of the Cumberland County Volunteers joined the Twelfth New Jersey Volunteer Infantry as Company K. The Twelfth was commanded by Colonel Robert C. Johnson of Salem. His Lieutenant Colonel was J. Howard Willets, a Cape May native, and his Major was Thomas H. Davis of Camden.

On August 14, 1862, Captain Richard S. Thompson, First Lieutenant Daniel Dare, and Second Lieutenant William E. Potter received their commissions from Governor Olden. At Camp Stockton the recruits began to learn the art of soldiering.

Camp Stockton, Woodbury, N.J.
August 17, 1862

My dear Sister and Brother,

On Tuesday next I propose going to Cape Island in the boat, provided I can get off. There is some talk of the Regiment moving on Thursday. If this is done I cannot come down, but will write you and you can come to Philadelphia and see us off. I suppose Em is with you and hope to join you all this week sometime. Yesterday Mr. and Mrs. James Scovel, Cort, Kate, and Jim's sister visited the camp. Things are not very inviting here as there is much dust and the Regiment is filling up with new men who make some confusion. Our Company is said to stand first and [a] company from Woodstown stands second. Our Company officers are now all commissioned and things are settled. Tell Frank if he can raise a company he will (in my opinion) find no difficulty in getting a commission. Tell him they are now trying to raise a company in Bridgeton and for him to write to Nixon asking him about the matter. I write in some haste as I have other letters to write, and duties to perform. I will not attempt to describe our camp but will leave it to your own judgment, as you must certainly come down before we leave. The most serious enemy at present is the dust. Have no fear about your living or board for our hotel keeper can boast the best public table in the state. But I will see you at Cape May and write you to come. Much love to the children and remember me to the friends. With much love and in great haste, your affectionate brother,

Richard

Near the end of the month John F. Starr, president of the Bank of Camden, gave the Twelfth a regimental flag. The giving of a flag was to become a standard ritual for every new regiment. It was common in the Union army, but many Confederate regiments also had flag presentation ceremonies. This banner became the symbol of the regiment and a rallying point in battle, second only to the nation's flag. The regimental flag, usually hand-sewn by mothers, wives and sisters of the men, also became the symbol of the home and communities they swore to defend.

On August 28th, over 2,000 south Jersey citizens visited the camp at Woodbury, Thompson's brother-in-law, Coleman Leaming, among them. Patriotic citizens prepared and donated food for a huge outdoor feast to celebrate the event. After they had eaten (to excess in many cases), Colonel Johnson assembled the men to receive officially the silk standard.

Thompson's superior officers selected him to receive the flag on behalf of the regiment and make the appropriate remarks. The ceremony was written up in local newspapers, "Captain Thompson, of Company K, received the flag of the Regiment. Captain Thompson is quite a young man, but he gave evidence of the possession of superior abilities as a speaker. He was perfectly self-possessed before the immense concourse of people and soldiery, and enunciated his statements in a clear, distinct manner, with an ease and grace, which many an older speaker might envy."[11]

Unfortunately, he had just started to speak when a heavy rain began. In the sudden downpour, he was forced to cut his address short. The newspaper noted that his audience stayed on in the rain for a few moments but becoming "soaked to the skin," fled for shelter.

On September 4th, the Regiment of 850 officers and men was mustered into the service of the United States Army by Captain W. B. Royall, of the Fifth U. S. Cavalry. Thompson was now an officer in the Union Volunteer Army. He immediately had his picture taken and sent copies home.[12]

The Regiment left New Jersey on September 7th and went to Baltimore. From there they were sent to Ellicott's Mills, a small Maryland village, where they went into camp. While he was stationed at Ellicott's Mills, Thompson began a daily diary of his camp life. He also wrote home as often as his duties permitted. It is primarily from these sources that his story is presented.[13]

Notes

[1] Price, W. H. (1961) *Civil War Handbook*. A Civil War Research Association Series, Fairfax, VA, Pp. 33-40.

[2] John Stevenson became a captain in Company A, 152nd Regiment of the Pennsylvania Volunteers. On February 17, 1863, the unit, with others, became Company A, Third Regiment, Pennsylvania Heavy Artillery, under Colonel Joseph Roberts. Stevenson was in the Peninsula Campaign when Major General George B. McClellan landed his Army of the Potomac near Fort Monroe, Virginia, on April 1, 1862, as a prelude to the taking of Richmond. That failed, but the Union Army kept its foothold on the peninsula, a constant threat to Richmond's security. After the area was secured, the stability of his assignment permitted Emma to be at the Fort Monroe Regimental Headquarters with him, where they remained for three years. Company A was mustered out on July 11, 1865. See Taylor, F. H. (1913) *Philadelphia in the Civil War 1861—1865*. Philadelphia, Pp. 152-153. For more insight into the significance of the Peninsula Campaign, see the synopsis in Jones, A. (1992) Military Means, Political Ends. In Boritt, G. S. (Ed.) *Why the Confederacy Lost*. New York, Pp. 53-56.

[3] Chapman Biddle (1822-1880) was elected captain of an old Philadelphia artillery company begun in 1844 and revitalized first as Company I, a militia unit. On April 19, 1861, it enlisted as Company A, First Regiment, Lt. Artillery, a Philadelphia Home Guard unit. Many prominent and affluent citizens joined; his brother Alexander became his lieutenant. After both Biddles resigned from this company in August to recruit the 121st Infantry Regiment, Pennsylvania Volunteers, Henry D. Landis took over the company, becoming its captain. It then became known as Landis's Battery, listed officially as an Independent Battery, Militia Light Artillery. Mustered into service with the Army of the Potomac at Harrisburg, on June 19, 1863, for the "emergency" (invasion of Pennsylvania by the Confederate Army), they were mustered out July 30th. The 121st was officially organized in September 1862, Chapman Biddle eventually becoming its colonel. His brother became lieutenant colonel. The 121st was in the First Brigade, Third Division, First Corps. Taylor, *op.cit.*, Pp. 23-24, 135-136, 220, 248.

[4] From the collection of the authors.

[5] On the envelope, a note in Thompson's hand reads, "He was in my class at Cambridge. A warm friend. He was much older than I. RST." Taylor roomed next door to Thompson and Potter at Brattle House. Nelson Taylor of Connecticut (1821-1894) served during the Mexican War as a captain, first in New York, then in California. He stayed in California for a while after mustering out, then returned east to go to Harvard where he and Thompson met. At the start of the Civil War he joined the 72nd New York as a colonel, rising to the rank of brigadier general. He commanded troops in the battles of Seven Pines, the Seven Days, Second Bull Run, and Fredericksburg. He served until his resignation in January 1863 and returned to New York. There he commanded troops during the draft riots. He was elected to Congress from New York in

1864. He practiced law from 1869 until his retirement. See Warner, E. J. (1988) *Generals in Blue*. Baton Rouge, LA, Pp. 495-496.

[6] Thompson played chess with a friend, James Lancey of Philadelphia. It is uncertain when they met, but they continued to play chess by mail after each went their separate ways. Lancey moved to Boston to enter the firm of Wilson, Hawksworth, Ellison & Co. Thompson wrote out stratagems on the back of old envelopes. The games-by-mail came to an end when Thompson joined the army, but the correspondence continued at least until 1864.

[7] Potter at first planned to finish his education, then join up. Two years younger than Thompson, he, too, graduated from Harvard Law School in 1861 and was working on a Master's degree at the College of New Jersey. He wrote Thompson on May 26, 1862, asking him for a lieutenancy in the company Thompson hoped to recruit.

[8] Charles Smith Olden (1799-1876), Quaker governor of New Jersey from 1860 to 1863, was a Republican. He left office during the war because the state law prohibited him from succeeding himself. Joel Parker (1816-1888), a Democrat, and member of a local militia, succeeded Olden in 1863. He left office in 1866 but was reelected in 1872.

[9] The Twelfth was one of the few outfits whose initial roster was almost entirely made up of local men. South Jersey sent more than 77,000 men to the war.

[10] Camp Stockton was named for New Jersey's Adjutant General, Robert F. Stockton, Jr., whose farm was close to the railroad which served the camp. He had the rank of major general, but as he is not listed in any reference of active officers, this may have been a position of political patronage.

[11] The *Woodbury Constitution*, NJ, September 12, 1862.

[12] Clean-shaven during his college days, Thompson, like many of his fellow officers, grew the whiskers made popular by General Ambrose Burnside. Back in civilian life, the "sideburns" were modified and he wore a small walrus mustache.

[13] Background information for this chapter came from Longacre, E. G. (1988) *To Gettysburg and Beyond.* . . . Hightstown, NJ, and Long, E. B. (1971) *The Civil War Day by Day: An Almanac, 1861-65*. New York.

Chapter Three

The Fledgling Captain

I could never be satisfied . . . to remain inactive
while my country is in . . . danger

RST to Hannah and Coleman, January 14, 1863

As would be expected, Thompson's diary entries are short and sketchy while his letters, usually written in calmer moments, are more detailed and descriptive. On the day following the flag ceremony, Richard wrote Hannah explaining some details of camp life.

Camp Stockton, Woodbury, N. J.
September 5, 1862

My dear Sister Hann,

Your husband about whom you inquired so particularly is, no doubt, by this time with you.

We expect to move on Sunday day after tomorrow for Washington, D.C., and you must write me there directing "12th Regiment N. J. Volunteers, Washington, D.C. or Elsewhere."

I enclose you two photographs of each kind and wish you to place one of each among my photographs in the upper drawer. The others are yours.

I am well and in very good condition for a big supper to be given tonight to the officers of the Regiment.

By the way, I owe you an [apology] or rather an explanation for not meeting you at the depot at camp the evening you passed through. While at Philadelphia I looked for you [on] both trains and was disappointed, and the next day I was making arrangements for the "flag presentation" in the afternoon when the train passed through. I trust you will charge the fact to circumstances and not to my wishes or negligence.

With love to you and the children, not forgetting the Doctor, I remain in much haste,

Your affectionate brother,
Richard

[P.S.] We have had some 16 ladies visit my tent this day. I have played the agreeable until I find myself asking pardon of the confounded flies I brush from my face. Tonight I gave 50 of my good men furloughs until tomorrow as the last chance many may have to bid farewell to the loved ones at home.

Trusting you may all be both happy and well and that our country may soon rise from the troubles that now weigh her down, I remain,

Your loving brother,
Richard

At 8:30 a.m. on September 7, 1862, the Regiment left Camp Stockton by train, stopping in Camden where friends and relatives were gathered to say goodby. Thompson was able to visit with the Scovels.[1]

From Camden they crossed the Delaware River to Philadelphia, leaving the train for a meal at the Cooper Refreshment Hall.[2] After their meal they marched to the Broad Street Station and entrained for Baltimore where they arrived at 11:30 p.m.[3] They marched from one depot to another, each time expecting to board another train to continue their journey, but no train was there, or anywhere else. Because secessionist sympathy was strong in the city, the men had their guns loaded and bayonets fixed but the arms were not needed.

As no facilities had been prepared for them, the men were left to find food and sleeping quarters on their own. Some of the officers found rooms at hotels. Thompson, like most of the men, slept in the streets or on the wooden sidewalks. It was not until the afternoon of the next day that the regiment could board another train. Unlike the passenger model of the previous day it was made up of foul-smelling, filth-laden cattle cars. The men presumed they were going to the front; instead, they arrived at the village of Ellicott's Mills.[4] They remained at Ellicott's Mills for about four months.

Ellicott's Mills, Md.
September 9, 1862

My dear Sister,

We left Camp Stockton, Woodbury on Sunday morning at 10:30, arrived in Philadelphia, took dinner at the Cooper Refreshment Saloon, and proceeded to Baltimore, arriving at 11:30 Sunday evening. We slept on the street pavement and on Monday at 3 p.m. came onto this old settled town of Ellicott's Mills. The country here is mountainous and picturesque, about 5000 inhabitants, half Union and half not.

We took the ground for bed and the full moon sky for covering last evening. Am all right this morning.

We may stay here several days, as this town has to be protected. I cannot tell when to write me as our movements are rather uncertain. But I will try and let you know soon.

In haste from affectionate brother,
Richard

Union military leaders considered Ellicott's Mills strategically important because it lay along a route that Confederate General Robert E. Lee might possibly use to make a march on Washington. And Washington was very frightened by Robert E. Lee.

For a while, Thompson's duties kept him from writing home, although he kept up his diary entries. Possibly because of Thompson's legal training, Major General John E. Wool, at 78 years of age the oldest general on active duty, appointed him Assistant Provost Marshal on September 12th. The duties of a provost marshal included the care of prisoners and their transport, keeping law and order in the regiment, guarding wagons and supplies, and persuading deserters to return to their units. A natural leader and disciplinarian, Thompson enjoyed the assignment. Four days after his appointment, four companies, K included, traveled to Monocacy on freight cars. From there, they marched to Frederick, where Thompson got his first look at his enemy, as prisoners. Fourteen hundred prisoners were loaded into railroad cars and sent to Baltimore.

A note he wrote on September 17th gives an indication of the prisoners' condition, "Those comrades [Union soldiers] who were members of that guard [were] scratching themselves at the memory of the 'graybacks' with which the prisoners were covered." He wrote Hannah his impressions.

Baltimore
September 18, 1862

My dear Sister Hann,

I am now in Baltimore waiting orders. Four companies from our Regiment went to Frederick yesterday and brought down to Baltimore between 1400 and 1500 Rebel prisoners. They were the hardest looking white or black men I ever saw, no stretch of the imagination can picture a more wretched set. Some have been without hats or shoes for the last four months, covered with lice both body and head. We marched them seven miles in quick time and made them think of death by having loaded guns within a few feet of them all the way.

Our Regiment is still encamped at Ellicott's Mills doing picket duty. I was last week appointed Provost Marshal of our district and have been administering the oath of allegiance to the inhabitants. Ellicott's Mills is a beautiful place of some 5,000 inhabitants. I have placed several of its citizens under arrest and made more Union men than you could shake a stick at.

It is *rumored* in our Regiment that one of our officers is thinking some of resigning his position and that I am to be made Major of the Regiment. This is mere rumor and, of course, you will keep the thing still. I will write you again soon. Love to all. Remember me to Dr. and the children and think of me,

Your affectionate brother,
Richard

Camp life followed the usual military routine. Like most officers, Thompson had a servant who cooked his meals, did his laundry and other chores. He spent off-duty evenings visiting fellow officers or the townspeople, especially the admiring ladies.

A diary entry for Wednesday, October 8th, reads,

Mor[ning] in Camp. Afternoon with Lieut. Davis and guard. Made demand on Mr. Archer, Pres. of the Female Institute for arms and have quite a time.

Sometime later he added the following, in pencil,

Interesting time, the search of the Female Institute—
oh my!!—for *arms*.

Some arms were found stashed under the stairs leading to the
second floor. On October 10th he recorded an amusing little event.
"A little before midnight, a captain [probably Thompson] observed some
of the men sprinkling something along the company street in a line
which ended in one of the Sibley tents into which tent the men
disappeared. The Captain investigated and found a line of shelled corn
had been laid reaching fully a hundred feet from that Sibley tent; his
curiosity led him to take a seat in his tent and keep an eye on that line
of corn. In about half an hour several plump looking pigs came along
and when [they] struck that line of corn they followed it up until one
of them got about his head and shoulders within the flaps of that Sibley
tent, there was a slight thud and balance of that pig disappeared into
the tent and Captain went to bed. The writer is credibly informed that
Captain had fresh pork tenderloin for his breakfast and that he ate it
and asked no questions as to where it came from."

For three days beginning with the 1st of October, a large boil
appeared on Thompson's neck, which bothered him considerably.
However, his own strong constitution and some medical treatment
brought about a quick recovery. A more untoward event took place on
October 11th. His hastily written diary entries used creative abbre-
viations and grammar. The notation reads (punctuation and spelling
copied as is),

> Saturday, October 11, 1862 Mor. Rains. Afternoon
> start out to search the house of Mr. Gaither.[5] take
> Lieut. Potter, Sergt. Dubois[6] and 3 men in two-horse
> carriage. find nothing at Mr. Gaithers Coming home
> as we drive down the hill at Ellicott's Mills, the breast
> strap slip[ped] and let the carriage [press] on the
> horses—they ran down the hill until the carriage
> upset and we [are] all turned out—smash the carriage,
> etc. I hold the horses and bring them up on the fence.
> Came near flogging the livery stable man. take an
> oyster supper and come to camp with my hand pretty
> well smashed and my back strained.

Several days later, he wrote a long letter to his doctor brother-in-law
relating the accident. He knew Coleman would read the letter to
Hannah to assure her that, although shaken up, he was not seriously
injured.

Camp Johnson, Ellicott's Mills
Headquarters
12th N.J. Regt.
October 19, 1862 (Sunday)

Dear Doctor,

I will endeavor to answer your kind letter as well as a man may whose hand is wrapt up in flaxseed poultice.

Last Saturday week, I received my wound which if not done in battle was certainly in the service. Acting as Provost Marshal, I took Lieutenant Potter and four men of my company and proceeded in a two horse carriage to the residence of Mr. Gaither, a very wealthy and influential citizen of Howard County, to make an examination into his domestic arrangements. He treated us with much respect, and our search for army clothing in his house proved useless. While returning home, the breast straps gave way and the horses started on the full run down a very steep hill. On one side of the narrow road was rough rock, on the other a ravine of some 35 or 40 feet. As the breast straps were broken, we had no control of the horses and they gave unmistakable evidence of dislike towards having the carriage run against their heels. To end a long story, as well as a long ride, the carriage upset and we were smashed up among loaded guns, pistols, swords, wagon top, rocks, etc., etc. I retained my hold on the horses and after being dragged from under the rubbish regained my feet long enough to run the horses into some posts and thus bring [them] up. We were all slightly injured; my hands being cut against the rocks, hence my poultice fingers and bad writing. But as one of the men (who is somewhat of a wag) remarked on gaining his feet, "It's all for the flag." One of the men when we picked him up had a rifle in each hand and sword under one arm. The wag said of him that he, seeing danger, had "fell out under arms." Our escape was Providential; we have been favored by a visit from Mrs. Colonel Johnson and Miss Thompson of Salem, sister of Richard P. Thompson. They have returned to New Jersey and from the manner in which they enjoyed themselves will I am sure report favorably of the 12th. Now I think you had better make up your mind to pay Maryland a visit, and am sure that should you and sister propose the matter to Ch. Ell [?] and wife they would accompany you, as well as Mr. and Mrs. William Nixon. Don't you think a small party could spend a few days as well as dollars very pleasantly among us?

Dr., this is, to me at least, a very singular life. Think of my living upon the tented field, doing picket duty. When at night I wrap my blanket around me and lie down on the ground under an old tree, and during the day, it may be, play the agreeable to some little Southern girl to pay for my supper. As the other day, being on picket at a place called Elchester, a train of cars ran over two cows and so injured them I took the responsibility of having one of my men who understood butchering kill and dress them. When the lady to whom they belonged heard who had done this, she sent for me—introduced me to her charming daughter and offered me bed and board during my stay at that post. The bed and board I refused, but spent a very pleasant eve with the daughter, who played and sang for me and was as sociable as ever I could wish. The family is very old and respectable, by name Ellicott. After their ancestors this place takes its name.

As to my installment, I shall have to ask you to arrange it as best you may, and use any money of mine that shall be paid you. Please send me a little account of my receipts and expenses, both as to the installment and the Neat Marcy note, as well as all others. I am glad to learn that both these subjects are likely to be so favorably arranged.

As to Albert Walker, he has received one months pay, $13; Cumberland County bounty, $30; U.S. bounty, $25; and the enlistment bounty, $2; total, $70. All the bounty promised in advance, leaving the $75 to be paid when mustered out of service and the $6 per month to the widowed mother.[7]

There is one other Cape May man in the Regiment whose name and certificate I will send you; I think his name is Hand, but I will write of that again. Wishing you may think of me often and write soon, I remain with love to all,

Your affectionate brother,
Richard

No correspondence remains from this period until December 6th. His diary indicates his military duties kept him quite busy. On October 25th, he acted as counsel for Josiah Davis of Company E. (While no Josiah Davis is listed in the roster of Company E, a Corporal Joseph Davis is.) Davis was brought before a Court Martial where

Thompson defended him and won. It was the first such case for Thompson.

November 2nd, the Provost Guard, Thompson included, entered a local saloon which had been selling liquor to the soldiers. They emptied 85 gallons of whiskey into the street. Drunkenness was one of the problems of camp life and the army forbade personal possession of liquor.

From the 12th to the 15th of November, he worked directly for General Wool (see Appendix B) or spent time in drill and picket duty. During their off hours officers and men alike added to their diet by hunting squirrel and rabbit. Most of the men were quite adept as they had hunted small game since childhood. Thompson had had his own gun since his Bordentown Seminary days. To add further variety to his soldierly routine, he was often invited to have dinner with several of the townspeople, especially the Ellicott family.

Later in the month he and some of his men had an encounter with several Maryland women, Southern sympathizers, who were hiding contraband to be sent to the South. For three days from the 24th to the 26th, his men had scouted some 15 miles into the countryside. During this foray, they killed a dog and arrested the women who had collected and hidden two large wagonloads of arms and accoutrements from the Battle of Antietam,[8] intending to send them to the Confederate Army. He quotes them as saying, "They would like to see my damned *Yankee* throat cut."

On December 6th the regiment received marching orders. They were to move out on the 10th. Thompson wrote home a letter detailing a little more of his life in the Army of the Potomac.

> *Camp Johnson, Ellicott's Mills*
> *12th N.J. Regt.*
> *December 6, 1862*

Dear Sister and Brother,

Today we received "marching orders." We strike tents and move to Washington, thence to *no man knoweth*. "The wind bloweth where it listeth, and no man knoweth whence it cometh or whither it goeth"—'tis thus with our order to march. We have some three inches of snow here and cold weather.

I will send some money home to be placed to my credit if any opportunity offers.

Everything is now in the shape of a family breaking up housekeeping.

We (my Company) have been on picket duty for the past two weeks, and during that time we scouted 25 miles from camp, captured 2 horses, 2 mules, 15 rifles, 30 overcoats, 25 blankets—10 tents, worth $200, and clothing to such an amount that it took six horses to drag them to camp. Had to sleep wherever we found ourselves. At night we lived in the woods, had plenty to eat and corn stalks to sleep under. Killed at my post (when I had 20 men), 40 rabbits, 20 squirrels, 4 turkeys, 10 chickens, and also 3 dogs. Had women tell me they would like to see my "damned throat cut" and other like pleasant expressions to aid me in the enterprise. Other women proved more kind and gave me bed and board.

At night when we had returned to our Picket Headquarters, the slaves from the neighboring plantations would come in and sing, play on the fiddle, banjo, bones, etc., while the men would dance straight fours[9] round the campfire. We enjoyed the moonlight nights, and many is the hard story told as we sat on logs with our feet to the fire smoking our pipes. I have attended ten dance parties and find that the Southern women are rather fond of a blue coat and brass buttons.

Thursday last was "pay day" and that evening we saw a high time among the whiskey shops. We shut up several and yet there were too many left. In fact this whole place is one honeycomb of whiskey shops.

Give my love to the children when you write. I received your last letter. I will write you again when I can send any account of my whereabouts.

With much love, I remain your brother,
Richard

Leaving Ellicott's Mills on December 10th, the Regiment boarded a troop train for Washington where they were billeted in an uncomfortable, run-down barn of a barracks called "Soldiers' Rest." It was a drafty place and the food was served cold. But here, the old Austrian rifles they had been using were exchanged for Springfield muzzle-loading percussion muskets. The Springfields, although outmoded, were an improvement on the foreign-made guns. They were smoothbore weapons that fired a round of one metal ball and three charges of buckshot. This was the buck-and-ball ammunition that the gallant Twelfth would make famous at Gettysburg.[10]

Washington, D.C.
December 12, 1862

My dear Sister,

I have just finished a good breakfast with Major Davis at Brown's at the Metropolitan as you call it. We are waiting here for new guns, and today or tomorrow morning will commence a march for Liverpool Point a distance of 64 miles. We are to report to Major General Burnside.

Will write again soon. Love to all. I shall send my trunk home as we are only permitted to carry 60 lbs. baggage. The key I will tie to the back of the straps under the cover so you may find it.

Remember me to all kindly, and when you get this think of me as in the mud of old Virginia.

Richard

They were ordered to leave Washington on the 13th. They expected the usual train, but this time they had to use the army's standard transportation, their feet. It was a 60 mile march, some of it in mud. Many of the men, wearied by the long march, emptied their knapsacks along the way, disposing of items they would later need. On the evening of the 15th, when they stopped for the night, they were in Matawan Swamp. Exhausted and footsore, they slept in the mud, many a man wishing he had kept his extra coat or jacket to protect himself from the marshy ground.

Their lot was hard but the lot of the major portion of the Army of the Potomac was worse. After crossing the Rappahannock River on December 11th to occupy Fredericksburg, Burnside's army engaged in a bitter battle for that city on the 13th. It was a debacle for Federal forces; they withdrew back over the river on the 15th, discouraged and defeated.

While the weary Army of the Potomac was returning to camp at Falmouth, Virginia, to lick its wounds, the Twelfth New Jersey was making its way to join them. They arrived in the late afternoon of December 16th at Liverpool Point on the Potomac River. The next day they crossed the river in a steamboat, arriving at Aquia Creek, Virginia, in the snow. They stayed here two days, again in the open, with only blankets for shelter. On December 19th, they marched about 20 miles to the north bank of the Rappahannock to the camp north of Falmouth, nearly opposite Fredericksburg. They were placed in the Second Brigade (Colonel Robert C. Johnson) of the Third Division under General William Henry French of General Edwin V. Sumner's Right Grand Division of The Army of the Potomac. Major General Ambrose Burnside was commander over all.

For the next ten days the camp, except for the usual reviews, was quiet. Lieutenant William Potter was appointed Chief of Ordnance for the Division. They happily received the first mail since leaving Ellicott's Mills 17 days earlier.

The Regiment now was established in a more or less permanent camp. It would be an especially snowy winter and an uncomfortable one for the troops. It was an uncomfortable one for Burnside, too. His assault on Fredericksburg was a costly failure, for which he blamed his subordinates. Lincoln called him to Washington for a conference. The army sat. To while away the time, Thompson wrote long letters home.

> *Headquarters*
> *12th N.J. Regt.*
> *Near Falmouth, Va.*
> *January 4, 1863*

Dear Coly,

Your letter of the 26 December I received on 1 inst. We received no letters from the time we left Ellicott's Mills until the day on which yours came. You may imagine the mail was a large one. The account was very satisfactory. Should you find a balance is likely to remain in my favor, please make a payment on your note if not already paid and also on Uncle['s].

Well, today being the first day I have been off duty since our arrival here, I took Dr. Gilman's[11] horse and rode over to the 6th, 7th, and 25th N.J. Vols., who are stationed about five miles from here—saw Joe Holmes and the rest of the Cape May boys in the 25th. They are all sick of soldiering and anxious to return home. Joe Holmes is in rather better spirits than the others.

In the 7th Regiment I saw Lieutenant Smith and Corporal Cooper of Cape Island. They are well and laugh at the homesickness of their friends in the 25th. I dined with Larry Wiley of the 6th N.J. He is much changed since I last saw him and looks like an old stager. The change has been an improvement. Frank Hand[12] is sick with heavy cold, and Dr. Wiley informed me he was endeavoring to obtain a furlough for him, so you will most likely see him in Cape May within a week or so.

Frank is low spirited and I truly pity him. He looks badly and I doubt his ability to endure the hardships of camp life. He threw away his dress coat on one of their marches and in speaking of it today said, "I had enough to do without carrying that darned thing." So you see he is Frank Hand still.

I believe I told you of my Christmas. Well, New Year's day I dined on an inch of pork fat, two army crackers, some molasses, and a cup of tea. I trust you at least thought of me while eating your fine things at home.

We only have four Captains on duty, and as our Colonel is in command of the Brigade and our Lieutenant Colonel is General Field Officer and the Major [is] sick I am in command of the Regiment and have been for the past five days. This together with being Officer of the Day once every four days and doing picket duty keeps me pretty busy. Lieutenant Potter has been detailed to the position of Ordnance Officer of our Division, which leaves me only one Lieutenant for duty. Lieutenant Potter is still my 2nd Lieutenant, only he is not on duty in the Regiment.

My health continues good, and I have not been off duty from sickness since I enlisted. I have not received a letter from Hann since we left Ellicott's Mills. Mary wrote me and you; none of my other friends (home friends) have had time to write me even a line. I ask you whether I have cause of complaint, considering I have written two or three times to Hann, Bell and Em?

Burnside has returned to Headquarters and we are all waiting to receive orders, either to go into winter quarters or for a movement. It is not likely things will long remain as they now are. Albert Walker is fat, healthy, and in good spirits. He makes a fine soldier, and I am much attached to the boy.

You must write me often and please remember a letter directed 12 Regt. N.J. Vols. via Washington will always reach me. At present you may direct 12 Regt. N.J. Vols., French's division, Burnside's Army via Washington D.C.

Send my love to the children when you write.

With much regard to yourself and love to Hann,

I remain, your brother,

Richard

Headquarters
12th N.J. Regt.
Near Falmouth, Va.
January 14, 1863

My dear Sister and Brother,

I sometimes fear my writing so much will weary you for what have I to write about but the war and myself and I am sure everyone is wearied of the war and anything connected with it. And again when I have matters of interest, it is like an indifferent reader with a good story, so the case is but little bettered.

My letters must offer savor of our living, a repetition of the same hard fare. Our Army still remains in *status quo* and we are yet on pork fat and sheet iron crackers. The table on which I write is a pine board; my candle is stuck to the table by its own grease; my ink is gunpowder and vinegar (why not with language dangerous and sour); my chair, a valise on end; my carpet, the ground; my bed, solid earth; my house, a nine-by-nine feet tent, with a good prospect of a reduction to a muslin one, six-by-four feet, or it may be "two paces of the vilest earth." Such is the "pomp and circumstance" of war. Our "chap," [clergyman] became disgusted and went home to preach against the ungodliness of soldiers and the unholiness of soldiers' living, or in other words not quite so clerical grub. At Aquia Creek he sat on a log all night and if report does him justice, said many things not found in his prayer book. On our march he slept under wagons, and in fact he became so well satisfied that we were becoming savages, resigned and went home—the best thing for himself and the Regiment, as he sinned in neglecting his duty, and the men sinned in damning him.[13]

My health remains good, and that is the best news a soldier can write those who love him. Poor Frank Hand can answer for this. Did you receive my letter acknowledging the receipt of the account? And also speaking of Frank, I have heard nothing from him since.

This life will teach many a man the value of home and the blessings of peace. Think not I am discontented, wishing to be home; I never could be satisfied, a single man and young, to remain inactive while my country is in such danger. And though my nightly prayer is for peace, yet 'tis for an honorable peace. I would rather live a soldier for life. Yes! Rather see this country made a mighty sepulcher in which should be buried our institutions, our nationality, our flag and every American that today lives, than that our Republic should be divided into little *nothings* by an inglorious and shameful peace, to suit political purposes for the advancement of political fiends. We are now suffering more from these fiends at home than the Rebels south. The Devil laughs as he calls them his children, and European powers rub their hands for joy to witness the success of their infernal plans. We are today 900,000 loyal men, men who have left the comforts of home to endure the hardships of war through our loyalty to this Government and through the determination to maintain it. And while we are absent, the sympathies of our enemy and cowardly politicians at home are making political capital of our absence—preparing to give up the rights we are fighting to preserve, and this over the heads of the living and bones of the dead soldiers. We have had no vote, shall have no representative in the coming Congress. We are the bone and sinew of the nation and we know it, and the solemn question that now hangs like a pall over this country, is, will 900,000 armed men, made desperate by sufferings already borne, submit to this? You may know my answer without the expression. I have suffered much, will suffer more, it may be sacrifice my life. And have a right to hate, and do hate, with a bitterness my soul never before dreamed of, the sneaking villain who is low enough to use his influence to dishearten our army and play a hidden game for his own personal advancement to the sacrifice of his country. I beg you will pardon this wandering of my pen from the happening of circumstance to the expression of sentiment. My pent up enthusiasm will at times boil over. Don't think we grow rough or crazy. In the utterance of a just indignation I forgot for the moment I was writing a social letter. I know you would pardon the language could you see the suffering I have witnessed and then think of those good easy souls sitting in comfortable chairs, writing articles that act like firebrands upon us, taking away the idea of permanent peace.[14] But enough, too much perhaps, of this. I have received no letter from Bell or Em since long before I left Ellicott's Mills. I trust they have not forgotten they have a renegade brother on these barren hills of Stafford.

I rejoice that a railroad to Cape Island has become so near a certainty. When next I come to the Capes I shall most likely do so by railroad. That sounds strange, notwithstanding so much talk of the thing for years.

'Tis reported through camp that our Colonel is like[ly] to be made a Brigadier General. . . . This would make several changes in the commissioned officers of the Regiment. As yet the thing is merely rumor, yet each officer has a little pet ambition and each is wide-awake for any chance that may offer to take another step in military honor.

The wind is blowing very hard. I dislike wind more than any rain, snow, or cold. It makes our tents unruly and gives one a sense of the insecurity of his house.

Now, please write me very soon; direct as I have told you. Mention whether my letters reach you and believe me your affectionate brother,

Richard

The camp abounded with rumors—one, that General Joseph Hooker had replaced General Burnside, turned out to be true.[15] Burnside had made another attempt at Fredericksburg on January 20, 1863. While he was planning the new assault, the weather had been cold but clear. As the army began to move, rain began to fall. It fell all day for the next three days, turning the countryside to mud. The clay soil of Virginia, when thoroughly wet, develops exquisite adhering qualities. The men tried to march in the sticky substance. They tried to pull, push and/or prod animals, wagons, and heavy guns through the mire. They could not.

His officers asked Burnside to reconsider the attack; they were all stalled—stuck in the mud. Burnside would not yield. He sent a letter to Washington demanding the resignation of three of his subcommanders, including General Joseph Hooker. Lincoln refused the request.

When, on the 24th, a final cold and heavy rain and snowstorm pelted the soaked and frustrated troops and it was apparent, even to Burnside, that this maneuver was impossible, the soggy soldiers were permitted to return to camp. The aborted attack went down in history as the Mud March.

Two days later, on January 26th, a joyful Joseph Hooker took command of the Army of the Potomac. Lincoln, still hoping to find the right man to lead the army, replaced Burnside, who was then assigned to the Department of the Ohio.

When Thompson was able to write again, he first mentioned the deaths of some of his men. The case of typhoid was only one of many that would follow as a result of poor water and sanitation. Writing to tell a family they had lost a loved one was one of the hardest duties any officer had to face.

Headquarters
12th N.J. Regt.
Near Falmouth, Va.
February 1, 1863

My dear Sister,

I am unable to say, from writing so often, whether I have answered your letter or not. Our Army has had many changes since writing you or anyone. Burnside's gone, Hooker in command, and several other changes in officers, but we remain in the same position. The snowstorm was against us, and in my opinion we are now only waiting for good roads. This afternoon Dr. Wiley[16] called. He is going home to the Capes tomorrow. He tells me that Frank has already started. Dr. is looking well, and the prospect of seeing his family makes him in even better than his ordinary good spirits. He will tell you how I am looking and in what condition we are situated. While Dr. was here, Mr. N. B. Aaronson (formerly of Cape May) called. He is the state agent for forwarding boxes and such things from New Jersey to the N.J. Regiments. His office is No. 203 Chestnut Street, Philadelphia.

I mentioned in my last that Cort Scovel has a Rebel sword I sent home. I also have sent a coat which will be sent you soon. I cannot write anything of interest saving that I continue to enjoy good health.

Since leaving Ellicott's Mills, I have lost two of my privates by death, one Francis Husted by inflammation on the brain, and W. D. Hendrickson a very fine young man of 20, by typhoid fever. Hendrickson's death is a very sad case. He leaves a widowed mother who depended entirely upon him for support. My men have resolved to pay the expense of sending his body home. He was buried with military honor here. The Company, with reversed arms, accompanied his body to the grave keeping step to the "Dead March" played by the band, and after the service three salutes were fired over the grave. There is much more solemnity connected with such funerals than any other.

There is very little sickness in our Regiment compared with those around us; some bury two or three everyday or so while we have only lost some seven or eight since entering the service.

As to my mention [of] friends or *friend*, I hear about once every three weeks from them. They are all doing well and the change from Bordentown to Bloomington seems to have been a happy one.[17] 'Tis been so long since I saw a woman I have even forgotten how they look, but suppose they are as changeable, pretty and spunky as ever. I have not received a letter from Mary or Em for a long time, though I have written them several times. Our band is now playing the "Red, White, and Blue." I wish you could hear them. We are blessed with good music four or five times each day, and that is a thing we never tire of hearing. I often think what a proud day it would be to return to our homes after an honorable peace. I think the blood would thrill through the heart as we march to the national airs played by our band through the streets of Philadelphia.

I should like to hear Frank Hand's opinion of things in general, and you must write me as near his language in the description of his soldier's life as possible.

You never have told me whether my trunk arrived and whether you found the key. Answer this.

I will now close wishing you all the happiness your own soul would wish, and prayer for the success of our arms.

Your affectionate brother,
Richard

On February 8th, Lieutenant Colonel Howard Willets went home on leave. Eight days later, General French appointed young Captain Thompson a Judge Advocate of a General Court Martial which remained in session until March 11th. This was a more or less permanent appointment. Court duty prevented him from serving on the picket line or marching and maneuvering in the deep snow. Also during this time, Colonel Johnson resigned and Lieutenant Colonel Willets returned to duty.[18] Thompson took time off one evening to write Hannah a long letter, the final pages of which have been lost.

Headquarters
12th N.J.Regt.
Near Falmouth, Va.
February 24, 1863

My very dear Sister Hann,

I am just returned from General Court Martial, where two poor fellows were condemned to six months hard labor without pay at the Rip-Raps.[19] I am officiating as Judge Advocate, under an appointment from General French. This will excuse me from picket duty for several weeks, a matter of no small moment during this kind of weather. The snow is some eight inches deep. Fine time for sportive young people at home. Your welcome letter of the 17th inst. is received. I must say by way of prelude that I appreciate your letters for many reasons, and among them that you do not wait for me to reply but write whenever opportunity presents. And this convinces me that 'tis love, not rule, that brings me so many kind and interesting letters from Woodside. I trust you may continue in this good calling as my epistolary powers are in abeyance and my pen no longer that of a ready writer. Em has not yet written me; Bell wrote me a short note under the following circumstances. I sent my card and a request for a letter by one of my men who went home on a furlough. She was well. . . .

As to the "little insects," the inhabitants of body and head, I will say, letting the "honest truth," I have never had any on me as yet though I have met with them in abundance. My Company are free from them, though every sunshine day may be seen on the sunny side of the hills men from other regiments picking them from their clothes—a very interesting sight. As to Frank or the Doctor, "deponent sayeth not."[20]

"Looking for me home." Now there are only two officers permitted away at a time and then only for 10 days. Nearly all the officers of my regiment have "put in" for "a leave of absence," and I would have to wait until they had been home and returned. But some of these fine days it may be I will pay you a flying visit, only don't think of it for two or three months at least.

Frank don't like snow in camp. Well, I prefer snow, cold, rain, or heat to wind. I don't like dust and to hear a. . . .

[Remainder of letter is missing.]

The week after Thompson returned to his regiment from court martial duty, the Irish Brigade exuberantly celebrated Saint Patrick's Day with races, games, and contests. More entertainment followed on March 21st, when Lieutenant Colonel Willets was commissioned as a full Colonel and Major Thomas H. Davis as Lieutenant Colonel. The officers had a party and the men got a whiskey ration. The majority was still open and Thompson longed to fill that position himself. He wrote home.

Camp near Falmouth, Va.
March 25, 1863

My dear Sister,

I had thought that I would not write you again until I could either name myself as Major or else tell who was the man, but I will write a few lines tonight if only to say that I still love you and often think of you all at the old homestead.

Colonel Willets and Lieutenant Colonel Davis have received their commissions, and still the Major's position remains unfilled. There are many aspirants and among them some influential *Democrats*. You can understand the meaning of that word. 'Tis a very doubtful question, though Brigadier General [Alexander] Hays has said he can unmake Majors as fast as Governor Parker can make them until he appoints one to his liking. That has its meaning.

I received a letter from *injured* (?) Em. She, of course, has either forgotten my letter or thinks I have, and that she can put on the injured. It won't do.

Before I forget it, have you ever received my [illegible] overcoat, sent home since my arrival here? Don't forget to answer this question. My letters want interesting matter. They are not equal to those written amid the hurry and exhaustion of rapid marches or the intoxication of victory or anything that tends to give life to them, but they are nevertheless live letters from the Army. When I think of this Army as now and when we came here, I can but rejoice. Men are awake and stirring. We have racing of horses and other games all tending to enliven the men. While at the time of arrival everyone was sad, even the lice had a downhearted demeanor and the mules looked on the style of the old cows standing tail to windward in a northeaster.

There is a late order that the men of the different divisions shall have emblems of some kind to distinguish them,[21] and indeed General Hooker has so changed things that we are not what we were.

All we now ask is that our friends at home shall bear us out and not disgrace us. Let the Copperheads be put down and let not the good and loyal citizens sacrifice sincerity for a cowardly complacency and we are all right yet.

I received a very interesting and lengthy letter from Kate yesterday. She is well and wishes to be remembered kindly to you. Nelly is there.

I enclose a letter from Mr. and Mrs. Dr. Fish, written some time ago, which please put among my letters in the drawer. I have no chance to take care of these things here. We have received orders that anything of value we are unable to carry upon our persons had better be sent home as transportation hereafter will be very uncertain. This shadows rapid movement somewhere and looks like bidding farewell to baggage. Now a horse to ride would be very pleasant under these circumstances. Don't you think so?

Nathaniel Holmes, Jr. is still here in the army selling marking plates.[22] Poor man, he looks sad and I do pity him from the bottom of my heart. I have lost another of my men by death—Henry Howell, the only child and a child of old age. His parents were about 50 and 60 when he was born. The Company will send his body home. They did this to the other man who died.

With much love, I remain your brother
Richard

Camp near Falmouth, Va.
April 12, 1863

Dear Sister,

I am just returned to camp after 24 hours picket duty in front of Fredericksburg. The pickets are placed on the edge of the river within about 100 yards of each other, Rebs on one side and ours on the other. I enclose you a written paper and a printed one sent over by the Rebs on a little boat.[23] This sending things across the river goes on when the officers are absent. They send over tobacco and our men return coffee. You cannot imagine how strange it looks to see the outposts of these contending armies sitting within easy pistol shot of each other day after day and yet no firing. The Rebs are very poorly dressed and are sadly in want of provisions. You must retain these papers as interesting documents.

The weather for the past three or four days has been warm and the roads are improving rapidly. It is now commencing to rain. What effect it will produce on the roads depends entirely upon how long it rains.

Frank Hand called on me on Thursday. He does not look well by any means and I hope he will be discharged. Lieutenants Potter and Dare are both here. I cannot tell as yet whether I shall get a leave or not. Should I receive a commission as Major I will come home; if not, then I shall remain a little while longer until after a movement. Everything here looks encouraging and I believe this army will yet gain a glorious victory. God grant that it may.

Give my love to the children and Dr.

I have not yet heard whether the sword and coat I sent home ever arrived. Don't forget to mention this in your next. I am now living in a log hut and find it much more comfortable than a canvas tent. Lieutenant Dare will reach Bridgeton tomorrow morning (Monday the 13th inst.) and leave the last of this week (Saturday).

Em wrote me a long letter last week, and from its style I judge she is enjoying herself. Bell, of course, I have not heard from. Received a long letter from Kate this week. She is well and says that Jerry and Hattie[24] are going to try farming. They intend to remain on the farm for one year and if they are pleased will continue farming. The rest of the family are well.

I was offered the position of Brigade Inspector (a staff appointment) but declined. I shall remain with this Regiment if I can for the Majority, but if not then shall try for some staff appointment. I have concluded 'tis better to have six legs than to go it on two. Write me soon, and long, very long. Tell me everything and anything. John Stevenson is still a Captain and still at the Fort.[25] He added a P.S. to Em's letter, but did not write in good spirits. I think he is getting tired of that position in that place. God bless and protect you all is the evening prayer of your brother.

Richard

Notes

[1] The Scovel party included Kate and her parents along with State Senator James (Jim) M. Scovel, who helped support laws to aid volunteer soldiers and their families. He also supported a proposed law to give volunteers the right to vote in the next presidential election, but the law did not pass.

[2] Officially, the Cooper Refreshment Hall was the Union Volunteer Refreshment Saloon and Hospital, but was popularly called the Cooper Rest or Refreshment Hall. A large building, it had been a cooper's (barrelmaker's) shop and here thousands of meals were served to men passing through Philadelphia on their way to the front. In the offices, a few cots had been set up for special cases of wounded men to rest on their way home or to other hospitals. Smith, A. W. (1911) *Reminiscences of an Army Nurse during the Civil War*. New York, Pp. 66-67.

[3] Details for this trip and later camp life come from the 1862 diary of RST and Longacre, E. G. (1988) *To Gettysburg and Beyond. . . .* Hightstown, NJ.

[4] Ellicott's Mills, a small Maryland village about ten miles to the southwest of Baltimore, was located on the Patapsco River. It was founded in 1774 on the site of flour mills erected in early colonial days, and descendants of the old Ellicott family still lived there. Thompson had occasion to deal with Mr. Ellicott and his daughter several times while at camp. Today it is known as Ellicott City.

[5] According to the Census of 1850, there were 14 males with the surname Gaither living in Howard County, Maryland. No further identification is possible.

[6] Edward M. Dubois, originally a sergeant in Company K, became a lieutenant in Company I. By war's end, he had become a lieutenant colonel.

[7] Walker enlisted as a private in Company K. He must have either worked for the Thompson family or was the son of someone who did. Thompson reported so regularly through his sister as to Walker's welfare that it can be assumed he promised the family to "look out for Albert." Walker survived the war, advancing to Corporal.

[8] The Battle of Antietam, or Sharpsburg, was fought on September 17, 1862. The Federals lost many men killed, wounded, or captured.

[9] Straight Fours is a figure in a country dance. Originally known as "Straight Hay for Four," it was derived from earlier English and Scottish dances, the Scottish version being called Straight Reel for Four. See Millar, J. F. (1991) *Country Dances of Colonial America*. Williamsburg, VA, Pp. 22-23.

[10] Thompson made a notation on the face of the Regiment's quarterly return, "This shows the change from Austrian rifles to smoothbore muskets— Buck & Ball—Dec. 12, 1862." The return was transmitted to the Chief of Ordnance, Washington, D.C. on June 13, 1863, and signed by Richard S. Thompson, Capt. Co. K 12th N.J. Vols. Commanding. On the reverse Thompson states that the return exhibits a correct statement of the public property in his charge. See Appendix B.

[11] Doctor Uriah Gilman was the regimental assistant surgeon.

[12] Franklin Hand (26/Sep/1836-1/Nov/1887) was a Cape May Court House farmer who enlisted as a private in Company H, Sixth New Jersey Volunteers. He served from September of 1862 to January of 1863 when he was discharged due to poor health. He may have tried to return to the Army of the Potomac sometime later. He and Thompson may have been distantly related; Thompson's maternal grandmother was Hannah Hand Holmes. He died of tuberculosis, leaving no direct descendents. An extensive history of the Hand family may be seen at the Cape May County Historical and Genealogical Society Library.

[13] William B. Otis had been rector of Salem, New Jersey, Episcopal Church. He conducted services at Camp Johnson but was very unpopular with the men of other denominations. After he left the Regiment, he returned to Salem. He was not replaced; there was no official regimental chaplain from then on.

[14] Like his comrades in arms, Thompson kept abreast of the political situation at home through the newspapers. His reference in these paragraphs is to the political group called Peace Democrats, also known as Copperheads because they identified themselves by wearing a copper penny in their lapel. They agitated for an immediate peace, accepting the legitimacy of the Confederacy. Thompson became incensed when he read the sentiments of the Copperheads published in the paper. The *Chicago Times* was especially sympathetic to the Copperhead cause. The soldiers from New Jersey were all so angry they held protest meetings in every regiment. Thompson and Potter, whose oratorical talents were well-known, spoke at a mass meeting on April 2nd. They both spoke fervently against the Peace Democrats and for the right to cast absentee ballots in the fall election, which had been opposed by Democratic Governor Parker. Thompson denounced the governor in all his speeches. See Longacre, *op. cit.*, Pp. 71-72.

[15] After McClellan's downfall, General Ambrose Burnside commanded the Army of the Potomac. Burnside's disastrous defeat at Fredericksburg in the previous December led to Lincoln's appointment of Joseph Hooker to this highest command. Hooker reorganized the army on a corps level, doing away with Burnside's "Grand Divisions."

[16] See Chapter One, Note 9.

[17] Thompson means the Scovel family. They moved from New Jersey to Bloomington, Illinois, sometime in 1863. He was not to see Kate again for two more years.

[18] Colonel Robert C. Johnson had not been happy in the army. While at camp at Ellicott's Mills, he wrote a friend that he was "bored to death" with much of the routine. He was also unhappy with the poor condition of the horses and mules and the old Austrian rifles they had been issued. See Johnson R. C. (September 11, 1862) Letter to Major E. A. Acton. *Lewis Leigh Collection.* Book 8. Carlisle Barracks, PA. Colonel Johnson resigned on March 8, 1862, giving his repeated bouts of lumbago and rheumatism as the reasons.

[19] Rip-Raps are unevenly broken stones used in walls or breakwaters. The men were punished by either having to break up large boulders to make these stones or by using them to build foundations. There was also, in the harbor at Hampton Roads, an artificial island called the RipRaps, which was made in the way described above. It is not known if Thompson refers to this place or a general area where large rocks were broken.

[20] Thompson uses an archaic expression here; a *deponent* is one who asserts under oath.

[21] General Hooker devised badges for the various corps. This helped both in identification of a corps and in the fostering of corps pride. Among the devices selected were the Maltese cross, diamond, and trefoil. The Second Corps adopted the trefoil, which at once became a "club." First Division badges were red; Second were white, and Third were blue. As part of the Third Division, the Twelfth New Jersey was a "Blue Clubs Regiment." Soon the boys were rallying with the shout, "Clubs are Trump!"

[22] Nathaniel Holmes, Jr., was a distant relative on Thompson's mother's side. The marking plates he was trying to sell may have been metal stamps with a design on them that could be impressed into damp writing paper, or metal stencils the soldiers could use to brush their names on to personal property. He may have been trying to make a living from this activity.

[23] These documents have been lost.

[24] Jerry and Hattie were Jeremiah and Harriet Scovel (or Scoville) Leaming who had moved to Illinois about the same time as Kate and her parents.

[25] Stevenson was promoted to Major on August 5, 1863. He was unhappy in the army even though his assignment permitted Emma to be at Fort Monroe with him. He asked for leave often to go home on personal business, some of which involved Emma's inheritance.

Chapter Four

At Chancellorsville

We have passed through three days of hard fighting.

RST to Hannah, May 4, 1863

Until Chancellorsville, the Second Corps[1] had seen little duty outside of the camp at Falmouth. The Virginia winter had been especially snowy, rainy, and muddy, preventing major military movements. The Army of the Potomac was beset by political interference and ineffective leadership.

The Twelfth New Jersey Regiment was still composed of green troops. Any "action" they had seen so far was in reviews or picket duty. Governor Parker reviewed the Regiment on April 27, 1863, after which he asked to meet Captain Thompson. It may be that the governor had heard about Thompson's April 2nd speech and thought to placate the young and vocal Republican. He offered Thompson a commission as a major in another regiment. But Thompson, despite his strong desire for a majority, was loyal to the Twelfth and his convictions. He declined. Parker gave the majority of the Twelfth N.J. Volunteers to John T. Hill, who had been a captain in the Eleventh New Jersey Volunteers.[2]

Spring brought the action the men thought they wanted to see. General Hooker began his spring campaign with a plan to move a column along the Rappahannock River far enough above Fredericksburg to cross without being detected by the Confederates. Having served under Burnside, he knew only too well that Lee's position in the city was nearly impregnable. The planned route was to descend rapidly along the northern bank of the river, covering the fords closest to the city. This maneuver would enable the bulk of the army to attack Lee's flank, making him leave his shelter. Hooker planned to meet Lee in the open in one of the large clearings near the crossroads where the Chancellor family had their home, roughly ten miles southwest of Fredericksburg. The surrounding terrain was thickly wooded, a veritable wilderness of oak and scrub pines laced with thick underbrush.

Thompson's brigade was ordered out of camp on April 28th. They marched to within two and a half miles of Bank's Ford and bivouacked. Some of the men were detailed to build a corduroy road, giving them no time to rest. The next day they marched six miles to pitch their tents in a field opposite United States Ford. It rained during the march and most of the night. The dry, brick-hard soil of Virginia once more became a heavy, clinging, slippery mass. It was made even worse by the churnings of thousands of marching feet. These feet finally stopped marching and slogged along doggedly in the miry mess. The men were soaked and miserable.

On April 13th, under more rain, they moved closer to Bank's Ford. Bone-tired, they bivouacked and rested from eleven in the morning until six in the evening. Thompson's brigade crossed the river on a pontoon bridge. They were given a two hour rest, then marched about five miles to a farm at the edge of the woods a short distance from the Chancellor House. By then it was ten o'clock at night. They slept as best they could.

At ten-thirty the next morning, May 1st, the brigade marched out past General Hooker's headquarters and down a plank road toward Fredericksburg. They heard artillery fire around noon, indicating a battle was in progress not too far away. Along the march, Lieutenant Colonel Davis became so ill that he was sent home. The men were marched back to their old bivouac at the farm where they remained all night.

The Twelfth, now very well trained, was ready for battle, and they got one. They came under attack on May 2nd. Around six o'clock in the evening, the Twelfth was ordered to advance. They formed behind a battery near the Chancellor House but the Confederates withdrew, so they were ordered to another position. While on the march they came under fire for the first time. Two men were wounded. When they arrived at their new position, they were moved closer to the front and placed in line of battle, where they remained all night. Thompson's diary reads,

> May 2. Morning our artillery opens. Heavy fighting [at] the Brick Chancellorsville House all day. Afternoon at 6 o'clock fight opens on the right. Our Brigade

at 7:15 [p.m.] pass[ed] down the Plank Road and other
Regts., 8th N.Y. Regt. on left, 30th Pa. next to the left
of the road. Several of our Regt. wounded. Our Brigade
in line of balls [and shells] all night. Artillery and
infantry firing over us.

The Confederates pounded them with artillery and musketry. The
men of New Jersey were stunned by this first encounter with the
enemy and they were also impressed by the sound they made. It was
the first time they had heard the unnerving Rebel yell. Yet they
endured, steadfastly remaining in position.[3]

Hordes of the gray-coated enemy seemed to be behind every bush
and every tree. The thick trees formed a natural screen for the
Confederates. They poured bullets on men trained only to fight on
open ground. The untried infantry was in trouble. This day, the
Twelfth learned the definition of the word *war*.

The next day, as the battle began once more, the Twelfth was sent
to rescue a part of Brigadier General Daniel Sickles's Third Corps that
was being pushed back by the Confederates. As the fighting progressed and men and officers fell dead or wounded, morale wavered.
Colonel Willets fell wounded; Color Sergeant William R. Walton of
Company B fell dead.[4] When on their right, the Fourteenth Connecticut suddenly broke and fled rearward, Company F of the Twelfth
began to follow, despite the efforts of their officers to stop them.

The exodus became contagious. The 108th New York Volunteers
and three New Jersey companies, including K, were separated from
the regiment by the 130th Pennsylvanians running through their lines
in great eagerness to the rear. As the only officer in this isolated group,
Thompson held the position for about 30 minutes. The Jerseymen,
however, followed the Pennsylvanians; they, too, broke and ran
through the woods to safety. Thompson followed his men.

Thompson's notes and his diary entries give a part of the picture.[5]

Sunday, May 3. At daylight the Confederates open
fire. We were under artillery fire until 7:30 a.m. A
Brigade of 5 regiments charged on our right flank. The
14th Conn. gave way and the right of our regiment was
forced back in a hand-to-hand fight; the left companies
under my command changed front and occupied an old
sunken road and with the 108th N.Y., which changed
front and joined on the left of our men in the old road.
We repulsed the Confederate brigade, which made
three charges, and held the position until our troops

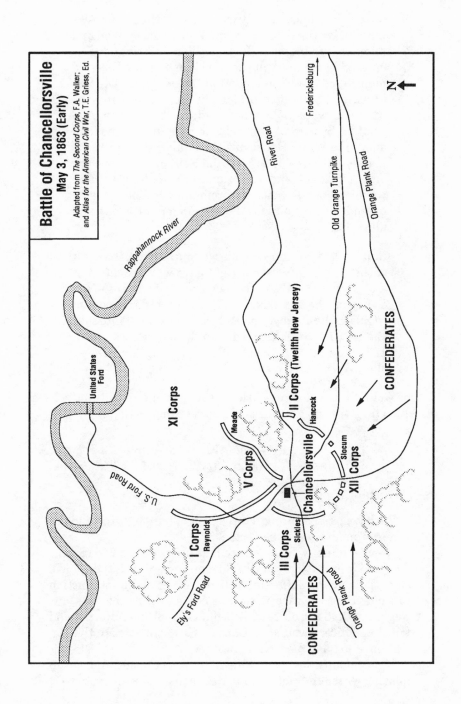

Battle of Chancellorsville
May 3, 1863 (Early)

Adapted from *The Second Corps*, F.A. Walker;
and *Atlas for the American Civil War*, T.E. Griess, Ed.

N

Fredericksburg

River Road

Old Orange Turnpike

Orange Plank Road

Rappahannock River

United States Ford

XI Corps

U.S. Ford Road

II Corps (Twelfth New Jersey)

Hancock

CONFEDERATES

Meade

V Corps

Chancellorsville

Slocum

XII Corps

I Corps
Reynolds

III Corps

Sickles

Ely's Ford Road

CONFEDERATES

Orange Plank Road

in the field about the Brick House retired. Then we
marched to the field where the White House stood and
rejoined our brigade. (List of killed and wounded as
entered in my diary at the time is as follows: Enlisted
men killed: 24, wounded: 133, missing: 22. Officers
killed [or] wounded: 6 and missing: 2.[6] Among the
wounded were Col. Willets, Adjutant Franklin, and
Captain Stratton.[7] Our Brigade remained in the field
about the White House until after all the other troops
had left it. Then at 11 a.m. the Rebs opened artillery
on our Brigade and we returned to the woods where
we joined our Division and remained in line of battle
behind the rifle pits for the remainder of the day and
all night.

Sunday, May 3. Our Brigade was outflanked, the right
of the 12th N.J. Vols; our right gave way. 2 Regts. left
and part of the 12th. The remainder of the 12th N.J.
Vols. and the 108th N.Y. Vols. held their ground and
repulsed the enemy. The 12th N.J. Vols. went into that
charge with 64 exhausted men. Killed, 24; wounded,
133, missing, 22. Col. Willets wounded. . . . I was
slightly wounded on wrist.[8]

The wound was not serious. He makes no mention of it in the letter
in which he gives the account of his part in the battle.

> *Battlefield of the Army of the Potomac*
> *Chancellorsville, May 4, 1863 (6:30 a.m.)*

My dear Sister,

We have passed through three days of hard fighting and the
victory remains yet to be decided.

Our Regiment was under fire four hours on the 2nd (Saturday) and from daylight until 7:30 a.m. yesterday (Sunday). We
were flanked and suffered much, but we have the satisfaction
to know that we gave them as good as they sent. We (our
Regiment) had one officer killed, our Colonel and Adjutant and
four line officers wounded. Captain Stratton, shot in the leg,
will have to have his leg amputated.

My company lost two killed, nine wounded, and seven
missing. After the right of our Regiment broke and retired, I

took command of the left wing and fought it for 35 minutes. We checked the Rebel's advance and had we been supported would have driven them. The Rebels lost 5 killed to our one—they are in some places lying one dead on another. Old soldiers say this is the hardest fought battle of the war and General Hancock says it's the greatest battle of modern times. The Rebels must have been fed on gunpowder and whiskey and are more like fiends than men. Jerseymen have lost none of their former glory.

Yesterday after our Brigade had been reformed on an open field, we remained the last on the field through neglect of the Colonel commanding the Brigade, and were lying down when the Rebels planted a battery on our flank and gave us the benefit of canister and shell until we had double quicked into the woods, some 200 yards away. Many men wounded, Captain Mattison for one. A shell struck within three feet of my head and bursted; it fairly lifted me off my feet and I was not long in putting on steam for the woods with the balance of the Brigade. Our new Major (a Captain Hill from the 11th N.J.) is not much and the line officers are now left to themselves.

I have commanded the Regiment three times since our Colonel was wounded. Our Lieutenant Colonel is sick and in hospital.[9]

Governor Parker when here offered me a commission as Major in another three-year New Jersey Regiment which I declined. How the matter of majorship will result, I know not. Please write to Mary and Bell and Em. Tell them that thus far I am, through God's great mercy, saved harmless. Will write again soon as opportunity offers.

Enlisted Men, 12th Regiment lost: 22 Killed, 126 Wounded, and 48 missing. Line Officers: 1 Killed, 4 wounded, 2 Missing, Colonel wounded and Adjutant wounded.

Albert Walker is all right. Pardon me in writing on such paper in such style, but I am writing on my knee on a single sheet in the rain.

From your affectionate brother,
Richard

May 4th and 5th brought them under fire again. Thompson's notes read,

May 4th. Still in same position. Rebs shell us at intervals during the day. Capt. Schooley wounded in hand. At 4 p.m. Rebs opened with artillery and infantry but are soon silenced. At 10:30 p.m. infantry opens at our front.

May 5th. Remain in same position all day. Orderly Crook, Co. K, sick, sent to hospital. In afternoon infantry opened in our front. A mere skirmish. Heavy rain starts in the afternoon. At 2 a.m. leave our position in rain and silence and move through a newly cut road to the pontoon bridge at U.S. Ford which we crossed at 5:15 a.m. and continued our march until 9:30 a.m., when we reached our old camp, wet, muddy, tired, and low spirited. Co. K lost, killed—Serg. Shuman, Privates Ward, A. Randolph, Josiah Garrison, Swinney, S. Harris; slightly wounded—Hall, Pancoast, McHenry.[10]

On May 6th, the Twelfth joined the general retreat from Chancellorsville. It was a disheartened army on another difficult and muddy march, with stumps, logs, and rocks hampering their way. With Colonel Willets wounded, Major Hill commanded the Regiment. They marched all day and most of the night, finally reaching Falmouth in the predawn darkness. Once in camp the men came to grips with what had happened. They had experienced a resounding defeat and the first loss of officers and comrades. All this and the way they conducted themselves in their first battle changed them from green troops to combat veterans.

What motivated Hooker to give up the initiative and not risk an attack of any kind may never be known. He boasted he would defeat Lee, but he did not. He had many more troops than Lee, yet seemed afraid to use them all. Low spirits and depression gripped the entire army.

On May 10th, Thompson requested a ten-day leave which came through two days later. On May 15th while he was gone, the Twelfth moved to a new location on higher ground two miles south of where they had been. They named it Camp Willets after their wounded Colonel. Since Willets would not be in command for some time, Major John T. Hill acted in his stead. Men were promoted to fill the places of officers wounded or killed. Lieutenant Potter left Company K for duty as Division Ordnance Officer. When Thompson returned from leave, he was given several opportunities for field command, but not the desired promotion. He acted as field officer until July 27th.

Chancellorsville gave Lee another victory but cost him his friend and outstanding officer, Lieutenant General Thomas J. (Stonewall) Jackson. Jackson's like was never to be found again.

To the Federal troops, the Confederate army must have seemed nearly invincible. Once more, Lee's superior generalship triumphed. Had Hooker kept his fighting spirit, Lee might not have won. With the win at Chancellorsville the South was more confident than ever. The Confederate government hoped this news would encourage England to enter the war on their side. While Lee laid plans to capitalize on his victory and invade Pennsylvania, the Union Army settled down in the camp at Falmouth for about six weeks of regrouping, refitting, and rehabilitation.

Thompson resumed his letters to Hannah on June 1st, telling her how he spent the rest of his leave.

Camp Near Falmouth, Va.
June 1, 1863

My dear Sister Hann,

My time in Philadelphia after my return from Cape May was spent in a very pleasant manner saving the few hours in the dentist's chair. On Tuesday while walking over 15th street on my way to A. I. Fish's dinner, I met for the first time in nearly three years Anna, Nettie, and Jennie Ford. They spoke and then stopped and we had quite a long conversation. They quite insisted upon my calling before leaving the city and seemed so kind that on Thursday afternoon I called. They were as of old, and all treated me as kindly as it was possible for them to do. I have the vignettes of Anna and Jennie.

On Tuesday eve I took tea with Mrs. Duckel, a friend of Lt. Davis, who has been very kind in sending me things since we have been in the service. Wednesday eve Bell and I took tea with Dr. Fish. Em came up and spent the evening.

I left Philadelphia Friday eve at 12, arrived in Washington at 6:30 a.m. on Saturday and through the negligence of the cab driver got left and had to remain in Washington until Sunday morning. I visited my sick and wounded men at the hospitals.

Upon my return to camp I found it changed to a much more agreeable location. The day after my return we had division drill under Major General French who placed our Major Hill under arrest for not bringing out the band. This left me in command. We are now having Regimental Drill every morning at 5:30 o'clock and brigade drill every afternoon. Our Major has been released from arrest.

Saturday and Sunday I was on picket. The weather is quite warm in the middle of the day.

Tell Dr. that I left $200 with A. I. Fish and if he can advise me what to do with it, I will invest it. I also have one share of C & A stock; the January dividend has never been drawn.

I am in doubt whether our army will make a forward or backward movement, but think a movement will soon be made somewhere. There are orders to hold ourselves ready to move at 30 minutes notice.

You must write me often and much. Colonel Johnson, the Provost Marshal of the 1st District of New Jersey, asked me who should be appointed to enroll the names of the county for draft. I gave him Frank Howard's name. I suppose he has been appointed. He will receive $3 per day and that will repay him.

Love to all from your brother,
Richard

Thompson was Brigade Officer of the Day on June 4th. The next day, Colonel Smyth ordered brigade inspection. Afterward, Colonel Smyth gave Thompson's Company K high praise for their military manner. The memory of Chancellorsville began to fade, and the men's spirits revived. They regained their battle-ready status. On June 7th, Thompson again served as a judge at a court martial. Two days later Lee pulled his army out of Fredericksburg and began to move north.

Notes

[1] The Twelfth New Jersey was now in the Second Brigade, under Brigadier General William Hays of the Second Corps, commanded by Major General W. H. French.

[2] Colonel Johnson had resigned March 1st. Lieutenant Colonel J. Howard Willets now became a full colonel; Major Thomas H. Davis became lieutenant colonel. John T. Hill, was from Boonton, Morris County, in the northern part of the state. Although a combat veteran (Fredericksburg) he was given his majority by Governor Parker just to fill the vacancy in the Twelfth. The men resented this, believing the governor was playing politics. He was; Hill's father

was a state assemblyman. Hill served until February 24, 1864, when his recurring bouts of rheumatism could no longer be ignored. He resigned on that date and left the Regiment, having earned the respect of the men. Thompson filled his position. Longacre, E. G. (1988) *To Gettysburg and Beyond.* . . . Hightstown, NJ, Pp. 81 & 172.

[3] *Ibid.*, p. 95.

[4] Foster, J. Y. (1868) *New Jersey and the Rebellion.* . . . Newark, NJ, Pp. 302-303.

[5] After the war, Thompson used old envelopes and scraps of paper on which he made additional notes and copied excerpts from his diary to help refresh his memory prior to writing a full account of his wartime activities, which he never completed.

[6] The records put the count at one officer, Lieutenant Joseph Pierson, and 23 enlisted men killed; six officers and 26 men wounded, with 22 missing. See U.S. War Department. (1880-1901) *The War of the Rebellion: A Compilation of the Official Records of the Union and Confederate Armies.* Series I, Vol. 25, Part. 1, p. 378 (Hereafter abbrievated *OR*); and Longacre, *op. cit.*, p. 99.

[7] Edward L. Stratton was captain of Company F.

[8] His notes, written years later, are from the collection of the authors. "I had my right wrist bruised by a piece of the same shell that wounded Captain Mattison [Captain Hamilton A. Mattison, Company H] in the foot."

[9] The officers of the Twelfth had a number of health problems. Colonel Johnson resigned his commission on February 27, 1863, after a fall from his horse injured his back and made his already painful rheumatism worse. Lieutenant Colonel J. Howard Willets replaced him and was shot in the right arm at Chancellorsville. Major Thomas H. Davis also suffered from rheumatism and was often hospitalized. Thompson was called upon to do Davis's duty from time to time.

[10] Captain William H. Schooley of Company C; Sergeant John P. Shuman; Privates William H. Ward, Asa A. Randolph, John G. Swinney, George A. Harris, Edward C. Hall, Thomas H. Pancoast, and George McHenry. *Ibid., Pp. 368, 394-396.*

Chapter Five

On the Road to Gettysburg

I would rather fight than make a forced march....
RST to Hannah, June 20, 1863

Hooker's attempts to break through Confederate positions around Fredericksburg and march on Richmond failed. Encouraged by this failure the Confederate government finally accepted Lee's plans to invade the North. They hoped a decisive victory on northern soil would encourage England to recognize the Confederacy's validity as an independent nation. Also, they hoped that such an invasion would force Federal troops to withdraw from around Vicksburg and Chattanooga, relieving the pressure there. On the 3rd of June, Confederate forces started to move out of Fredericksburg.

By June 9th only Lieutenant General Ambrose P. Hill's Corps was left to defend Fredericksburg. On the 13th, Hooker moved the bulk of his army northward in pursuit of Lee. The Second Corps, including the Twelfth New Jersey, was left behind to bluff the Confederates into thinking the camp was still at full strength. The men now had to be actors as well as soldiers. The Second Corps bustled about, pretending to be all eight corps of the Army of the Potomac.

Camp Near Falmouth, Va.
June 12, 1863

Dear Brother and Sister,

We are again on the move and where, or for what, is a question. The whole army is engaged in the movement. Yesterday received your double letter and the enclosed from John

W. Candy. Tell John (should you think proper to sell) that my terms are "cash up and no trust."

Lieutenant W. E. Potter is and has been for some time Ordnance Officer of this division. The position is one of trust, and he has done himself honor. He still remains a 2nd Lieutenant in my company and is merely detailed in that office. 'Tis called "Departmental Staff."

I suppose you have seen that the Rebel loss in the Battle of Chancellorsville according to their published list of names, has amounted to 25,000 killed and wounded. This beside[s] the prisoners and missing shows we were not idle while over the river. In reply to the enemy and home traitors who claim the victory of that hard fought field, we might ask, as was asked of the English after the Battle of Bunker's Hill, "how many such victories their army could stand?" In my opinion (if one so low in military life may venture an opinion) the Rebels were defeated but God did not intend us to succeed. As a nation we put too much trust in our own power, too much confidence in human skill. Had we been entirely successful, we would have called it Hooker's Victory, and forgot God.

As at the Battle of Waterloo the destinies of the universe were turned upon a rain in the morning, the directing finger of a convoy to Bülow, the shake of a peasant's head when asked by Napoleon of the sunken road of Ohain.[1] So with us God has demonstrated to any thinking mind that so far as man was concerned the battle was fought and won by us and yet we gained nothing. God was not recognized in victory. He forced a recognition in the failure of our enterprise. Let those at home pray that the nation and army may trust in God.

So then there is in truth an engine, a railroad engine in the County of Cape May; that is good news and to think of a ride from Philadelphia to the Courthouse in three hours is a cause of pleasure though we travel it but once a year.

I have not heard from Em, Bell, or Mary since my return. Em is certainly at fault about writing. Captain or Major Stevenson[2] rather got the start of me in going to Richmond.

Remember me very kindly to the children when you write.

Yes, Hann, Anna was kind, so were they all, kind, and it reminded me of old times to see them all. I have a very pretty vignette of Anna, and think from the picture of that said Lieutenant he must be slow, very slow.

With many kind wishes, and in the hope of hearing from you soon, I remain,

Your affectionate brother,
Richard

The Confederates under Hill left Fredericksburg on June 14th. The Twelfth left Falmouth at nine o'clock that same night, marching until eleven-thirty. For the rank and file soldiers this march would be their most grueling; its end, their most momentous. They did not know they were on their way to Gettysburg.

June 15th was a miserable day for marching. The men in their woolen uniforms suffered greatly from heat; the temperature reached 102° by afternoon. Mercifully, they were permitted to rest during the hottest part of the day, commencing again as the evening began. They marched more or less constantly for the next five days when on the 20th they passed by the old battleground of Bull Run (Manassas). Thompson made this diary notation, ". . .see shells, balls, large quantities of human bones, men half-buried. . . ." It must have been a disturbing sight.[3]

When they arrived at Gainesville in the afternoon, they set up camp and stayed for two days. Thompson wrote Hannah, mistakenly giving the place name of Centerville. At this time, as acting major, he was entitled to ride a horse and was grateful for the privilege.

Bivouac at Centerville, Va.
June 20, 1863

My dear Sister Hann,

Our Corps left camp near Fredericksburg on Sunday last and marched to this place, a distance of some 57 miles. We came via Stafford Court House, Dumfries, Bristoe Station near Fairfax Station, etc. The march has been a most difficult one. On Monday we marched 22 miles and the thermometer stood [at] 102°.

Where we are to go now, I cannot tell. I had rather fight than make a forced march, a thing known little of by persons who have never made one, never forgotten by those who have. To see men fall from exhaustion, clothes wet, faces and teeth black with dust, lips parched, eyes sunken, feet blistered, and then driven on at the point of the bayonet. This is a forced march.

This maneuver of the Rebels will I think wake up the sleeping North and result in good to our arms.

I will write you from time to time when opportunity offers. I am still acting as Major and therefore will continue to move on six instead of two legs.

I am quite well. Received letter from Em the other day. Mrs. Fish had given Bell my vignettes, one for you. Write me soon.

Written in haste in much love by,

Your affectionate brother,
Richard

By the 26th of June they were at the Potomac which they crossed on a pontoon bridge the following day. They enjoyed a little respite from the perilous heat and humidity of the march. Thompson's diary makes mention of a swim he and several others took in a millrace on the evening of the 28th. The next day his regiment was given the duty of guarding the baggage train; they marched about 32 miles in nearly 12 hours. Thompson and his regiment were on their way to the most unforgettable days of their lives.

Hooker planned to deploy his men around Frederick, Maryland, cut Lee's lines of communication, and stop the Confederate invasion of the north. He was in position on June 28th, but he did not get the opportunity to put his plan into action. In Washington, Lincoln's patience with Hooker was exhausted. He had waited for McClellan to act, had suffered Burnside's failures, and had hoped with Hooker. For a number of complex reasons all of his generals had failed. Lincoln wanted and needed a decisive leader for the Army of the Potomac, so, on June 28th, while Hooker waited at Frederick, Lincoln replaced him with Major General George Gordon Meade. Unlike Hooker, Meade would fight. He was unable to avoid it.[4]

Notes

[1] Thompson refers here to seemingly inconsequential events of chance that led to Napoleon's defeat at Waterloo. Friedrich Wilhelm von Bülow, Count Dennewitz (1755-1816), was a Prussian general who participated in defeating Napoleon in three battles: Dennewitz, Leipzig, and Waterloo. He commanded the Prussian IV Corps, encamped at Liège during the Battle of Waterloo. Ohain was a tiny hamlet located below the swampland near the plain of Waterloo. See *Encyclopedia Britannica*, (1910) New York, Vol. 4, p. 795; and Expilly, J. J. d' (1767) *Dictionnaire Geographique Historique et Politique des Gaules et de la France*. Amsterdam, Netherlands. p. 294.

[2] Thompson alludes to Major Stevenson's participation in the Peninsula Campaign. (See Chapter Two, Note 2 and Chapter Three, Note 25).

[3] The first Battle of Bull Run (Manassas) ended in a rout. Union survivors could not get away fast enough, neither could the burial parties. They placed the dead in shallow graves, some of which were uncovered by rains, and some, sad to say, by souvenir hunters. The Confederate dead were not buried much more carefully. Families from both sides later came to disinter their loved ones for reburial at home. In their grief, they were often careless of other graves.

[4] Near the end of June, Hooker had asked to be relieved. After he was replaced, he was sent to the West, where in September he was given command of the Twentieth Corps, a combination of the remnants of the Eleventh and Twelfth Corps.

Chapter Six

Gettysburg

The fight was a serious matter.
The ground in our front is actually covered with dead Rebels.

RST to Emma and Isabella, July 4, 1863

During the next three weeks Lee moved through Maryland and into Pennsylvania by way of the Shenandoah Valley, while Meade made his way into Maryland around the city of Frederick. Due to the lack of intelligence from General J. E. B. Stuart's cavalry or Lieutenant General R. S. Ewell's Second Corps, Lee did not know the exact location of the Union troops. Despite this handicap he went ahead with his plan to invade Pennsylvania and capture Harrisburg. He then planned to march across the state to Philadelphia and perhaps attack Washington. During the evening of June 28th, he received word through Longstreet's spy, Harrison,[1] of the position of Federal forces. This knowledge forced him to concentrate his forces close to the Pennsylvania-Maryland line, in the areas of Cashtown and Gettysburg. General Meade's plans were to work through Frederick toward Harrisburg. Like Hooker, he hoped to sever the Confederate lines of communication and prevent Lee from threatening Washington.

Both sides were seeking the other with no definite battleground in mind. The Confederates had heard a rumor that a large quantity of shoes and other supplies were to be found in Gettysburg, a town made strategically important by the intersection of a number of important roads.[2] Many Confederate soldiers had worn out their shoes during the long march; their supply wagons had no replacements. General J. J. Pettigrew's brigade of Major General Henry Heth's division moved into Gettysburg intent on a shoe-foraging expedition. In the morning of the 1st of July Federal General John Buford's cavalry division,

which was in the town on June 30th, came upon Pettigrew's First
Brigade. Buford gathered his men together to defend the little town.
Armed with new Spencer carbines, his troops dismounted and held off
infantry attacks by Heth's and W. D. Pender's divisions which had also
converged on the village.[3]

Meanwhile, General John F. Reynold's First Corps and O. O.
Howard's Eleventh Corps rushed up to assist Buford. Before any real
defense could be made, a Rebel sharpshooter shot and killed Reynolds.
Union forces took heavy casualties and pulled back. The stronger
Confederates captured McPherson's Ridge and moved toward Semi-
nary Ridge. While the Confederates prepared for another assault,
Ewell's Corps arrived and prepared to attack the Federal north flank.
The beleaguered Federals called for help. General O. O. Howard's
Eleventh Corps was ordered to come up quickly to strengthen the
Union line, yet the Federals were driven back through the town. By
the end of the day, The Army of Northern Virginia held the village of
Gettysburg. Thompson recorded in his diary,

> 1863–July 1, Wednesday. I am acting as Field Officer.
> At 7 a.m. marched through Trevania (prettiest place
> seen since we left Washington), continue[d] march
> through Taneytown & other burghs to near Gettys-
> burg. Near Gettysburg met some of our army wounded
> from the Battle of Gettysburg this morning. We
> crossed the Pennsylvania line at 5 p.m. Bivouac in a
> field some two miles from Gettysburg village.

The 2nd day of July brought more action. The two forces again faced
each other, with the Confederates occupying Seminary Ridge and the
Federals, Cemetery Ridge. Between them was a mile of shallow,
rolling valley with open fields, bounded by woods and the Emmitsburg
Road. Thompson wrote,

> 4 o'clock a.m. continued march towards the front. At
> 5 a.m. the first gun was fired, no reply. We go into line
> of battle on a gentle incline (left center). We witness
> the formation in the valley between the two armies
> which is in plain sight of both lines. At 4:45 p.m. the
> artillery on both sides opened fire and continued on
> our left until dark.

Thompson's contribution in the Battle of Gettysburg was his role in
the capture and destruction of the Bliss barn.[4] This action, virtually

ignored in later history, was of pivotal importance to the outcome of the day's events. The Bliss farm became the prize in a deadly tug-of-war between the two armies.

During those fateful July days, William Bliss's farm was in the worst possible location for the safety of the family. Located in a swale between rolling slopes, it was about 500 yards from the main Confederate line and ideally located for the Rebels. The Confederate army, massing in the woods along Seminary Ridge, used the house and the barn as a forward post. The large barn, some 75 x 35 feet, with a lower level of fieldstone and an upper level of oak, was as strong as a fort. In the stout oak walls of the overshot upper story its long, narrow "loophole" windows supplied perfect cover for Rebel sharpshooters.

Around four in the afternoon of July 2nd a group of Confederate infantrymen left the wooded ridge and occupied the farm. These men belonged to a Mississippi brigade of A. P. Hill's Corps under the command of Brigadier General Carnot Posey. Sharpshooters took their places at the upstairs loopholes. Other men occupied the house and outbuildings or took positions in the farmyard. From there they began firing at skirmishers from the Twelfth New Jersey who had been sent out in front of part of the Second Corps massed on Cemetery Ridge.

Colonel Thomas A. Smyth, commanding the Second Brigade (to which the Twelfth belonged), had positioned his men on the rocky and weed choked ground behind the low stone walls of the rise above the Emmitsburg Road. The men of the Twelfth had the First Delaware Infantry on their left, with the Fourteenth Connecticut next on *their* left. To the right was the 111th New York Infantry and behind them up the partially wooded slope known locally as Ziegler's Grove was the 125th New York.[5] To afford themselves more protection, the Union troops had torn down rails from nearby farm fences and laid them atop the two feet high stone walls.

With Posey's Mississippians in control of the farm the men of the Second Corps were pinned down. Pender's and Mahone's brigades could ready themselves for the planned attack on Cemetery Ridge by moving up to this position, using the farm buildings as a shield. Throughout the day, the Rebels harassed the Second Brigade's position. By 6:00 p.m., Brigadier General Alexander Hays, commander of the Second Corps, Third Brigade, had lost several good men and his patience. He ordered Colonel Smyth to send some men to put a stop to the unfriendly fire.

Two companies of the 106th Pennsylvania from Brigadier General William Harrow's division were closest to the farm. They were sent under the command of Lieutenant Colonel W. L. Curry along with a company of Minnesota sharpshooters to dislodge the Confederates. They could not. The Minnesotans withdrew, but Curry deployed his Pennsylvanians as skirmishers. General Hays saw how strong the Rebel position was. He next ordered most of the Delaware troops under Lieutenant Colonel Edward P. Harris to relieve Curry's men. Colonel Smyth ordered part of the Twelfth New Jersey in to the support of the Delaware men. Major Hill called on Captain Henry F. Chew[6] and his Company I. Around 7:00 a.m. these troops connected with the Pennsylvanians who, relieved, returned to their former position.

From inside the barn and house, from behind trees, hedges, and fenceposts, the Confederates fired on their new attackers. Under the blistering summer sun the Union troops endured a blizzard of minie balls. To add to the deafening noise and confusion, farm animals Bliss left behind now ran amok, adding their assorted noises to the din. With his men falling wounded, Lieutenant Colonel Harris lost his nerve and ran. His Delaware troops panicked with him, broke and ran also. (Harris was later cashiered.)

Major Hill ordered more Jerseymen to help Company I, which was now stranded. He sent Companies B, E, G, and H with Captain Samuel B. Jobes of Company G in command. They moved out from the far side of the Bryan barn,[7] which was just a little to the right of their line and down the slope a few hundred feet. This maneuver kept them from any direct fire from the upper windows of the Bliss barn. But as they charged down the slope, fire from the Bliss house and farmyard caught them. Captain Charles K. Horsfall of Company E was killed. Captain Jobes and Lieutenant Stephen G. Eastwick were wounded. These events notwithstanding the Jerseymen surged forward, bravely holding their fire until nearly on top of their target. Then they let loose a storm of the murderous buck and balls. Facing this new assault, the Mississippians took their turn to run. Those who stayed, surrendered. The barn was captured. Ninety-two of Posey's men, including seven officers, were sent up the slope to the Union lines. The Twelfth lost 40 men, killed and wounded.

Despite their valor, the Twelfth New Jersey held the barn for only an hour or so. Confederate artillery rained down, pulverizing the small out-buildings and making the larger ones a trap. More of Posey's men began moving off Seminary Ridge toward the farm. It was growing dark by now and it seemed a prudent idea to withdraw. The New Jersey soldiers left their hard won prize and climbed back up to the safety of their own lines.

The Rebels were not ready to give up such a strategic position. They waited until the early hours of the morning, then quietly returned to the empty barn. At dawn sharpshooters again began picking off their targets. Thompson recorded the action in his July 2nd diary entry.

> Companies B, G, H, & E of our Regt. 12th N.J. charged an old stone barn and captured 67 privates, 18 non-commissioned officers and 7 officers and returned to our regiment. Our Regt. is in line behind some stones and fence rails. In this charge on the barn Capt. Horsfall was killed and Lt. Eastwick was wounded. Our loss (in 12th N.J.V.) was 14 killed and 36 wounded and 9 missing.

At 7:30 a.m. on July 3rd Captain Thompson, still doing temporary duty as a major, was ordered to charge the barn. He chose companies A, C, D, F and his own Company K. They leaped over the wall, charged down the slope, crossed the road, and pushed their way through the trampled stalks of grain to their objective. After strenuous fighting they finally retook the barn, but 20 or so men were wounded, including two lieutenants. Thompson was unhurt. A Confederate major and ten men were captured. Despite their gallant efforts Thompson's men needed help to keep possession of the hard won buildings.

Colonel Theodore G. Ellis and four companies of the Fourteenth Connecticut relieved Thompson and his men, who then returned to their position behind the wall. General Hays, aware that yet another fight for the barn would take place, ordered it burned. At 10:00 a.m. he called for a volunteer to carry the orders to Colonel Ellis. Sergeant Charles A. Hitchcock of the 111th New York responded. Running through the stalks of grain as best he could, Hitchcock delivered the orders and the matches. As the Connecticut men were setting the hay and straw afire in one corner of the barn, a shell from a Confederate battery exploded on the roof setting it aflame. Hitchcock and the rest of the men fled for safety back up the ridge, but before leaving the area, Hitchcock picked a bunch of flowers growing in the barnyard and presented them to the general when he reported back! Hays immediately promoted him to Lieutenant.[8] The sergeant was wounded in the arm but the troublesome barn and house, now burning to destruction, were no longer a haven for the enemy.[9]

Had the barn remained standing, it might have played a significant part in the outcome of Pickett's charge. Left in Confederate hands it would have been a place of relative safety behind which the men could have gathered to re-group and re-form for a second attack on the Union

Battle Field of Gettysburg Pa —

July 5 1863.

My dear Sister Hann — I am well & uninjured — dirty & hungry. Our Corps arrived here early on the morning of 2nd inst Thursday — We were under cannonading all day. at 6 P.M. four of our Companies charged a house & barn occupied by Rebel sharp shooters — We lost our Capt Killed several men, and one Lt. & about forty men wounded — They captured 69 men — 18 non-Com: officers & 7 commissioned officers —

On the 3d inst Friday at day light the battle opened The Rebels tried the right & left, & then the centre

at 7.30 am I took command of five of our Companies & led the charge upon the house & barn occupied by the Reb sharp shooters — We lost some 25 men & two Lts — captured a Reb major & four men Our Regt was greatly praised by Gen Hays comde of our Div his words were that the "12 Regt is the only one able to take that barn". The others objected to leading their men against what they called certain death — We took it twice — at 11.30 am the Rebels brought one hundred and sixty cannon to bear on our position & shelled us until 2.45 P.M. They silenced our two batteries that our division was supporting & then charged with

An Excerpt from RST's Letter to his Sister, Hannah Thompson Leaming, commenting on the Battle for the Bliss Barn at Gettysburg.
(*From the Authors' Collection*)

line. Sharpshooters would have had the opportunity to cut down more Union defenders up on the slope before the charge was made. (See Appendix C)[10]

Following the action at the Bliss barn Confederate artillery began a merciless bombardment of the Union lines, while infantry units gathered for a massive assault. The shells of the 150 guns that were trained on the Union position went over the heads of the men in the most forward lines. They fell in the rear, damaged the Bryan farmhouse and barn, splintered the apple trees in Ziegler's Grove, and came uncomfortably close to General Meade's headquarters behind the crest of the hill. After several seemingly endless hours the firing finally stopped. In the oppressive silence men waited for the next move. The Confederate infantrymen, in line since ten in the morning, were given the signal at three in the afternoon.

Soon after moving out from the shelter of the trees, Confederate infantry came to a low depression in the land where they dressed their lines and started their march, going past the smoldering ashes of the Bliss barn to their fate as part of Pickett's charge. In close formation, battle flags flying, nearly 15,000 men in gray began walking up the rise, then trotting, then running, all the while shouting their terrorizing "Rebel yell."

The Twelfth New Jersey were in splendid position to absorb the assault. They faced Pettigrew's men deployed on the left of the Confederate assault force. They learned later these men were the same North Carolinians and Mississippians who had defeated them so effectively at Chancellorsville, then part of a division under Major General Isaac R. Trimble.

As the men came up the slope under the broiling sun, the Twelfth held their fire until the Confederate front ranks were within 50 yards of their wall. The Twelfth's old muskets did not have any effectiveness at long range but were quite lethal at close range.[11] Under ordinary circumstances their ammunition was one round ball that fit the bore of their muskets and three small buckshot. While awaiting Pettigrew's advance, they tore open their cartridges, threw the balls away, and loaded their guns with as many as 25 buckshot pellets. At close range this was accurate and deadly. As the Confederate lines neared the wall, the men of the Twelfth rose up and fired as rapidly as they could, at nearly point-blank range. It was as if the Jerseymen were taken by a mass madness; they fired over and over and over. The dead and wounded piled up like cordwood. Survivors of this withering fire who tried to run or crawl back down the hill were shot in the back. After annihilating the front ranks, the Twelfth turned to Pettigrew's flank,

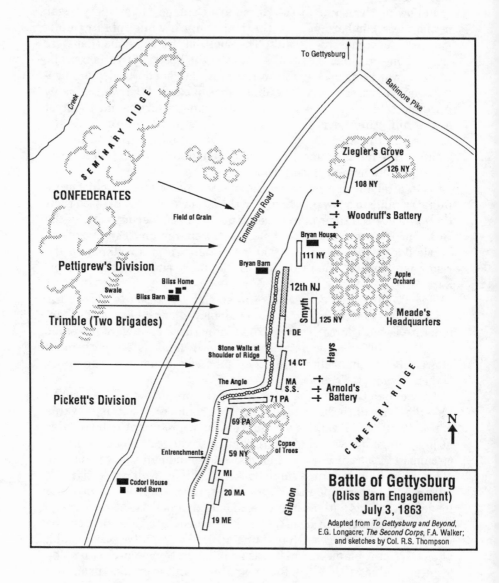

To Gettysburg

Baltimore Pike

Creek

SEMINARY RIDGE

Ziegler's Grove

126 NY

108 NY

CONFEDERATES

Field of Grain

Emmitsburg Road

Woodruff's Battery

Bryan House

111 NY

Bryan Barn

Pettigrew's Division

Apple Orchard

Bliss Home

Swale

Bliss Barn

12th NJ

Smyth

Meade's Headquarters

125 NY

Trimble (Two Brigades)

1 DE

Stone Walls at Shoulder of Ridge

14 CT

Hays

Pickett's Division

The Angle

MA S.S.

Arnold's Battery

71 PA

CEMETERY RIDGE

69 PA

N

Copse of Trees

Entrenchments

59 NY

7 MI

Codori House and Barn

20 MA

Gibbon

19 ME

Battle of Gettysburg
(Bliss Barn Engagement)
July 3, 1863

Adapted from *To Gettysburg and Beyond,*
E.G. Longacre; *The Second Corps,* F.A. Walker;
and sketches by Col. R.S. Thompson

which was trying to reach the clump of trees behind the wall in front of Gibbon's[12] division (now under Hancock's command). They next turned to fire on Pickett's men.

Confederate attacking fire was heavy; the Federals took many losses. Colonel Smyth was wounded in the face but remained in command. He reported later that some Rebels had come to within 30 or 40 feet along the entire front. Some New Jersey soldiers later remembered a young man who fell dead within 20 feet of their line and another who reached the little Bryan barn at their right. He managed to get off one shot before falling. The Twelfth captured two battle flags in the encounter.

The hot July sun shone on a scene that it had never before seen in this land nor would ever see again: thousands of countrymen attempting to kill each other while infant fruit was taking shape on the apple trees in the grove behind them. By evening Gettysburg was filled with wounded and dying men from both armies. All field hospitals filled to overflowing, and all available church buildings in town were converted to serve as hospitals. The Lutheran Theological Seminary, for which Seminary Ridge was named, served as a hospital for Confederate wounded.[13] Other wounded were housed in stores, private homes, barns, makeshift shelters and tents, or left to lie in the open.

The men of the Twelfth received commendations from their superior officers. Colonel Smyth's report stated, "The officers and men behaved with the greatest coolness and endured this terrible [artillery] fire with much fortitude. As the fire . . . slackened, their infantry moved upon our position in three lines . . . Major John T. Hill, commanding Twelfth New Jersey Volunteers, directed his men to retain their fire during the charge of the enemy until they were within twenty yards, when, at his command, so tremendous a fire of buck and ball was poured into their ranks as to render it impossible that one of them should reach the breastworks "[14]

After noon of the next day, July 4th, a severe storm struck with the intensity of a cloudburst. Although it made those wounded left in the open totally miserable, it had a cleansing effect on the land, washing away blood and other evidence of the carnage.

While part of the Twelfth was on duty tending to casualties and burying the dead of both armies, Thompson, huddled under a blanket in the pouring rain, penned a letter to his sisters Emma and Isabella revealing that he was still under the stress of the battle. He also drew a small map showing his position at the time of the attack called "Pickett's Charge."

Other members of the regiment were on a skirmish line which proved to be lively duty, as firing from the Confederate lines was brisk. Still others were sent out to collect armaments left behind. Potter, in charge of ordnance, reported 2,500 pieces of arms were collected from the dead or wounded, and at least another 1,000 left uncollected when darkness fell.

Battlefield Near Gettysburg, Pa.
July 4, 1863.

My dear Sisters Em and Bell,

I have only time to say I am uninjured and well though dirty to an extent never before known to my small body. Our Corps arrived here on the 2nd inst. early in the morning. We at once went into position on the front [and] were under fire from Rebel batteries all day. At about 6 p.m. four of our companies—B, E, H, and G—were ordered to charge a stone barn situated between the lines, from which the Rebel sharpshooters were troubling our skirmishers. They charged. We lost one captain killed, one lieutenant and about 40 men wounded, but they took the barn and captured 97 prisoners. Yesterday morning at daylight the battle opened at 7:30 a.m. I, in command of five of our companies (K among them), charged the barn and house again. We lost two lieutenants and some 20 were wounded, took the barn and house driving the Rebels out, captured one major, and some privates. There were quite a number of Rebels killed.

At 11:30 a.m. the Rebels brought to bear on our position 160 cannon and continued the fire until 3:30 p.m. This was considered by old officers the hardest field cannonading ever known in this country. They silenced two of our batteries and then charged us with a division and a half of infantry with bayonets fixed. We let their three lines come up within short range and then our boys opened on them with buck and ball. The fight was a serious matter. The ground in our front is actually covered with dead Rebels. Our regiment took over 500 prisoners, captured two stands of colors. Our division captured 15 stands of colors. Our loss was quite small. I cannot write a description of their charge or of our fighting. The ground is covered with their dead.

We have lost about 120 in killed, wounded and missing. Our position is this [here he drew a small map]. Our division is immediately upon the apex of the angle and where the great battery fire is given for our amusement. You must remember in reading the account that we are 2nd Corps, 3rd Division, 2nd Brigade, 12 N.J.V., and I can safely say we have no reason to be ashamed of our name.

You will see accounts of the heavy artillery fight on Friday the 3rd inst. It was upon our position they concentrated the fire of 160 guns.

I must close. It is raining very hard and I am writing under a blanket covering my head and body. That God will give us the victory and peace is the prayer of your affectionate brother. Remember me kindly to Mr. and Mrs. Dr. Fish and Mrs. F.

Richard

On the following day, while his men were burying more of the numerous Confederate dead, Thompson, now more composed and able to write in greater detail, wrote the following letter to his sister Hannah. In it, he tells the story of his action at the Bliss barn and of the hopeless charge that resulted in the debacle of death at the copse of trees.

Battlefield of Gettysburg, Pa.
July 5, 1863

My dear Sister Hann,

I am well and uninjured, dirty and hungry. Our Corps arrived here early on the morning of 2nd inst., Thursday. We were under cannonading all day. At 6 p.m. four of our companies charged a house and barn occupied by Rebel sharpshooters. We lost one captain killed, several men, and one lieutenant, and about 40 men wounded. They captured 69 men, 18 non-com officers, and 7 commissioned officers. On the 3rd inst., Friday, at daylight, the battle opened. The Rebels tried the right and left, and then the centre.

At 7:30 a.m. I took command of five of our companies and led the charge upon the house and barn occupied by the Reb sharpshooters. We lost some 25 men and two lieutenants, captured a Reb major and four men. Our Regiment was greatly praised by Gen. Hays, Commander of our Division. His words were that "the 12th Regiment is the only one able to take that barn." The others objected to leading their men against what they called certain death. We took it twice. At 11:30 a.m. the

Rebels brought 160 cannon to bear on our position and shelled us until 2:45 p.m. They silenced our two batteries that our Division was supporting and then charged with their infantry in three lines of battle, the rear line with fixed bayonets driving on the other two. This commenced immediately after the silencing of our batteries. We let them come up within easy range and then opened fire. They came up to our line, but only to die. They were driven back. Not over one-sixth of the Rebels who made the charge led by Longstreet and Hill went back. The ground in our front is covered with their dead. We are at this moment burying them. Our Regiment captured 600 prisoners and two stands of colors. Lieutenant Richard Townsend, son of William Townsend of Dennisville, was shot dead.[15] He joined our Regiment on the 30th of June. Our Regiment went into this fight with 345 men and officers. We have lost in killed, wounded, and missing, 140. Albert Walker is well and all right. Remember in reading the accounts of the battle that our regiment is 2nd Brigade, 3rd Division, 2nd Corps. We are proud of our name and have lost nothing in honor during this fight. General Pickett in person commanded the charge upon our division.[16] We occupy the centre, the apex as it were of our line of battle. Lee's plan on the 3rd was (so the prisoners tell us) to demoralize us with the artillery and then make a determined charge, but we were too many for them. Jackson's old command were the troops who charged us. There are more dead and wounded in our immediate front than we have men in our Regiment, two to one. Our loss was quite small considering the fire we sustained.

I am writing on Rebel paper taken from their dead. I enclose a flower from the battlefield. Yesterday, 4th inst., we had nothing but skirmishing. General Hays attempted to charge again the old stone barn and his old brigade refused to go. He came to our Regiment and took K and I, but after approaching near the barn concluded not to charge. Our boys have never yet refused to do their duty. I enclose a Rebel note taken from a dead lieutenant.[17] Write to Mary. I wrote to Em and to William Townsend. Please save the notes as curiosities. Trusting that God will soon give us the good result of peace as he has given us the victory, I remain your loving brother,

Richard

Confederate firing began to dwindle as the day wore on. At dark General Hays ordered Company K to push as close to the enemy lines as possible to determine why. Thompson took his men down the wet and slippery slope in the darkness, stumbling over abandoned weapons and corpses remaining in the field. They were not far from their lines when they were fired upon, not by Confederates but by their own nervous pickets on the ridge. Thompson quickly moved his men rearward as they were now in more danger from their own men than from the enemy. Safely regaining their old position, they settled down behind their familiar stone wall. Meade waited all day for another attack that did not come. Lee, heartsick and weary, had withdrawn his forces out of Pennsylvania and was on the road back to Virginia. The battles at Gettysburg were over.

The Twelfth New Jersey lost nearly one-fourth of its total complement, 115 volunteer soldiers. Two officers and 21 men were killed; four officers and 79 men were wounded. Nine men were missing. Thompson's Company K lost two privates killed and five wounded, one of whom died a few hours later. Two privates and a sergeant missing during the Bliss barn engagement died in 1864 as prisoners at Andersonville.

The action at the Bliss barn is often given little attention in the general history of the Civil War, yet it was of pivotal importance to the outcome of the Confederate charge. A few questions remain: (1) If the barn had remained undisturbed and in Confederate hands, how many Union officers and men would have been killed by the sharpshooters at its windows? (2) If the barn and house had not been destroyed, would Pickett have used the farm as his command post instead of the Codori farm, almost a mile away? (3) If the Bliss buildings had not been taken, would the farm have been a staging area or a haven for men to re-group?

The Bliss barn engagement had many heroes. Men from several companies showed extraordinary courage braving the fire which poured down on them from its windows and behind its walls. Several men gave their lives to secure this farm. Thompson's part in this action was of short duration, yet he and his command flushed out the last of the Rebel soldiers trying to maintain control of this vital position.[18]

Notes

[1] The spy Harrison was originally identified in 1970 as James Harrison, a Richmond actor. However, later research indicates him to be Henry Thomas Harrison, who served as a Mississippi scout in the early days of the war. He was later a special agent of John A. Seddon, the Confederate Secretary of War who sent him to the Gettysburg area. He was paid $200.00 per month *in*

United States currency for his espionage activities. See Sifakis, S. (1988) *Who Was Who in the Civil War.* New York, p. 287.

[2] Coco, G. A. (1987, 1989) *On The Bloodstained Field* and *On The Bloodstained Field II,* Gettysburg, PA.

[3] Heth and Pender were part of A. P. Hill's Corps. Heth was acting contrary to orders when he led his four brigades against Buford's cavalry. He was severely wounded in the action. Pender was mortally wounded July 2nd and died July 18th at Staunton, Virginia.

[4] The farm of William and Adelina Bliss was situated some few hundred yards west of the Emmitsburg Road. The house and barn were quite close together. When the Rebels occupied the property, the family fled to safety in Gettysburg taking few possessions (some books, the family Bible, and some livestock). After the war, Bliss applied to the government for compensation but received nothing. He was told his loss was one of "the fortunes of war."

[5] Toombs, S. (1888) *New Jersey Troops in the Gettysburg Campaign from June 5 to July 31, 1863.* Orange, NJ, p. 284. ". . . at a distance of fifty yards from the grove [Ziegler's] near Bryan's well, a stone wall had been constructed on the natural rock, and continued for about three hundred and fifty yards. Hays' division of the Second Corps occupied this position . . . in two lines of battle . . . [the] One Hundred and Twenty-fifth New York of the Third Brigade were immediately in the rear . . . on higher ground which enabled them to fire over the front line."

[6] Henry F. Chew was wounded at the Battle of the Wilderness. He was promoted to major when Thompson became lieutenant colonel and was later promoted to lieutenant colonel himself. Longacre, E. G. (1988) *To Gettysburg and Beyond. . . .* Hightstown, NJ, Pp. 189 & 233.

[7] The Bryan property, on the ridge above the road, was a farm of about 40 acres. The small barn was on the right flank to the north of the Twelfth's position, affording some good cover for the New Yorkers. Behind them and further up the slope to their right, was the two-room farmhouse with a loft room upstairs. The ground underfoot was rocky, uneven, and overgrown with weeds. An apple orchard known as Ziegler's Grove ranged up the hill. A well was a short distance from the house and to the rear of the Jerseymen's position. The Bliss farm was about 600 yards west of Bryan's farm.

[8] Fleming, G. T. (1913) *General Alexander Hays at The Battle of Gettysburg.* Pittsburgh, PA, Pp. 16-17.

[9] Coco, *op.cit.,* Pp.80-81.

[10] Justly proud of their small but vital action during the battle of Gettysburg, years later men of the Connecticut and New Jersey regiments erected markers at the site of the barn. There is now no way to approach the site of these markers on foot, but the National Park Service has recently made an effort to restore the area to more accurately represent the appearance of the site in 1863. To this end trees in the Peach Orchard and Ziegler's Grove have been planted anew, and it is hoped the Park Service will mow a path through the field and clear away the brush and poison ivy that has grown up in the area where the barn once stood.

[11] The Twelfth New Jersey, armed with old .69 calibre smoothbore muskets had to hold their fire; these old guns were highly inaccurate, even within one hundred yards.

[12] John Gibbon (1827-1896) was loyal to the Union although he had been reared in North Carolina and three of his brothers fought for the Confederacy. Warner, E. J. (1988) *Generals in Blue*. Baton Rouge, LA, Pp. 171-172.

[13] The main building of The Lutheran Seminary, finished in 1832, was known as "Old Dorm." It was a sturdy brick structure with a cupola that made a fine observation tower. Emmanuel Ziegler, steward of the college, had living quarters on the first floor. Classrooms and dormitories took up the other floors. On July 1st, it was used as a hospital for Rebel wounded. Later it became a Union hospital; the Confederate wounded there became prisoners. By July 6th, 173 wounded were crowded into the building. The nearby home of the Reverend Dr. Charles B. Krauth was also filled with wounded. Hospital tents were pitched on the ground between Old Dorm and the Krauth home. Coco, G. A. (1988) *A Vast Sea of Misery*. Gettysburg, PA, Pp. 6-8.

[14] Toombs, *op. cit.*, p. 304.

[15] Richard H. Townsend was promoted to second lieutenant a few days before the battle; shot through the heart, he died in his first battle and his first command.

[16] Thompson is mistaken. Throughout the assault that bears his name, Pickett remained at the Codori Barn. Generals Lewis A. Armistead and James J. Pettigrew led the charge; Pettigrew's men being closest to the Twelfth's position. When Armistead fell mortally wounded, the Federal soldiers who carried him to the rear thought he was Longstreet.

[17] Both the flower and the Rebel note (Confederate paper money) have long since disappeared.

[18] Background material not specifically noted in this chapter came from Longacre, E. G. (1988) *To Gettysburg and Beyond. . . .* Hightstown, NJ and

Christ, E. W. (1993) *The Struggle for the Bliss Farm at Gettysburg, July 2nd and 3rd, 1863*, Baltimore.

Chapter Seven

Bristoe Station

I thank God for his mercy in sparing my life. . . . .
RST to Hannah and Coleman, October 15, 1863

It was as if the bloody and grisly battlefield of Gettysburg was a doorway through which the war-weary soldiers stumbled only to find more hardship on the other side. Both armies learned something valuable. The Union now knew that Robert E. Lee was not invincible; the Confederates now knew the Union troops would stand fast and fight. It would be a different war from now on. There would be more and bloodier battles, more dead, more wounded, more prisoners taken, more money spent, more land devastated, and more families torn apart.

The armies would change. For the Confederates, recruits coming to face the Union forces were either older men or young boys; many were conscripts and some were bounty men. Union ranks would be partially filled with conscripts and bounty men, too. New volunteers included many who were foreign-born. The English and Irish boys had little trouble learning the American form of English, but the French, Germans, Hungarians, Poles, and Swedes who joined the army had some difficulty. There were a number of foreign-born officers whose European military training made them eligible for command in the Army of the Potomac.

For the rest of July the order was not to do battle but to move. The two armies headed southward—Lee in retreat, Meade in desultory pursuit. On July 14th at Williamsport, Maryland, Meade had the opportunity to engage Lee in a final battle that could end the war. Lee had reached the Potomac River, dangerous with high water from recent rains. But Meade hesitated and Lee's forces made their escape, with a difficult but successful crossing. Had Meade attacked, Lee's army, tired and depleted, could not have withstood the Union push. Skirmishes were fought along the nearly parallel routes taken by the two armies, but no major battles. On July 17th General Pettigrew, commander of the left at Pickett's charge, died of wounds sustained on July 14th at Falling Waters.

When Lincoln learned of Lee's escape, he was enormously displeased and disappointed. Major General Henry W. Halleck, general-in-chief of all the Union armies, sent a dispatch to Meade stating that the President was upset with his failure to engage Lee. A disheartened Meade offered to resign his command but Lincoln refused to accept it.[1] Only a few military and political leaders knew of the tension between Meade and his superiors in Washington. Lincoln was frustrated with Meade's uncanny ability to miss every chance to attack Lee and finish the war. He chafed at Meade's inaction.[2]

Lee was back in the Shenandoah Valley by mid-July. Meade, with an army nearly double the strength of Lee's, had planned to attack him at Manassas Gap and cut the Confederate forces in half. He failed to do so because Lee moved his Army of Northern Virginia so rapidly that it had left the Valley and moved across the Rappahannock before the ever-cautious Meade could act. The last of the Union Army crossed the Potomac on July 19th. Lee, already at the Rappahannock, dug in. Meade then pushed his men on to Warrenton, Virginia, where they halted while he planned another strategy. For six days, from July 25th to the 31st, the Army of the Potomac was camped at Warrenton.

During the lull Thompson wrote Hannah a short letter commenting on the advent of a rail line from Philadelphia to Cape May, which was completed that year. Brother-in-law Coleman Leaming had been instrumental in promoting the building of this line; both men had invested in railroad bonds.

Bivouac Near Warrenton Junction
July 27, 1863

My dear Brother and Sister,

Your joint letter of the 19th inst. is received. Today we received a mail for the first time for some ten days. I can assure you the arrival of these home letters is the cause of more joy than the authors of them can imagine. I have little time to write, but will say that any arrangements you may make in regard to C. H. Depot will meet my approval. There is no man living in whom I have greater confidence in such matters than yourself, not excepting myself. Give your mind ease about my thinking strange or disapproving your action. I am rejoiced to know the road is so nearly completed.

We have been moving down on the Rebels slowly and trust that when we again cross arms with them they shall learn we are more determined to continue, through God's blessing, victorious. The glorious news from the other armies has helped to inspire our troops in this, and the Battle of Gettysburg was worth more in point of improvement to us than 20,000 recruits would be.[3]

The mail boy is about going and I must say that I still think of you as my brother and sister, for whom I have the greatest regard and from whom hope ever to merit love. Remember me to the children when you write.

> Your affectionate brother,
> *Richard*

Meanwhile, Lee crossed the Rapidan River about ten miles to the south. Once across, his men constructed extremely strong defensive works. They would be ready for any Union attack. Meade's next move was to Morrisville, about three miles north of the Rappahannock, where once more the army settled to re-group. As with every regiment that fought at Gettysburg, the ranks of the Twelfth had been thinned. To fill vacancies among the officers, several men were now promoted: Company K's First Lieutenant Daniel Dare went to Company E as its captain; Second Lieutenant William Potter became a First Lieutenant; Sergeant Charles A. Markley was transferred from a Pennsylvania regiment to take Potter's place.[4]

During the quiet evenings between the long, difficult marches, Thompson wrote all his friends and family. His old mentor Doctor Fish, fired with patriotism, replied at length.

> *1608 Vine Street*
> *Philadelphia*
> *July 16, 1863*

My Dear Richard,

Having a few leisure moments this evening, I have determined to devote them to you. I trust I may not be interrupted more than a half dozen times before I finish this sheet. I was much delighted the other day on receipt of your last missive.

I began to feel quite uneasy about you, not having heard for some time. I thought that General French was still your division commander and possibly you were in the fight. I feel thankful and congratulate you that you are again unharmed by Rebel bullets. I feel glad that you were in this battle as the sequel proves you are not injured. In future it will be considered a great honor, as it should be, to say that you belonged to the noble Army of the Potomac.

The Battle of Gettysburg I suppose was one of the most hotly contested and sanguinary conflicts of the War. I am delighted that the Rebs received such a severe handling; they have been taught a bitter lesson from the last sad experience; how terrible is their defeat, when they attempt to invade free territory. This is the second invasion of Pennsylvania by General Lee; I presume he returns with his shattered and partially demolished forces, a wiser, would that I could add, a better man. His prestige is gone, he will soon be numbered among the fallen mass of the bogus Confederacy.

My heart burns with shame and indignation. I feel deeply humiliated that the citizens of this great commonwealth, my adopted state, should treat even with the slightest indifference, the lowest private in the Union Army, who have come with generous hearts and strong arms to protect our lives and property from the ruthless invaders.[5] Such conduct on the part of men that would be freemen (and with this miserable slave forces utterly abolished) is more damaging to our righteous cause than 100 defeats.

Then again, the recent avowed resistance to the draft in New York by an infuriated mob, who would by their violence and wanton destruction of valuable lives and property subvert all law and order, is disgraceful to us as a nation.[6] It is reported tonight that all is quiet in New York City. Heaven grant it may be so, and this may be the first and last outbreak of the kind. The conscription act is a law of the land and we should, as loyal and law-abiding citizens, respect it and yield obedience to all its provisions. Is it not ignoble, unmanly, unjust—nay cowardly—to object to any legal measure that will favor the crushing of this mighty rebellion, or bad faith to the tens of thousands of noble fellows who have volunteered and are now suffering the hardships [and] privations of the tented field and exposure in the field of battle. All mobs from whatever cause and of whatever character should be summarily dealt with and quickly suppressed. The moral effect alone of the great metropolis of [the] continent being for three days under the control of an ignorant and excited populace is beyond calculation.

That General Lee should have escaped once more into Virginia we feel disappointed, but I did not entertain any idea that his entire army would be captured. After such a severely fought battle as the 1st, 2nd, and 3rd of July, with the necessary physical exhaustion to our troops, forced marches, etc., it seems next to impossible that the result should have been otherwise; there is yet a great work for the Army of the Potomac to accomplish. I know they are both ready and willing, and may the next contest be the final and fatal blow to this accursed rebellion.

Mrs. Fish wrote you a letter a few days since, which I enclose. Let us hear from you whenever you have the leisure to write. What a terrific fight you had in storming the barn with Rebel sharpshooters; how miraculous your escape. May God protect you from all harm in any future battles your regiment may be engaged in. Let us hear from you soon again. Good night,

Your affectionate friend
A. H. Fish

As July ended and August began, Meade's forces left the Morrisville area, marched north about seven miles and established a new camp at Elk Run. After a few days they left the Elk Run camp and marched back to the Rappahannock, where they camped between Rappahannock railroad bridge and Warrenton.

It was not an entirely peaceful time; skirmishes developed with Confederate cavalry on scouting patrols. There was action at various points, including several at Brandy Station and one at Bristoe Station, small stops along the Orange and Alexandria Railroad (now called the Southern). Meade used this line to supply his troops from the large military supply depot at Alexandria; Lee used it to move supplies and troops south of the Rapidan.

At last, sultry August ended and September began. The Army of the Potomac camped for about ten days at Culpeper, situated about halfway between the Rapidan and the Rappahannock. There was some skirmishing at Culpeper Court House on September 3rd, but most of the month was spent in motion, not in action. The men devoted days to the crossing and recrossing of rivers and streams for (to them) no apparent reason. Meade, however, was looking for the opportunity to fight at some place other than those sturdy works the Confederates had built up along the Rapidan.

Early in September while the Union Army commanders began preparations for a campaign, Thompson and his regiment had little to do; the Second Corps was being held in reserve. When Hancock was wounded at Gettysburg, Brigadier General John C. Caldwell was given command of the Corps. After the engagement at Brandy Station Major General Gouverneur K. Warren[7] was given command. He served until March 1864 when Hancock returned to duty.

On September 16th, the army camped at Stevensburg, about four miles to the south of Brandy Station. The next day they moved to the junction of Crooked Run and the Robertson River, a tributary of the Rapidan, to stand ready for action. Action did not come. They sat there while Washington made some changes. After the Union defeat at Chickamauga and Lincoln's order to Meade to reinforce the Army of the Cumberland, Howard's Eleventh Corps and Slocum's Twelfth Corps were sent out for duty in Tennessee. Meade lost two corps, but Lee had lost his most capable general, James Longstreet, whose corps had been transferred to Tennessee just prior to the Battle of Chickamauga. Both Washington and Richmond were moving their pawns over the chessboard of war.

With a skirmish at Bristoe Station on the 24th, September's engagements ended. The next day the army began to march. On September 27th when Lee's scouts alerted him to the movements of the Union troops, he decided to attack. His bold plan had its drawbacks. He had only about 45,000 poorly fed and equipped men to Meade's well fed and smartly equipped 76,000. In Lee's favor, however, was Meade's zealous caution and the Union Army itself. Many of the men were raw recruits, given uniforms, weapons, and minimal training, and then sent off to the front. Their patriotism was shallow at best. They arrived on the field with attitudes far different from the volunteers of two years ago. The naive enthusiasm of the volunteers of two years past was killed at Gettysburg. Desertions were rampant.[8]

Lee proceeded with his plan despite heart problems that troubled him in early October. By the 8th and 9th his men had crossed the Rapidan and were ready to harass Meade. He began his offensive on the 10th, with skirmishers firing along the river. The firing continued on the 11th and 12th, becoming more intense each day. So began the Bristoe Campaign.

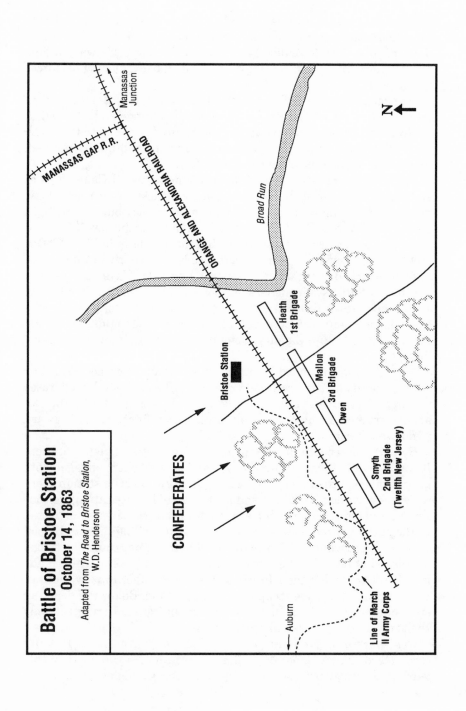

Battle of Bristoe Station
October 14, 1863

Adapted from *The Road to Bristoe Station*,
W.D. Henderson

CONFEDERATES

Manassas Junction

MANASSAS GAP R.R.

ORANGE AND ALEXANDRIA RAILROAD

Broad Run

N

Bristoe Station

Heath
1st Brigade

Mallon
3rd Brigade

Owen

Smyth
2nd Brigade
(Twelfth New Jersey)

Auburn

Line of March
II Army Corps

Sometime earlier, Meade's signal corps had broken the Confederate code. Learning that the Confederate cavalry was ordered to draw three days' rations, Meade realized Lee was on the move. He was, and he pressed forward; Meade fearing a trap, pulled back, moving his forces northward.

October 13th was a difficult day for the Twelfth New Jersey, in fact, for the entire corps. They marched along the Orange and Alexandria Railroad, crossed the Rappahannock to Bealton, went on to the south bank of Cedar Run near the village of Auburn,[9] and finally camped, exhausted, about nine o'clock that night.

By daybreak of October 14th Meade's men crossed Cedar Run at Auburn. Units of J. E. B. Stuart's cavalry attacked rear units of the northward moving army near the flour mill. A short but serious fight took place; eventually, survivors of both sides withdrew.[10] The engagement took place on an unnamed hill the men later dubbed "Coffee Hill," since they had been brewing coffee when the Confederate cavalry attacked out of the fog. General Alexander Hays deployed the 126th New York as skirmishers, supported by the Twelfth New Jersey. The Confederates drove the New Yorkers into the Jerseymen, who opened fire. Among the Confederates killed was the commander of the First North Carolina Cavalry, Colonel Thomas Ruffin of North Carolina.

After the fighting ended at Auburn, the Second Corps, acting as rear guard, moved along the railroad to Catlett's Station. The Confederates followed along on an almost parallel route. Fighting between the two armies erupted all along the way until Union forces turned toward Manassas Junction.

By early afternoon Meade's men approached tiny Bristoe Station. It was a small village before the war and several short engagements in previous months had nearly destroyed it. Around the station there were a few ruined buildings and a little scrubby vegetation; neither army could depend on the terrain to offer protection in case of battle. In the outlying area, however, pine woods and rolling country helped conceal any movement. Commanders of both armies could see troops moving—but not all of them nor exactly whose they were, which made it difficult to deploy their forces to best advantage. Finally, here at Bristoe Station, Meade stopped to make a stand. Below the depot an embankment ran along the west side of the rails, offering the only shelter available; they deployed here.

Confederate Major General Henry Heth's division of A. P. Hill's corps faced Union Generals William Hays and Alexander S. Webb. During the artillery action shells from the Confederate batteries

caused such casualties that Colonel Smyth was ordered to silence
them. He called on the First Delaware, the Fourteenth Connecticut,
the Seventh Michigan, the 108th New York and the Twelfth New
Jersey to do the job. It was a difficult and dangerous assignment. The
Twelfth charged with muskets and fixed bayonets, coming to within
yards of the enemy before firing. They nearly captured several cannon,
but despite their heroics other members of the brigade captured the
guns first. Although they were under heavy fire, the Twelfth lost only
one man killed and six wounded.

Colonel Smyth recalled his men as the Confederates fought back to
regain their position. Heth's men followed the retreating troops but
were cut down by the defenders on the embankment. It was a fierce
fight; the Federals won. (See Appendix D.) At dark they quietly
withdrew. Thompson wrote a detailed account the next day.[11]

Battlefield of Bull Run, Va.
October 15, 1863, Friday Morning

My dear Brother and Sister,

Fearing you may be over-anxious as to my welfare, I will
write a few words by way of parenthesis. In graver matters
the 2nd Army Corps to which I am proud to belong has, during
the last week, now more bright laurels. After leaving Elk Run
on the 12th September our Corps was the advance of the Army
to cross the Rappahannock and follow the Rebels to beyond
Culpeper C.H. From there our Corps alone advanced 12 miles
from the remainder of the Army and took position on the bank
of the Rapidan, where we remained until the 6th inst. when
we returned to Culpeper C.H., where we remained until 10th
inst. Then [we] advanced again to the front three and a half
miles, remained in line all night, and on the morning of the
11th inst. at 12:30 (early morning) we commenced march[ing]
to [the] rear. [We] crossed the Rappahannock and, at Bealton
Station rest[ed] for the night (distance marched that day, 18
miles). On the following day (12th inst.) we return[ed] again
to the Rappahannock, cross[ed] the river and advance[d] in
line of battle three miles, following our cavalry and artillery
as they drove back the Rebels. At 12 o'clock midnight on the
12th inst. we again marched back across the river and
march[ed] to within five miles of Sulphur Springs, then
change[d] our direction and march[ed] towards Warrenton,
continued marching until 9 p.m. and bivouac[ed] near Cedar

Creek about five miles from Catlett's Station. At daylight the following morning we commenced [the] march again and had only moved part of the Corps from camp when a brigade of Rebel cavalry attacked our Division, thinking us a mere wagon guard. We soon gave them to understand better and after a short sprinkling of artillery charged them with infantry. They gave us evidence of how mistaken they were by running like mad in every direction, some even ran into our provost guard in rear of the Division. We laughed a little, disposed of the killed and wounded, and continued our march to Catlett's Station where we rested until 1 p.m., then resumed our march along the railroad until we reached Broad Run. Here we met worthier game. Hill's large corps, almost double ours in number, were waiting to cut us off and capture us before we could reach the main army. They made the attack with a suddenness and determination which looked like ending this glorious little corps. Their position was well chosen and everything ready. Many of our men were cut down [in] the first fire, but they had no flying Dutchmen to deal with. [12]

With a good hearty cheer that made the blood tremble we received their infernal lead and iron and sent back the battle cry of the 2nd Corps. Our badge is a Club (♣) and "clubs are trump." The instant the Rebels fired, we charged them at double quick, drove them from their position, captured nine pieces of artillery, [and] over 2,000 prisoners, and placed many a poor soul in his long "winter quarters." May God pardon the sins of the dead! The Rebels returned but a little and then charged us three times and three times were repulsed and as they gave back, they were followed with cheers of the bullets of the Blue Jackets. I thank God for his mercy in sparing my life and permitting me to live to see the corps I love and the cause I pray for succeed as we did on then 14th of October. The fight continued until after dark and then, being unable to get reinforcements, continued our march to Bull Run arriving after a forced march at 2:30 a.m. the next morning. The enemy was not aware of our leaving and had made his calculations to attack us in the morning.

Prisoners state that the Rebels were never so handled by a force so much smaller than their own. General Warren commands our Corps and mark me, he will yet, should God spare his life, command an Army. I lost one killed and one badly wounded from my Company. The [one] killed had joined me that morning, he being a straggler from the 3rd Corps. Well, to go on, the same morning we arrived at Bull Run. The rest of the Army, that had been waiting our arrival, left and we were again attacked in the afternoon and repulsed the enemy. [See Appendix D.]

The mail is going. I am well. Write to Em and John.

> From your affectionate brother,
> *Richard*

From Bristoe Station the fatigued men marched rapidly to the old Bull Run (Manassas) Battlefield. They stumbled across, kicking up the bones of the dead from their shallow graves. The next day, October 16th, they crossed Bull Run itself and halted at Blackburn's Ford. They positioned themselves behind the old breastworks that were abandoned at the first two battles of Bull Run. When the Confederates attacked, they could not dislodge the steadfast Twelfth. After three tries and three failures, they quit. When evening came, they gave up and left. The tired but relieved Union troops returned to the camp at Warrenton.

Thompson wrote home from camp. His letter indicates he would be away from his regiment and he made plans accordingly.

> *Camp Near Warrenton, Va.*
> *November 5, 1863*

My dear Sister Hann and Brother Coly,

Why so silent? Were I not sure of your affection, I might say to myself, "thy friends and family have forgotten thee," but I know you have not done this. I now write only to say that I desire you to send the following named articles of "clothing, camp, and garrison equipage" to the office of A. I. Fish, Esq., No. 6 Mer. Lib. Building, 5th St., below Chestnut, Philadelphia, Pa., there to be called for. You had better address Asa to this effect. No. 1. My thick pilot cloth blouse (or sack coat) that I left in Philadelphia last spring. No. 2. Any little article you may think I require put in the pocket. The bundle will be opened and some things put in in Philadelphia.

Now the above is one want. Here is another separate and distinct. Send up to Bell and tell her to keep them in Philadelphia for me. My black cloth pants, balmoral shoes,[13] three or four pairs of white socks, two or three white pocket handkerchiefs. For should any such good fortune await me as a leave of absence or an order home for any purpose, I will require these last mentioned articles upon my arrival in Philadelphia. There is no immediate hurry as regards the things to be sent to Bell, but the sack coat I desire sent immediately as it will be called for in a few days.

Our 2nd Corps still remains near Warrenton. We have had nothing worthy of note to happen lately. There is some talk of Colonel Willets resigning and if he should do so, the old subject of promotion will again come under consideration.

I wrote you soon after the Battle of Bristoe Station. You saw by the papers how our Corps can fight. Our Regiment in that engagement lost only a few killed and wounded; 1st Lieutenant Lowe was killed.[14] We had quite a number of stragglers in our Regiment at the time (they having been compelled to join us) and the loss among them was fearful. Our Regiment now numbers about 300 for duty. Only two captains on duty, and after today there will only be one. Our whole Brigade only numbers four captains for duty (I am one of the four).

There is much speculation in camp about winter quarters. People at home I suspect are anxious for us to go on, but they know not what suffering this cold weather work brings on. We have been on the "go" ever since the last of May, and such marching as it was thought impossible to accomplish has been our usual employment.

I wish you would write me soon. Mary says the Court House husbands and wives are forming into two parties. Jane and Smith I believe she mentioned. Come tell me all the news and domestic talk that is going on.

Colonel Willets has not joined in. He is on court martial in Washington, D.C.

With much regard and love, I remain your affectionate brother,
Richard

As he hinted in his letter, a respite from duty in the field came early in November when he served once more on a special court martial. He also invested some of his military pay in United States bonds. He trusted this business to Asa Fish, who reported to him.

No. 6 Mer. Lib. Bldg.
Philadelphia
November 18, 1863

My Dear Richard,

I send you, as requested in your note to Dr. Fish, three packages by Captain McComb.[15] Nothing has as yet reached me from Cape May.

I have invested $800 for you in the U.S. 5.20's and still have $150 in hand which I design to use in the purchase of a share in Col. RR as soon as they get somewhat lower, perhaps, in January unless you direct otherwise.

I am glad to hear by Captain McComb that you enjoy good health and that your regiment is in good fighting trim.

Trusting that the same good fortune may attend in the future that Providence has vouchsafed to you in the past.

Believe me, my dear sir, very truly yours,
A. I. Fish

Thompson returned to duty in time for the four days of battle at Robinson's Tavern on November 27th and at Mine Run November 28th to 30th. He wrote nothing more that survived until the first of the year.

From December 26, 1863, to May of 1864, he was on detached service to the Draft Rendezvous at Trenton, New Jersey. Stationed at Camp Perrine, Trenton, he was in charge of recruiting. Once more his talent for persuasion kept him from danger.[16] During his absence, Company K was led by First Lieutenant Frank M. Riley of Company G. Riley had been one of Company K's original sergeants and knew many of the men well. Once settled in his new location, Thompson began writing home again.

Camp Perrine, Trenton, N.J.
January 3, 1864

My dear Sister Hann,

My wants are only equaled by my continued asking for their answer. I wish you to send me my small trunk marked "Capt. RST" and I do *not* want the pants, but want the small pistol I sent home from Washington in my trunk. You can have the trunk expressed to me under the following directions: Capt. Richard S. Thompson, Camp Perrine, Trenton, N.J. Don't put the regiment on the direction as it may go to the Army.

I received the shoes Doctor left at 1205 but as I did not arrive in the city until near 8 p.m. was unable to see him. Tomorrow I take command of a detachment going to Ft. Monroe and will return about Friday.

I should like very much to see you all and hope that when you visit Philadelphia you will come to Trenton and send me word that I may come up and see you as this camp is no place to receive ladies.

I will execute the deed sent by Doctor and send it to him tomorrow. I am thinking this being here on duty is a very fat thing, and will endeavor so to conduct myself as to remain. 'Tis a grand improvement on camp life in the field. Write me soon.

Love to all from your brother,
Richard

He was happy to be less than 90 miles from home. His recruitment duties included signing the men up, placing them in the various regiments as needed, and escorting the new soldiers to camp to insure that they did not desert. Thompson's duties kept correspondence at a minimum.

Alexandria, Va.
January 19, 1864

Dear Sister Hann,

Your letters, one to army and the other to Trenton were received. The trunk arrived all right. I will call at Burlington the first opportunity. I am at present on escort duty taking a detachment to the Army of the Potomac.

My duty at Trenton is simply to escort recruits and drafted men to the army. I most likely shall remain there until March. I intend making an application to the War Department as I return to Trenton for a 15 days leave of absence, and if successful, will go west and then on my return will visit Cape May. You had better delay your visit to Philadelphia until you hear from me again as we might otherwise miss seeing one another.

I will write you when I will be at Cape May upon my return to Trenton, say in three or four days. I wrote you that I should visit Fort Monroe. Well, I did, saw Em and John. Em was looking better than when I saw her last, yet I think she lives upon excitement only. I pity her! And pray that all may yet be well. Will write you more another time.

And with the hope of seeing you soon, say goodnight for the present.

Richard

Camp Perrine, Trenton, N.J.
February 19, 1864

My very dear Sister Hann,

Only a few lines to acknowledge your kind letter and thank you for it. I have but just returned from the Army where I took some 120 recruits for New Jersey Regiments. I trust you will write me at once upon your arrival in Philadelphia, or that you will come immediately to Trenton. I think Mrs. Fish would come with you. You can now come to the camp with some propriety, we having made a change in our arrangements.

Will not trouble you with any more poor writing at present, only say that I trust soon to have the pleasure of seeing you and we will then talk over matters and things. Pray do come soon and telegraph me from Philadelphia telling me where you are stopping and etc. Remember my time is not my own and I have to take a leave when it best suits higher rank to give it.

John Stevenson still writes to sell the *Constitution*,[17] he says $600 for Em's quarter. This is more than I think he will be able to obtain. He says Em's well.

With regards to all and love to Coly and yourself,

I remain as always your affectionate brother,
Richard

While he was at Trenton, the Twelfth New Jersey was in an engagement on the Rapidan at Morton's Ford. It was a short, bitter, and inconclusive fight resulting in senseless casualties. Fording the icy water caused or aggravated many existing illnesses. Major Hill's rheumatism became so debilitating that on February 24th, he resigned his commission and left the Regiment. This left Lieutenant Colonel Davis as the Twelfth's only field officer. Colonel Willets, wounded severely in the right arm at Chancellorsville, was still unable to return to his command.

In March, Thompson got a 15 day leave and went home. While he was home, the government began conscription, which eventually sent about 50,000 often reluctant men to fill the many gaps in the ranks. The attitude of the people toward the war had changed. Volunteers were now a far different breed from the enthusiastic young patriots of 1861. Some were deserters from one corps who simply reenlisted in another to get the bounty money, then deserted to do it all over again. The new men displayed no great enthusiasm for the war. Some soon deserted, or gave minimal service; some showed cowardice and lack of discipline. Meade finally resorted to fear and punishment, and the number of courts martial and executions of all soldiers increased.

The Army of Northern Virginia had problems, too. Lee suffered from heart disease. Officers and men alike suffered under higher than usual August temperatures and lack of proper food. Horses, so vital to the cavalry, lacked adequate fodder and shoes. In addition, hoof rot, an equine disease, took numerous animals out of service. Morale fell among the troops while desertions climbed. Courts martial grew in ratio. Lee sent cavalry units out looking for deserters skulking in the woods, trying to go home. He instituted a religious revival in the army, asking the chaplains to work harder to help lift the men's spirits. He also began a system of rewards. To men who remained on duty, he gave two week furloughs. To deserters, he offered amnesty if they returned to their regiments within 20 days.

While at Camp Perrine Thompson learned the Army had a new commander, Ulysses S. Grant.[18] Change filtered down to Thompson, too. Among his papers he preserved a copy of the letter that would make him a major, a promotion for which he had waited two years.

Headquarters
2nd Brigade
March 2, 1864

To His Excellency
Governor J. Parker

Sir:

As the majority of the 12th Regiment N.J. Vols. is now vacant, I take pleasure in recommending to your excellency's notice the name of Captain Richard S. Thompson, Company K, 12th Regt. N.J. Vols.

He is a gallant officer, a strict disciplinarian, and as an executive officer he has few equals.

His assiduous attention to his duties has upon several occasions called forth the highest encomiums from his superior officers.

I have the honor to remain very respectfully your Obedient Servant,

Thomas A. Smyth, Colonel Commanding,
2nd Brigade, 3rd Division, 2nd Army Corps

On March 14th, Thompson wrote his friend and chess opponent, James Lancey, commenting on Grant's tactic of sending successive waves of men in frontal assaults against entrenched Confederate troops. Grant often planned attacks that other commanders would not have dared to envision. Thompson also expressed his concern that Grant's strategy was the cause of the rapidly increasing number of both dead and wounded. For the first time Thompson voiced the fear that when he next saw combat, he would be among the wounded. He was not wrong.

The character of the war had changed. Bristoe Station was one of the last engagements that was conducted traditionally, where the loser withdrew after a battle and the combatants rested. From now on there would be a relentless quality to the war. It would be more confusing, more bloody, more horrifying.[19]

Notes

[1] When Meade's offer of resignation reached Washington, the President may have been surprised. Whatever disappointment Lincoln may have felt, he admired Meade and had no viable replacement for him. When Halleck replied to Meade's letter of resignation, he changed the word "displeased" to "disappointed" and tried to mollify the situation. See Bache, R. M. (1897) *Life of General George Gordon Meade, Commander of the Army of the Potomac.* Philadelphia, Pp. 359-362.

[2] Henderson, W. D. (1987) *The Road to Bristoe Station. . . .* Lynchburg, VA, Pp. 51ff.

[3] He had just received word of the fall of Vicksburg to Grant's army on July 4th.

[4] Other officers were promoted besides those listed in the text. The regiment also received three new volunteers; more came later in the year.

[5] Dr. Fish refers to the newspaper accounts of the way some Gettysburg citizens mistreated the wounded, refusing them food, water, or shelter. The newspapers played up the attitudes of these callous and frightened civilians. For the most part, however, the population was very compassionate toward the helpless men, opening their homes and hearts to the wounded of both armies.

[6] On July 11th, the first names in the new draft lottery were drawn and angry New Yorkers took to the streets rioting and causing disturbances of all kinds. Troops were marshalled to subdue the rioters.

[7] West Point graduate Gouverneur Kemble Warren of New York (1830-1882) was an army engineer who became a brigadier general of volunteers in 1862; becoming a major general the following year. His talent for selecting the best terrain for a battle saved the day at the battle for Little Round Top on July 2, 1863, at Gettysburg. When Hancock resumed command of the Second Corps, Warren was made commander of the Fifth Corps. After the battle at Five Forks, clashes with Grant and Sheridan led to his removal. See Warner, E. J. (1988) *Generals in Blue*. Baton Rouge, LA, Pp. 541-542.

[8] See Henderson. *op. cit.*, Pp. 70ff.

[9] Auburn, sometimes called Auburn's Mills, located on the banks of Cedar Run, is about five miles northwest of Catlett's Station. It was the home of a flour mill which supplied the surrounding area. The skirmish that took place there on October 14, 1863, was considered a part of the Bristoe Station Campaign. On that day Brigadier General Joshua T. Owen's brigade of the Second Corps and the Twelfth New Jersey repulsed an attack by Stuart's cavalry. See *Ibid.*, Pp. 142-145; Longacre, E. G. (1988) *To Gettysburg and Beyond*. . . . Hightstown, NJ, Pp. 152-154; Boatner, M. M. (1959) *The Civil War Dictionary*. New York, p 132.

[10] For details of these movements, see Henderson, *op. cit.*, Chapters 9-11, and Walker, F. A. (1887) *History of the Second Corps in the Army of the Potomac*. New York, Pp. 331ff.

[11] Despite his heading there was no third battle of Bull Run. A notation on the envelope reads, "written on the battlefield of 3rd Bull Run October 15th and act. of the battle of Bristoe Station."

[12] He refers to the Eleventh Corps which broke and ran at Chancellorsville; most of the men were German immigrants, "Ich ein Deutsche" was what they called themselves, but the Americans immediately translated this into "Dutchmen" with little regard for accuracy.

[13] Balmoral was the name given to a high-topped shoe or boot that laced.

[14] Lt. James T. Lowe, from Camden County, New Jersey, was in Company G. He was wounded in the thigh and died October 30th. Longacre, *op. cit.*, p. 157.

[15] Captain James McComb of Camden was the second lieutenant of Company E then captain of Company D. He commanded the Regiment after Spotsylvania and was wounded on June 3, 1863, at Cold Harbor when a cannon ball struck his left leg. Dr. Alvin P. Satterthwait, the regimental surgeon, amputated the leg, but he died a month later in Washington. *Ibid.*,Pp. 207, 210, 217; and Foster, J. Y. (1868) *New Jersey and the Rebellion.* . . . Newark, NJ, p. 312.

[16] Camp Perrine was named for Lewis Perrine, who became a Major General in 1865. He was also Quartermaster General of New Jersey.

[17] This was a ship owned jointly by the Thompson sisters and Richard. Each had a one-fourth share.

[18] Lincoln had followed Grant's career in the Western Theater and was impressed. He nominated Grant for overall command of the Union Army with the newly created rank of Lieutenant General. Congress confirmed the nomination the next day. On March 8th, Grant was in Washington, where he met Lincoln for the first time. He received his commission on the 9th and was back in the field on the 10th. So many men from the First and Third Corps were lost at Gettysburg, that Grant simply dissolved these Corps and attached them to the Second, Fifth, and Sixth Corps. The Second Corps did not welcome all the changes, but they were glad to see Hancock return to duty. General Warren left the Second Corps for the Fifth Corps. The Second Corps was now organized as follows:
Major General Winfield S. Hancock
First Division, Brigadier General Francis C. Barlow
First Brigade,Colonel Nelson A. Miles
Second Brigade, Colonel Thomas A. Smyth
Third Brigade, Colonel Paul Frank
Fourth Brigade, Colonel John R. Brooke
Second Division, Brigadier General John Gibbon
First Brigade, Brigadier General Alexander S. Webb
Second Brigade, Brigadier General Joshua. T. Owen (later mustered out for misconduct)
Third Brigade, Colonel S. S. Carroll
Thompson's regiment was formerly in the Second Brigade, Third Division, with a blue Trefoil (club) as their insignia. They were now in the Third Brigade, Second Division and sported a white one.

[19] Additional background information for this chapter came from the following sources: Long, E. B. (1985) *The Civil War Day by Day, An Almanac*

1861-1865. New York; Longacre, *op. cit., passim;* Walker, *op. cit.*, Pp. 401-402; *OR,* Series I, Vol. 29, Part I, Chapter 41.

Chapter Eight

Problems around Petersburg

*The time is not far distant when some of their forts will experience
an exalted sensation as we have mined them. . . .*

RST to Hannah, July 18, 1864

In war's roundabout manner the way from Bristoe Station led to Petersburg. The long-sought "road to Richmond" was like the pot of gold at the end of a Yankee rainbow. Grant's plans to take the Confederate capital included Petersburg, situated about 20 miles to the south. It was the focal point for three railroads which enter from the south and one that went on to Richmond. With these rails under Federal control no new supplies or food could get into the capital city. Civilians and soldiers alike would go hungry, and presumably the demoralized inhabitants would pressure the government to seek peace.

Much more than Petersburg was involved. Grant's "Grand Strategy" required enormously detailed logistics. There were to be coordinated attacks on five fronts. General Nathaniel P. Banks was to move on Mobile, Alabama; General William T. Sherman on Atlanta, Georgia; Major General Franz Sigel[1] on Staunton, Virginia. In a two-pronged assault on Richmond itself, Meade was to come from Fredericksburg and Major General Benjamin F. Butler from Norfolk. Butler, moving up the James River, was to land at Bermuda Hundred, worry Petersburg, and attack Richmond from there.[2] It was absolutely crucial that the various commanders fully cooperate with one another. The plan also needed the cooperation of the Confederate Army, which was expected to fall back in disarray at every turn.

Butler was the key. He was given command of the new Army of the James, formed from various elements of the Army of the Potomac and several detached units. It was an army with no history or spirit of comradeship, yet it was expected to perform major military miracles. After taking control of the Bermuda Hundred region, Butler was to establish headquarters at City Point, about one and one half miles from the landing. Ten miles north and east of Petersburg, City Point lay at the confluence of the James and Appomattox Rivers.[3]

Butler brought his army upriver from Hampton Roads and landed at Bermuda Hundred on May 5, 1864, the same day the Army of the Potomac was fighting in the Wilderness. A year earlier at Chancellorsville, many of these same men had fought and lost. Now in the Wilderness, the Twelfth New Jersey fought in an agonizing engagement where Captain Potter and Lieutenants Riley and Dubois were wounded. Thompson remained on detached duty in the Trenton recruiting office (draft command).

While the Army of the Potomac was thus engaged, Butler was to move rapidly inland, destroying the railroads around Bermuda Hundred.[4] Lee had once stated, ". . . any disruption of the southern railroads would cause the abandonment of Virginia." This, of course, was Grant's goal. Yet, the cooperation necessary to the success of this plan did not develop. Butler's two subordinates, Major General William Farrar (Baldy) Smith, commanding the Eighteenth Corps, and Major General Quincy A. Gillmore, commanding the Tenth Corps, were often at odds with each other and with Butler. Smith was especially critical, Gillmore often reluctant to obey orders. In addition, the Confederate Army refused to cooperate.

Butler finally secured the periphery around Bermuda Hundred but was unable to go any further.[5] For awhile the Army of the James was stalled while the Army of the Potomac endured the bloodiest 30-day period in its history. From May 5th to June 12th it was a punishing routine of marching, fighting, and marching again. They fought at the Wilderness, around Spotsylvania Court House (where Lieutenant Colonel Thomas H. Davis lost his life), and Cold Harbor. The survivors got little rest; the Twelfth fought nearly every day out of 30.[6]

Butler meanwhile switched to the offensive and moved closer to Petersburg. After several abortive attempts, on June 9th he ordered Gillmore to attack the city, but that attack failed. While Butler was blundering around Bermuda Hundred and the Twelfth was struggling above Richmond, Thompson, at Camp Perrine, near Trenton, New Jersey, was promoted to Major (February 25, 1864). His leadership qualities would now be challenged, and he could ride instead of walk over Virginia's often difficult roads (no minor matter to the new Major). He was proud and delighted.

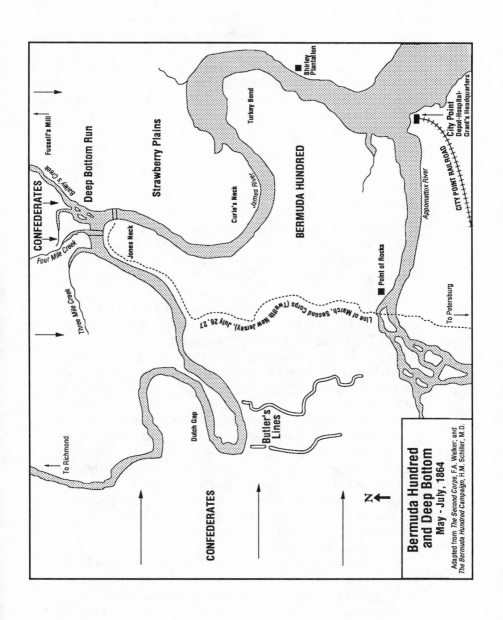

Bermuda Hundred
and Deep Bottom
May - July, 1864

Adapted from *The Second Corps*, F.A. Walker; and
The Bermuda Hundred Campaign, H.M. Schiller, M.D.

On April 5th he got orders to leave the Trenton office where he had worked since December, with the exception of a 15-day leave of absence. He was sent to the recruiting office in Camden, where he remained until June 2nd, when ordered to close up and return to his regiment. Conscription, begun again in March, had eased the man-power situation at the front.[7]

Before Thompson returned to his regiment, he asked for and received permission to stay in Washington until the 9th to obtain a proper uniform befitting his new rank. He arrived in Washington on June 8th and wrote Hannah, on the 10th.

Washington, D.C.
June 10, 1864

My dear Sister Hann,

With much useless shifting from post to post, I am now at Camp Distribution some three miles from Washington waiting orders to proceed to the front. I shall most likely be in command of a provisional brigade that starts for the front tomorrow.

I left Philadelphia on Tuesday and will not reach the Army before Sunday or Monday, so much for government transportation. The hundred days men[8] are being sent to the front. Many a man, who enlisted to enjoy the reputation of having been in the army and yet in reality do nothing more dangerous than guard some bridge on the safe side of Washington, will see sights he never dreamed of. And once in the front General Grant will probably use them during the hundred days in a manner that the nation shall be put to no useless expense on account of the shortness of their term of service. My Regiment has been badly cut up. Out of 16 officers there are only four left; and out of 500 and some men only 130 remain; and only 19 are unaccounted for. So you may see how the 12th Regiment has fought. There never was any discourse on their fighting.

Give my regards to the Doctor and remember me to the children when you write.

Of all the places under the sun to be in, Washington is the poorest. Dust, dirt, and high prices are the only things to be found in this city. If you stop at a hotel and inquire for a price, they will most likely charge you some fifty cents, and to look at a horse is considered just ground for charging a dollar.

I have nothing to write excepting my love for you. All is the same as ever and that you may remember me in your prayers. Pray for our country and myself is the wish of your affectionate brother,

Richard

In Washington Thompson was given orders to report to Brigadier General Henry S. Briggs at Alexandria. There he received further orders to board the steamer *Cossack* and proceed to White House Landing, Virginia, a Federal depot on the Pamunkey River, where he took temporary command of the Provisional Brigade Camp. The men he brought with him were a mixture of new recruits, substitutes, and transfers from the Reserve Veterans Corps. They were badly needed to replace the men lost during the May and June campaigns.[9] He now turned these new troops over to General Butler and prepared to rejoin his regiment.

On June 13th, Thompson reported to Brigadier General John W. Turner,[10] at Point of Rocks, Bermuda Hundred. Point of Rocks, named for the outcropping of limestone on the face of a bluff overlooking the Appomattox, was the site of Butler's headquarters. Thompson began his field duty as a major by commanding a provisional brigade here. Still on detached duty from the Army of the Potomac he was subject to orders from Butler. Unfortunately, a mix-up in the muster rolls kept his pay at a captain's level. After reading his new orders, he wrote a short note.

Point of Rocks on the Appomattox River
June 13, 1864

My dear Sister,

Am just arrived at this point. Am in command of a provisional brigade of some 1300 men, which I brought down from Alexandria, Va. We are waiting an opportunity to join our Regiment.

Will write again soon, as in great haste at present.

In much haste from your affectionate brother,
Richard

Grant, grimly determined to subdue Petersburg, ordered the Army of the Potomac to move from Cold Harbor, cross the James River, and move on the city. It took three days from June 14th to the 16th to move the thousands of Union troops over to the south side of the James. Members of Second Corps went first. Some were ferried over from Wilcox's Wharf to Windmill Point near Charles City Court House, while the rest crossed at Upper Wyanoke at North Bend, using a bridge consisting of 101 pontoons. Two thousand and two hundred feet in length, it was the longest such bridge ever built.

On the 15th, while the crossing was in progress, Butler sent Smith against Petersburg, now defended by General P. G. T. Beauregard.[11] About 3,000 Confederate troops faced nearly 9,000 Federals, and more were coming. The attack went on all day but as darkness fell, Smith called it off. Hancock, who arrived late on the scene due to various delays in moving his men, wanted to finish the assault with a night attack, but Smith refused. During the night Confederate reinforcements made their way into the city and the Union attack the next day made little or no headway. This was the last meaningful engagement of the Army of the James; the Bermuda Campaign, as such, faded away.

On the 17th another Federal attack against Petersburg was soundly repulsed by a strong Confederate counterattack. After several more failed attempts, Grant conceded that the city could not be taken by frontal assault, so he laid siege.

Meanwhile, Thompson had been at Point of Rocks for nearly ten days, expecting and hoping to return to the Twelfth at any moment. He had many duties but none that seemed newsworthy. He wrote home infrequently.

Headquarters
Camp Distribution
Point of Rocks on the Appomattox River
June 20, 1864

My dear Sister Hann,

Still at this place commanding what was a brigade but now turned into a camp of distribution. We are constantly expecting orders to join our regiments, but each day passes away and we find ourselves still within sound of every cannon that is fired by either army and yet in little or no danger. I am sending men to their different commands and receiving others to be distributed. How long this state of things may last is a question. I have nothing of interest to tell that is not far better told in the papers. The colored troops have been doing very fine fighting lately, and the Rebs are awakening to the fact that they will meet a brave enemy in ye Nig [Negro] in blue clothing. The Rebel prisoners are very fearful of being left to the charge of the colored troops as they fear their own acts of inhumanity will be repaid. The Nigs are all anxious to kill but not to take prisoners, and their cry is Ft. Pillow, [12]etc. when they are ordered to charge. Day before yesterday a Rebel among some prisoners refused to be marched to the rear by a Nig guard. One of the guard[s] ordered him to move on; he refused again, when without further words the Nig ran him through with a bayonet killing him instantly.

Butler reduced an officer to the ranks for cowardice, and yesterday an adjutant was marched through our camp with a board on his breast with "Coward" printed on it while a drum and fife played the rough march behind him.

From our camp we can see Petersburg and from the "look-out" we can see the tops of Richmond. How or when Richmond will be taken is a matter for greater military heads than mine. Petersburg is now under our guns and we can shell them out at any moment, but the Rebs have command of the city also with their guns and would shell our troops should they enter the city. Some mysterious movements are now going on and important results or failures will soon be reported. God grant us success and a decisive victory.

The prisoners say that they are willing to quit and that the only people to blame are the officers who have risked every-thing and who know that their only hope is in success of the Confederate Government. I am of the opinion that the ques-tion is reduced to one of endurance alone. The best man holds on the longest. From what we know of Grant, we have reason to believe he will stick while anything is left to stick to.

Remember me to my friends. Regards to Doctor and love to you from your affectionate brother,

Richard

At 11:40 p.m. on the same night he wrote Hannah, Thompson received orders to take his troops and report to Colonel Francis B. Pond for duty in the line. He also got similar orders for the next evening, the 21st. However, these orders were rescinded and he and his men were ordered to return to camp. (See Appendix E.)

To expedite the siege of Petersburg, Grant attempted to extend his lines westward and gain control of the Petersburg and Weldon Railroad, the most important of the railroad supply lines into the city. The Weldon ran about 60 miles due south of the city to Weldon, North Carolina.[13] Grant wanted to wreck the railroad all the way to Hicksford (now Emporia), Virginia.

On June 21st, Grant sent several detachments of noncombatants, mostly from the quartermaster's corps of the Army of the Potomac, on a wrecking expedition down the line. Commanded by Major General David B. Birney, the wrecking crew was guarded by infantry and some artillery, with support from units of the Eleventh Pennsylvania Cavalry led by Colonel Samuel P. Spear, under the command of Brigadier General August V. Kautz.[14]

The wrecking crews found themselves engaged in backbreaking labor. Their work went like this: "A brigade would be formed facing the road and the men would all seize hold of rails or ties or whatever came handiest and at the word of command all would roll over like a furrow from the plow. Then the rails were knocked loose from the ties, which were piled up and fired and the rails laid across; when the latter were red hot in the middle, the men would seize the ends and run and strike the middle against a tree or a telegraph pole and just lap the ends across each other completely ruining the rails for anything except old iron."[15] They managed to remove some of the rails and destroy some of the line.

To protect themselves from a possible Confederate attack, the men built a makeshift abatis or breastworks of fallen trees.[16] Confederate scouts observed all this activity and reported to Lee, who promptly acted to put a stop to the destruction. He sent part of A. P. Hill's division to engage the Federals. When the Confederates came out of the woods and attacked the working party and their guardians on June 22nd, they met with no serious resistance. After a short contest during which the little depot at Reams' Station[17] was burned down, the Union troops withdrew. The next day they regained some of the lost ground in an engagement near the Jerusalem Plank Road but could not control or keep it. They went back to the trenches of Petersburg; the Confederates moved back in and repaired the damage to the tracks within weeks. Grant, occupied with, among other things, the Petersburg Campaign and its corollary operation, Bermuda Hundred, did not initiate further action along the Weldon until August.

On the 23rd of June, Thompson was finally mustered as a major, succeeding Major Hill, who had been discharged in February.[18] He and his men left Point of Rocks and began a difficult march to a position closer to Petersburg, near Prince George Court House. While the distance to the city was not long, the heat was very intense and many suffering men dropped out along the way. Thompson rode his horse, but still felt the effects of the burning Virginia sun. Once at the new position he assumed command, taking over his duties with the Twelfth New Jersey, which had lost many men. Thompson's recruiting success and conscription helped fill up the empty ranks.

Caught between Union forces blockading on the outside and Confederates defending within, Petersburg was an armed camp. The city was ringed by nearly 20 miles of trenches and forts sturdily built of logs and earth. Men in both armies endured the same hardships. On dry days the sun baked them and they choked on the dust; on rainy days, the dust turned to mud and clung everywhere. They all swatted flies and picked off vermin.

Despite the efforts expended, the soldiers and citizens in Petersburg were not starving according to plan. After two months of stalemate General Burnside devised a scheme to undermine one of the forts ringing the city and give the Army of the Potomac a "gateway" into Petersburg. He enlisted former coal miners from the Forty-Eighth Pennsylvania to tunnel from the Union lines to one of the forts. The job was begun on June 25th. Enjoying a lull in his duties, Thompson wrote letters to family and friends. He brought Hannah up-to-date on army happenings.

Headquarters
12th Regt. N.J.
Near Petersburg, Va.
June 26, 1864

My dear Sister Hann,

On Thursday the 23d inst., I marched my Provisional Brigade from Point of Rocks on the Appomattox to Army Headquarters and after turning over my command and being mustered, I joined my Regiment.

Last Tuesday and Wednesday I was in Butler's entrenchments with my brigade doing duty. His works are the finest I ever saw and in my opinion are safe against any force that can be brought against them. Today I saw Dr. Wiley[19] [the Thompson family physician] at the 3rd Division, 2nd Corps Hospital. The bad luck of the 2nd Corps three or four days ago when we lost so many prisoners due to the troops that were placed in this corps from the old 3rd (Doctor's). They gave way without any cause and let the Rebels in behind the left of our division. Our boys say that the loss is the 3rd Corps' doings and there is a very bad feeling on account of it.

I received a letter from Kate in which she tells me that you had written her a good letter and she speaks of it in the highest terms and said she was about answering. I am glad you did write. Any friendship that exists between my sisters and the person I intend making my wife is, of course, a matter of happiness to me. You can understand this much better than I can express it and therefore I will say no more upon the subject.

On our march from Point [of] Rocks to this place about eight miles, three men died from sunstroke and three other men [were] pronounced past hope by the surgeon, so you may imagine how hot it was. But today is terrible and if the troops have to march, there will be many a poor soul start on its last journey. I have written you several times since I left Philadelphia and hope you have received them, if only for the purpose of convincing you that my intention was good if the letters were poor.

It is so warm that I have to place my pocket handkerchief between my hand and the paper or the sweat would ruin the paper. Give my love to the children when your write. I often think of them and wonder how they are getting along [in] this hot weather.

When you write, direct Major RST, 12th Regiment, New Jersey Vols., 3rd Brigade, 2nd Division, 2nd Corps via Washington, D.C., and let your doings be such that you will soon have need to use this direction. Letters are ever the nearest things to our actual presence, and to a soldier they are invaluable. Please write often and much. I know how hard it is to write and no one likes to perform this duty less than myself. But still you must not always wait for me to answer, and remember I have written several lately to which you have not answered. Give my regards to Doctor and tell him that his pen might do more work with some words. 'Tis so hot I am entirely melted and cannot write or think.

Pray God for the success of our arms and that peace may soon dwell among us, and for my own safe keeping, and believe me as ever your affectionate brother,

Richard

By now both sides were tired of war and morale was low, yet despite the many casualties and growing anti-war sentiment, more than

100,000 men reenlisted in the Army of the Potomac. While these reenlistments huddled in their Petersburg trenches, Sherman's men pushed on to Atlanta and Sheridan destroyed the Shenandoah Valley.

Thompson's military career took another step forward on July 17th when he was mustered in as Lieutenant Colonel Richard S. Thompson. He wrote to Hannah telling her the news and hinting at the building of the tunnel.

Headquarters
12th Regt. N. J.
Near Petersburg, Va.
July 18, 1864

Dear Sister Hann,

Your letter I have waited for so long, nearly six weeks, arrived last evening, and glad was I to know you have not forgotten your duty entirely.

Well, yesterday I received my commission as Lieutenant Colonel of this Regiment and today was mustered as such. So you see I have taken one more step, and thus relieved Major Stiles from his lamentable position of two Majors in the same family. Never saw you such dust as we have to live in here. It has not rained for seven weeks and when troops are moving, you cannot see a man ten yards distant. This is no figure of speech called "stretcher" but a solemn fact. Let all good Christians pray for rain to fall upon this army.

Yesterday a young gentleman, Lieutenant Brown on General [?] Staff, handed me a letter from Em. She is well and from what I can judge gay and happy. I should much like to visit her but that is out of the question at present. She states that Capt. Jones from Bridgeton, who used to be stationed at Ft. Delaware,[20] is now in the hospital at Ft. Monroe dying from a wound through the breast.

The other day while our division was working upon fortifications the Rebs saluted us by a few shells and a Whitworth[21] shot or two. But no great damage was done, excepting they kicked up much dust. The day is not far distant when some of their forts will experience an exalted sensation, as we have mined them and only wait the mining of others to try the effect of powder under their fortifications. I imagine it will have something like the effect the firecrackers did with the cat on our back porch.

Tell Doctor to write me as to the burnt timber and the action of the RR Co. Give him my regards and ask him whether the Cape May military powers are making due preparations to receive the *Florida*[22] should her crew conclude to spend a few weeks or days at the Island to refresh themselves. Mary has written me several times and had it not been through her I might have thought you dead. Kate wrote me a letter saying how much she was pleased to receive so kind a letter from you and that she had answered it.

I know of nothing of interest about which to write. Everything is now settled into a habit, as it were. The skirmishers keep up a constant popping and every few minutes a cannon throws a shot or shell, but we are so accustomed to this that we notice it but little more than one does the ticking of a clock, unless a stray shot comes within too uncomfortable a distance, or as once in awhile, several batteries open on some point at once.

Remember my instructions about my shoes, to put them in my trunk and also my overcoat. Don't let that become moth-eaten. In such times a coat of that description is an item in a poor soldier's hard-earned greenbacks.

With love to children, when you write, and remembrances to all friends, Fanny and Major Stiles included.

I am as ever your affectionate and loving brother,
Richard

Little went on in the trenches while the tunnel was being dug. Fearful that the Confederates would discover the mining operation before it could be completed, a diversionary action was set in motion. The Confederates knew there was a tunnel, but not its location. They had one or two of their own started, aimed at the Federal lines.

On July 25th and 26th, part of the Second Corps, including the Twelfth New Jersey, was sent to the north side of the James. Known locally as Strawberry Plains, it was an area which was cut by a slow-moving tributary of the James called Deep Bottom Run. Both sides of Deep Bottom Run were marshy and stump-filled; marching was difficult. No real action erupted until the 27th when about a mile from Deep Bottom and along Bailey's Creek, the troops met well-entrenched Confederates. They charged; a sharp fight broke out. As the mud from the swamps dried, the thick dust kicked up by the moving men hung like a curtain in the hot, humid air. More men fell from heat exhaustion and sunstroke than from bullets. The Twelfth, in the rear during this action, suffered little.

The next day when the battle resumed, portions of Hancock's forces fought Major General J. B. Kershaw's division—successfully at first, but when Confederate cavalry and five divisions of infantry showed up, the engagement came to a standstill. Hancock tried a flanking movement that was unsuccessful. He next tried a frontal assault, but the strong Rebel counterattack spurred the Union troops to seek the rear. Marching back to the James, they crossed over on the pontoon bridge they had used a few weeks earlier. The men were exhausted; they had done little but annoy Lee's troops and had failed to uproot the rail lines. Disheartened, they trudged back to Petersburg, enduring a forced march to be in position to support Burnside in the planned assault after the mine exploded.[23]

After nearly four weeks the tunnel was completed. Under the Confederate fort called Eliot's Salient, the miners laid four tons of gunpowder and the fuses to ignite it. The first fuse lighted on July 30th was defective, but the second one ignited, setting off the explosion at 4:30 a.m. Had it worked, Burnside's plan could have resulted in the conquest of Petersburg; what actually ensued was senseless slaughter. The gunpowder blew an enormous hole in the earth, 30 feet deep, about 70 feet wide, and nearly 200 feet long. The Confederates were stunned.

The next move should have been a massive Federal attack while the Confederates were still in shock, but precious time passed before any troops moved. Almost too late, nearly four divisions of the Ninth Corps (one of them black troops), went down into the huge crater, while others charged around it. Men who dropped into the crater could not climb out.

General William Mahone's Confederate defenders went to the edge of the huge hole and fired directly down on the heads of the struggling soldiers. Hundreds of injured men were butchered by clubbing or bayonetting. (See Appendix F.)

Consternation and charges of dereliction of duty filled headquarters that night. General Burnside was granted leave and never recalled to duty. Surprisingly, Thompson makes little mention of the disaster in his next letter to Hannah. The Twelfth New Jersey, held in reserve, was not directly involved. They saw the explosion and heard the noise of the guns; in fact, some shells landed among them, yet they had no inkling of the fiasco that followed until later. The Second Corps got orders to move out shortly afterward.[24]

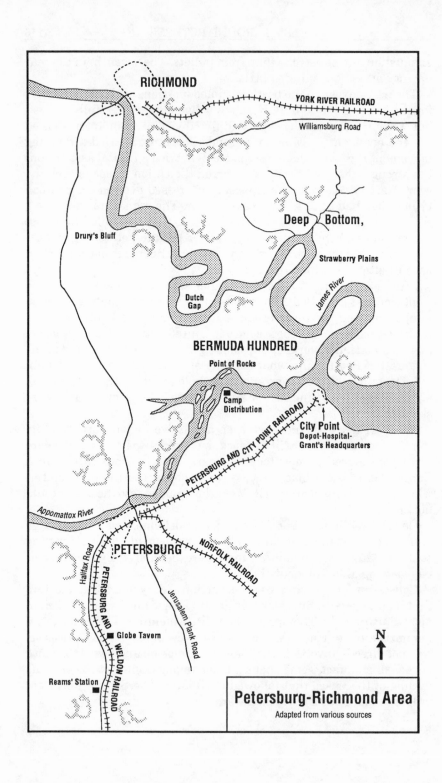

RICHMOND

YORK RIVER RAILROAD

Williamsburg Road

Deep Bottom,

Drury's Bluff

Strawberry Plains

James River

Dutch Gap

BERMUDA HUNDRED

Point of Rocks

Camp Distribution

PETERSBURG AND CITY POINT RAILROAD

City Point
Depot-Hospital-
Grant's Headquarters

Appomattox River

Halifax Road

PETERSBURG

NORFOLK RAILROAD

PETERSBURG AND

Jerusalem Plank Road

WELDON RAILROAD

Globe Tavern

Reams' Station

N

Petersburg-Richmond Area

Adapted from various sources

Headquarters
12th Regt. N.J.
Near Petersburg, Va.
August 3, 1864

My dear Sister Hann,

You are becoming very remiss in your letter writing, only written one letter in two months. Well, I will not ask you to write. I have done that in some six or eight letters written during that time and it amounts to nothing. I must tell you that Dr. Gilman[25] during this campaign has quite redeemed his character. He has even done better than most of his profession and been up to the front where few surgeons have dared to venture. I am sorry I ever said anything which might tend to injure him in the estimation of his acquaintances.

I wrote you of my promotion to Lieutenant Colonel. I beg you to pardon any faults of this letter as the flies are so thick that I have to keep one hand in motion all the time to prevent their covering my face and hands. At night I am actually tired from having my arms in constant motion and then the heat is such as to set ones body, brain, and temper in a flame. Oh! for a dip in the Atlantic or a good glass of ice water. I would give a dollar for a piece of ice the size of my hand and a hundred dollars to be fly proof.

Mary has collected the rent of the little house and lot of mine on Cape Island and I told her to pay it over to Doctor. Has he needs?

I shall send my old sword home the first opportunity. It is the one with which I originally came into the service and I have carried it now nearly two years as Captain, Major, and Lieutenant Colonel. I think it high time I had a new one. It is not a suitable sword for a field officer. Take good care of it for 'tis to me at least a thing of interest.

Albert Walker is now a Corporal and in good health. He is an excellent shot, and has distinguished himself for bravery and coolness. The general news is better told in the papers of the day than I could tell them. I had the pleasure of witnessing the terrible explosion of the mine under the Rebel fort and the artillery duel which followed on Saturday last. During that engagement we had one man wounded in our Regiment, none killed.

With much love and no patience to write more, I am ever,

Your affectionate brother,
Richard

Thompson wrote next to Coleman Leaming, trying to drum up more recruits for his regiment. Without actually saying so, he expressed his concern over the thinning ranks.

Headquarters
12th Regt. N.J.
Near Petersburg, Va.
August 7, 1864

Dear Doctor,

By today's mail I wrote Frank Hand the proposition of a 2nd Lieutenant for thirty (30) volunteers for this regiment. Whatever may be his action on this matter there must be haste as there are others who could and would avail themselves of such an offer. If you think there is no hope for him, discourage the young man at the start as nothing less than 30 will answer.

The impending draft may act as a very wholesome stimulant to volunteering, and I should imagine enough faith in the ill effects of delay had already been created in the minds of you good people on the Capes.

I received your letter. Give my love to the children and Hann. If there should be any volunteering, cannot some influence be brought toward throwing the men into this Regiment. As they will most likely enlist for one year, it may be an inducement to join a regiment that has about one year to serve. Our time is out on the 4th of September, 1865.

With much regard and many good wishes I remain your affectionate brother,

Richard

The blowing up of the Rebel fort and the artillery duel which followed presented a fine display of the effects produced by powder. Our position was quite safe during that engagement (30th July). We had only one man wounded. We were quite tired having but just returned from the north side of the James River. Yesterday we lost a few men while working on the entrenchments. There is much speculation upon our future movements. Rumor says Hancock has been offered the command of the Middle Department (Washington) and that he accepted on the condition that his corps should go with him and the troops there take their place in this army. But Grant would not permit this saying the 2nd Corps was his main dependence. We of this corps like to believe this as it tickles us.

[RST]

From August 13th to the 18th, the Second Corps (and the Twelfth New Jersey) found themselves again north of the James, involved in engagements at Bailey's Creek, Deep Bottom Run (again), and Fussell's Mill. These demonstrations were planned as diversionary tactics to draw large numbers of the Confederate Army away from Petersburg and Bermuda Hundred. Lee, however, sent only enough men to create a stubborn resistance and tarnish the waning reputation of the once mighty Second Corps.

Despite repeated charges by the Twelfth under Majors Chew and Thompson, the August 16th attack at Fussell's Mill was a failure, as was the one at Bailey's Creek. The Twelfth New Jersey was in position behind a hill (not specifically named, but it may have been New Market Heights, behind Bailey's Creek) between the main troops and a group of skirmishers. A Confederate artillery battery held them there; the shells caused little damage, but were a definite annoyance.

To capture the battery and put an end to the shelling, Thompson led his men to the hilltop and formed them for a charge down the other side. They got orders to halt just as they began the downward run, mixing with other soldiers and acting as skirmishers. When they reversed direction to regain the top of the hill, they became easy targets. Fortunately, most escaped injury and they withdrew with the rest of Hancock's force. Hancock was disappointed in the failure of his corps.[26] Death, injury, or capture had claimed too many of his once crack troops. Many of the new recruits were as eager to charge rearward as forward. Green troops and some of the immigrant soldiers often misunderstood orders.[27] Despite the exhortations of their officers most of the men fell back. As usual, the Twelfth could say with pride that they stood their ground.

After dark on the 20th, Hancock's army retreated over the pontoon bridge. With the enemy close behind, Hancock's men recrossed the James, with the Twelfth the last to cross. The troops moved as quietly as possible, having laid down a bed of straw to muffle the noise of marching feet. Crossing water on pontoons was a hazard in broad daylight, but after dark it was even more dangerous. Major Chew supervised the crossing while Thompson, as Officer of the Day, stayed in the rear to expedite the safe withdrawal of the pickets and skirmishers. Not a man was lost. Many years later Thompson wrote the following notes along the margin of a newspaper.

> This was the night of Aug. 20, 1864, when I was Corps officer of the Day and had to hold the pickets in line until 10 p.m. under the order of Genl. Hancock. The picket lines were in some places only 30 yds from the enemy line. We crossed the James River on [a] pontoon bridge. The enemy discovered our withdrawal and opened their guns throwing shells in the direction of this pontoon bridge. As soon as the last man was on the bridge, I ordered the ropes cut on the north side and the tide in the river swung the bridge to the south bank. We joined our Corps about sunrise.[28]

Because of his efforts in getting the men to safety, he received a commendation and a personal letter from General Hancock, complimenting him on the performance of his duty.

After the crossing, rain came down heavily during the march back. The heavy dust endured during the battle turned to thick mud. Tired, wet, dirty, and dejected, the Twelfth longed for rest. They were given duty digging more trenches and building up the earthworks.

Meanwhile, Grant once again turned his attention to the Weldon Railroad. Before dawn on August 18th he sent General G. K. Warren's Fifth Corps out with orders to destroy the line as far as possible. The corps set out down the Jerusalem Plank Road for a few miles then turned right toward the railroad, nearly four miles to the west. The Jerusalem Road was the only one in the area that was planked. Once they left it, the march became exceedingly difficult. Previous heavy rains and clinging mud prevented Warren from bringing along his heavy artillery and supply wagons. The troops slogged along as best they could; there were many stragglers. When they reached the Weldon near Globe Tavern, they began to tear up the tracks.

However, the Federals were met by Henry Heth's Confederate forces who protested their progress. A moderate engagement took place, but the next day A. P. Hill's division came up and a full scale battle ensued. The Battle of Globe Tavern lasted three days. The Federals held their ground; the Confederates conceded that the part of the Weldon line from Globe Tavern north to the city would remain in Union hands.[29]

General Warren had achieved part of Grant's goal to destroy the Weldon Railroad, but this did not satisfy the commanding general. He would send the Second Corps to finish the job. The Second Corps was on the march once again, but this time in battle, it would not be proud. And Thompson would be in his last field action.[30]

Notes

[1] Franz Sigel was a German born officer who came to America in 1862. He was not a military success, but had great influence on the many German-Americans who fought for their adopted country. So many Germans joined the army that there were several regiments composed entirely of the foreign born. They had their own song, written in dialect, *I Goes to Fight mit Sigel*. (A copy of this song may be found in Glass P. & Singer, L. C. (1968) *Singing Soldiers*. New York, Pp. 118–119.) Sigel was routed in the Shenandoah and was removed from field duty.

[2] Situated between Petersburg and Richmond, Bermuda Hundred was the name of the peninsula formed by a loop of the James River where its south side nearly meets the Appomattox. The designation *hundred* was derived from an archaic method of dividing county lands in England. The name no longer had any meaning in nineteenth century Virginia, but continued to be used. A small village of the same name was located on the James.

[3] After Butler secured the area, the army set up a major supply depot, a large military field hospital, and Grant's headquarters on the land opposite and south of Bermuda Hundred called City Point, a terminus of the City Point Railroad. Lincoln came to City Point in June and reviewed the troops there, staying at Grant's headquarters.

[4] From November 11, 1863, Butler commanded the new Department of Virginia and North Carolina territory held by the Union. Included in the Department was Fortress Monroe and the area around Norfolk north to Yorktown and south to New Bern, North Carolina. With his new Army of the James, he left this largely administrative post for a field command of primary importance. See Schiller, H. M. (1988) *The Bermuda Hundred Campaign, Operations of the South Side of The James River, May, 1864*. Dayton, OH, Pp. 23ff.

[5] Robertson, W. G. (1987) *Back Door to Richmond*. Baton Rouge, LA, Pp. 79-91.

[6] Cold Harbor was fought between May 31st and June 12th. Lee won this battle, but both sides sustained terrible losses. The losses suffered by the

Army of the Potomac could be replenished; Thompson's activity in Camden was to do just that. The ranks could also be filled by conscripts. The South did not have similar resources.

[7] His muster roll records show that he was detached from the Regiment on December 21, 1863, by Special Orders No. 333. He joined the Draft Command at Trenton on the 28th. While at Perrine he was promoted to Major (February 15, 1864), but not mustered in until he was back in the field.

[8] On May 16, 1864 Governor Parker called the militia of New Jersey into active service for a period of one hundred days, dating from muster into the service. They were armed and paid as United States Infantry volunteers and were to serve wherever required in or out of the state. They were given no credit against the draft and were paid no bounty. The governor hoped to raise five regiments but only two regiments, the 37th and 38th, became partially filled. They were consolidated on June 23 at Camp Delaware, Trenton as the 37th New Jersey Volunteers. They were sent to General Butler at Bermuda Hundred and went into camp at Point of Rocks on July 1st where they did commissary and entrenching work. They did picket duty in the trenches at Petersburg and were mustered out on October 1, 1864. After being mustered out, several officers reenlisted. They did not participate in any battles, but lost 18 men to disease and stray shells. Twenty-nine were wounded. See Foster, J. Y. (1868) *New Jersey and the Rebellion.* . . . Newark, NJ, Pp. 670-673.

[9] During May of 1864, the armies of the Potomac and James lost more men than Lee had in his entire army. Over 6,000 men were killed; more than 35,000 were wounded and many others were missing and presumed captured.

[10] Turner was commander of the Second Division of Gillmore's Tenth Corps.

[11] Pierre Gustave Toutant Beauregard had been commander of the reorganized Department of North Carolina and Southern Virginia. He replaced General Pickett, who had been detached from the Army of Northern Virginia after Gettysburg. The defense of Petersburg and Richmond was under the Department of Richmond, headed by Major General Robert Ransom, Jr. When Beauregard first took over his new command, he had his headquarters at Weldon, North Carolina. See Robertson, *op. cit.,* Pp. 44-49.

[12] Fort Pillow, along the Mississippi River in Tennessee, was held by about 260 black men of the 11th U.S. Colored Troops and Battery F of the 4th U.S. Colored Light Artillery, and almost 300 white soldiers of the 13th Tennessee Cavalry, all under the command of Major Lionel F. Booth. On April 12, 1864, Confederates commanded by Brigadier General James R. Chalmers and under the direct personal command of General Nathan Bedford Forrest attacked the fort and demanded its surrender. Major Booth was killed. Major William F. Bradford took his place and refused to surrender. The Confeder-

ates took the fort easily, killing nearly half the Federal troops, both black and white. The survivors claimed the Rebel soldiers murdered many of the black soldiers after they had surrendered and that tents in which there were wounded men were set on fire. The North called it a massacre; the South denied it. The words "Fort Pillow" soon became the rallying cry for black soldiers in the Army of the Potomac. Boatner, M. M. (1988) *The Civil War Dictionary.* New York, Pp. 295-296.

[13] The Petersburg and Weldon Railroad connected with other railroads that ran from the Carolina coast. Food from the farms in the area was shipped over these rails. Blockade runners brought in food, guns, ammunition and other needed supplies from England via Bermuda and other island ports to Wilmington, North Carolina. These supplies were then transferred to railroad cars and shipped to Weldon to be transshipped to Petersburg. The line ran through typical southern Virginia countryside: oak and pine forests, thick tangled scrub, and an occasional swamp. Here and there a farmer had fields of sorghum or corn. Weldon, North Carolina, today is east of Route 95.

[14] German born August V. Kautz and Brigadier General James Harrison Wilson had been raiding along the Southside and Richmond and Danville Railroads during this time. After completing as much damage as they could to their separate objectives, they attempted to return to Reams' Station on June 29th, but they found it in the hands of Confederate cavalry. *Ibid.*, Pp. 931-932.

[15] From a letter dated September 4, 1864, written by Lt. Laurens W. Walcott, Company D, 52nd Regiment, Illinois Infantry, 16th Corps. He described how the Montgomery Railroad near Lovejoy, Georgia, was wrecked. This was roughly the same method used by the Army of the Potomac on the Weldon. (Letter formerly in the collection of the authors.)

[16] An abatis (from the French *abattre*: to fell) was a defense made by felling whole trees and placing the root end toward the defenders, while the tops of the trees faced the enemy. If time permitted, the branches were sharpened into points. Having to pick through a tangle of twigs and branches could help slow down a charge. These works, built by the Sixth Corps, were used in August by the Second Corps.

[17] The station was named for a local family whose name was originally Riehm. They came from Winzingen in the Rhine Palatinate area of Germany and settled first in Pennsylvania. At least one member of the family fought in the Revolutionary War. Later they moved into Virginia, settled below what became Petersburg, and resumed the family profession of farming. They may have contracted with the railroad to stop there and pick up produce to be sold in the city. In his letters Thompson spelled Reams' as *Ream's*, but local use put the apostrophe *after* the *s*, and modern scholars have accepted this spelling. Archives of Virginia State Library.

[18] The rolls were dated back to May 12, 1864, but this was inaccurate. The date should have been March, which was the month in which he was promoted. When he applied for his pension, and tried to correct the error, it was denied.

[19] Doctor Wiley served in the 3rd Corps of The Army of the Potomac. See Chapter 1, Note 9.

[20] Thompson may have meant *Camp* Delaware at Trenton. See note 8 above.

[21] Whitworth was the name of a rifled cannon made in England. It was made of various calibre sizes that could use an explosive shell or solid shot. Some models were breech loaders and some muzzle loaders. With its great accuracy and long range, it was the Confederate artillery's most efficient weapon. In flight its shells produced a peculiar sound which Union soldiers learned to respect. *Ibid.*, p. 917.

[22] The *Florida* was a Confederate steamer commanded by Commodore John Newland Maffitt, famous as a blockade runner. She was captured in October or November by the U.S. ship *Wachusett* which had rammed her while she was in a Brazilian port. The *Wachusett* arrived at Hampton Roads in November with her prize, which sank shortly thereafter. *Ibid.*, p. 285.

[23] For the detailed story of the actions at Deep Bottom, see Horn, J. (1991) *The Destruction of the Weldon Railroad-Deep Bottom, Globe Tavern, Reams' Station.* Lynchburg, VA.

[24] For a telling narrative of the Battle of the Crater, see Catton, B. (1953) *A Stillness at Appomattox.* New York, Pp. 242-253.

[25] Lt. Uriah Gilman, Assistant Surgeon to the Regiment, was a graduate of Jefferson Medical School of Philadelphia. Whenever Chief Surgeon Satterthwait was not present, Dr. Gilman acted in his stead. Longacre, E. G. (1988) *To Gettysburg and Beyond.* . . . Hightstown, NJ, p. 28.

[26] For a detailed account of the Twelfth New Jersey's activities north of the James, see *Ibid.*, Pp. 234-242.

[27] See Davis, B. (1982) *The Civil War: Strange and Interesting Facts.* Averel, NJ, p. 90.

[28] This notation was written by Thompson on the inside of the front page of *The National Tribune* newspaper for December 15, 1910. The front page carried a long article by John McElroy called the "Wilderness Campaign" which dealt with the war after Gettysburg. Another article in the series was dated December 22, 1910. Thompson made pencilled notes over all of it,

recalling his part in the battles described in the article. It was only four years until his death, yet these scenes remained vividly in his memory.

[29] For detailed descriptions of this and other battles that took place over the possession of the Weldon Railroad, see Horn, *op. cit., passim.*

[30] Other source material for this chapter came from Garrison, W. (1992) *Civil War Trivia and Fact Book.* Nashville, TN; Long, E. B. (1971) *The Civil War Day by Day.* . . . New York, Pp. 555-558; Walker, F. A. (1887) *History of The Second Corps in the Army of the Potomac.* New York.

Chapter Nine

The Battle of Reams' Station

... the hissing iron and lead passed over us,
cutting off trees a foot and a half through. ...

RST to Emma, August 24, 1864

Despite all the effort expended, the Weldon Railroad, which kept Petersburg alive, was a thorn in Grant's side and he wanted it removed. He wanted to stretch Lee's line of supply so provisions to Petersburg would have to be carried over the Boydton Plank Road to the west of the Weldon, adding ten or more miles to the length of the route.[1] Before Butler went up the James,[2] a plan to attack the head of the line at Weldon, North Carolina, was proposed but not accepted. In June a wrecking crew was attacked and defeated by A. P. Hill's forces.

By mid-August as the Fifth Corps regrouped after fighting for the Weldon line at Globe Tavern, Hancock's Second Corps marched over roads "from Deep Bottom to Petersburg [that] were in miserable condition, even for Virginia."[3] The men were spent with fatigue when they finally reached their old position near a deserted house on the left flank of the Army of the Potomac.

On August 21st, the Second Corps' First Division, under the temporary command of Brigadier General Nelson A. Miles,[4] and the Second Division, under Major General John Gibbon, were put on fatigue duty in the rear. The Twelfth New Jersey, as part of Gibbon's division, was set to work digging trenches and otherwise improving the earthworks which they planned to inhabit for a while. They were given about one hour of rest, then Grant ordered both divisions and a cavalry detachment of 2,000 men under Major General David M. Gregg to proceed to Globe Tavern where they were ordered to construct a defense perimeter around the Strong House. Many of the men, too worn out from all they had been through, did not comply. Second Corps' new recruits were especially debilitated. Well-trained men could march 15 or more miles on easy roads, but these men, in wool uniforms, carrying guns and packs and not as disciplined or well-trained as the early volunteers, were taxed beyond endurance in the hot, sticky, Virginia August. Every regiment left behind exhausted men who just lay where they fell. Of course, Thompson and the other officers above the rank of captain did not have to march, but the heat also affected them severely.

They were then ordered to move farther down the Jerusalem Plank Road to the Williams House west of the road where it crossed Second Swamp. They arrived around three o'clock in the afternoon and camped in the rear of the Fifth Corps. The Twelfth's division finally rested, but Miles's troops moved further south along the Halifax Road, which paralleled the Weldon Railroad on the east. Their goal was Reams' Station, where they were to continue the work of destruction on the Weldon begun by Warren's men at Globe Tavern.

Reams' Station, about 12 miles south of Petersburg, was not much more than a crossing and depot, now burned.[5] The small station was west of the line. Thick pine woods around it kept the little building from being seen at a distance. Beyond the railroad to the east were the Halifax Road, Oak Grove Methodist Church, a couple of fields, dense woods, and a ravine, at the head of which Hancock established his headquarters. West of the railroad and south of the church was a part of the roughly horseshoe-shaped earthworks which had been thrown up on June 22nd during the earlier aborted attempt to wreck the Weldon. The northwestern leg of the works abutted the Jones Hole Swamp.

For the men who had fought at the Wilderness, this was a similar landscape—dense oaks and pine, with thick, tangled scrub, brambles, and an occasional swamp. But here, open fields and farmland punched holes in the forested area every now and then. The march down from Globe Tavern made itself memorable for misery. In addition to all their other hardships the men were desperately thirsty. Although they marched in intermittent rain, there was not enough to fill up the rills and springs so that the men could get fresh water. When it was not raining, the heat was intense and the dust rose in clouds. To add to their troubles, the marching men disturbed hordes of ticks, flies, mosquitoes, and other biting insects.

In the evening of the 21st, the men spent the night near the Aiken House, sleeping in the mud under a pouring rain. The new recruits were now somewhat disenchanted with army life. By August 22nd, Miles's working soldiers had destroyed the railroad track to about a mile and a half above Reams' Station while Gregg's cavalry had gone the full distance to the station. They did not find any Confederates there but scouts informed them that Brigadier General John Chambliss's cavalry brigade was at Tabernacle Church, about six miles west of them.[6]

When the new day dawned, it was raining so hard the men were given the day to rest. General Barlow, just out of City Point Hospital, returned to command around 11:00 a.m. His orders were to move on to Reams' Station, to cover the working party and occupy the area. Barlow sent Colonel James B. Lynch's First Brigade which arrived around noon. An hour later despite the weather, the remainder of the division arrived and began working at once.[7] As they moved along, there were skirmishes now and then with Confederate troops, who held a definite advantage. The road led through a thickly wooded landscape like the woods in which the Southern soldiers had hunted most of their lives. They moved swiftly through the forest disappearing into the trees after firing a few rounds at the Federals.

Responding to the news of cavalry contact with the enemy on the 22nd, Meade now ordered Gibbon's division and four artillery batteries to reinforce Barlow and Gregg at Reams' Station. He gave overall command of the operation to Hancock. From their camp near the Aiken House, Gibbon's still weary troops moved out late in the afternoon of the 23rd. They marched all night down the plank road, straggling into Reams' Station between 3:00 and 10:00 a.m. on the 24th.[8]

While the Second Division was en route, Barlow's men had been "working on the railroad," wrecking the rails from Globe Tavern to Reams' Station and trying to improve the old entrenchments. Around ten o'clock, the new arrivals relieved Barlow's weary soldiers in the shallow rifle pits or went down the line to help destroy more of the tracks. By evening they had gone three miles farther south.

Barlow deployed his men into the inadequate entrenchments and prepared for the next day's work, but his old wounds reopened and he was carried off on a stretcher. This time, Miles's assumption of Barlow's command was permanent. Miles sent part of his infantry, assisted by cavalry, to protect the working party of Gibbon's division which had been ordered to tear up the track down to Rowanty Creek, roughly eight miles below Reams' Station. The Twelfth New Jersey, armed with picks, shovels, and crowbars participated in this detail. Hancock now had nearly 7,000 men at Reams' Station and the surrounding area. In the intense heat and a warm, stifling rain which made the roads nearly impassable and work unendurable, it was virtually impossible to move artillery or supply wagons. More men in the ranks fell to heat stroke and exhaustion.

During his off-duty hours, Thompson wrote two letters, one to Emma and one to Hannah, relating his part in the action north of the James and musing on what would happen next. (It was just as well he could not see the future. Many soldiers had premonitions of being wounded or killed; often these premonitions proved correct.)

Headquarters
12th N.J. Regt.
Ream's Station
August 24, 1864

My dear Sister Em,

Today I received your letter and will answer at once. Our Corps returned from the James River, leaving there at dark on Saturday. I was Corps Officer of the Day and remained until midnight with the pickets. We were in some places only 25 yards from the enemy and this made the withdrawal quite difficult. Upon my reporting with the pickets at Headquarters, General Hancock, who had left staff officers to report the manner in which I conducted the matter, complimented me in person for the manner and success of my withdrawal. This, of course, repaid me for a long ride and a sleepless night. While north of the James we were under fire nearly everyday and some days nearly every hour. Still, in my Regiment the loss was very small. At one o'clock p.m. on the 16th inst. with my Regiment, charged the enemy's entrenchments on the supposition that they were only held with a small force, but were quickly undeceived by receiving a fire from a full line of infantry and canister from two batteries. We laid down and the hissing iron and lead passed over us, cutting off trees a foot and a half through and trimming up the bushes in a style peculiarly its own. There were troops about 150 yards in rear that suffered badly.

We are now at Reams' Station, immediately south of Petersburg, engaged [in] tearing up the railroad track. What our next move will be is doubtful to such as myself.

John [Stevenson] surprised me very much by calling on me previous to our late move. How much I would like to return the call your own heart can answer. If we go into anything like a permanent camp, I intend making an effort. Kate has gone west, and so ends our intended visit for her. I received a good long letter from Hann the other day. She and Mrs. Allen are quite regular correspondents. Hann has taken quite a fancy to her and is acting the part of a kind friend. Em, I sometimes think my life is strange, and when I think of it wonder much. Everyone may do the same, who knows?

Now I want you to write me a good long letter soon. If you only try, you can find a pleasure in writing me.

Excuse the envelope; hot weather affects them when carried in our pockets.

Affectionately your loving brother,
Richard

Headquarters
12th N.J. Regt.
Ream's Station
August 24, 1864

My dear Sister Hann,

I have only time to write a few lines. Yesterday I detailed Albert Walker for duty at Trenton, N.J., and he is now on his way there. This will give him a chance to visit home and secure him from Rebel bullets during this campaign. We returned from the north of the James River on Sunday last or at least I did with my command, which amounted to about two brigades. I was Corps Officer of the Day when the withdrawal took place and had the bringing in of the Corps picket line, which was no small matter as in some places our lines were within 25 yards of the enemy. A rain lent me its aid or I should not have been so successful. The Corps crossed the river at dark. We (pickets) remained until midnight. Upon reaching the Corps, General Hancock, who had left staff officers to report the conduct of my affairs, came out of his tent and in person complimented me upon the manner of my withdrawing and its success. That fully repaid me for the loss of a night's sleep and a long ride. See what kind words will do for a soldier.

We are now at Reams' Station on the W and P RR [Petersburg and Weldon Railroad] exactly south of Petersburg, tearing up the track and making sad work with green corn and apples. This country is so fully Rebel that this same corn rebels against the digestive organs of a loyal man's in many cases. For the past few days I have eaten but little else. While on the north of the James we were under fire nearly everyday and some days nearly every hour, yet our loss in the 12th was very small. We charged once by ourselves and met a full discharge of canister from two batteries and also a fire from a full line of musketry—we being deployed as skirmishers. Every man laid down and the death dealing iron and lead passed over us cutting the trees and bushes in a style that would make even an old soldier say "did you ever see the like." Trees a foot and a half through were cut off and fell to the earth with a crash. A line of support 150 yards in rear suffered severely.

I answered Em's letter. Your good interesting letter I have read some 50 times more or less and am most anxious to receive another. Love to you and the children.

Write soon to your ever affectionate brother,
Richard

When General Gregg moved his cavalry to Reams' Station the day before, he found that Colonel Samuel P. Spear's troops of the Eleventh Pennsylvania Cavalry had been skirmishing with the Rebels about a mile and a half from the Dinwiddie Stage Road to the west of the railroad. He reported this to Hancock. By the time darkness fell on August 24th, the men had destroyed three miles of track south of Reams' Station to Malone's Crossing.[9] According to orders, they still had five miles to ruin; it could be done in the next day or so if the Confederates stayed away. Enemy skirmishers harassed them but were driven off by 200 infantrymen. The destruction of track continued until dark, then both the work party and their protectors withdrew to the Station via the Halifax Road. Afraid of an attack the weary men slept in their shallow pits, guns loaded and ready. Colonel Spear's cavalry remained that night at the crossing.

The work on the railroad had attracted Lee's attention. Union lookouts reported the movements of large bodies of Rebel troops and cavalry in the area but could not deduce their intentions. Meade sent a report to Hancock at eight o'clock in the evening regarding infantry moving near the intersection of the Halifax and Vaughan Roads. From Army Headquarters General Andrew A. Humphreys alerted both Hancock and Warren of the possibility of a serious encounter. Hancock postponed the order to continue the destruction of the railroad and made plans to return to Globe Tavern at daybreak on the 25th; he did not wish to separate his forces for such a long distance. He felt his strength to be inferior to the 8,000 to 10,000 Confederates said to be lurking in the woods around them. Scouts reported the enemy to be moving along the Halifax Road south of Malone's Crossing. General Warren considered them to be Confederate repair parties and had no fear of an attack.

At dawn the alerted men were ready to move back to Globe Tavern. However, a report came in from Gregg that his cavalry had pushed the enemy back in at least two places, so Hancock changed his mind and moved Gibbon's work party on out. They had barely left when Colonel Spear reported that he had been attacked at Malone's Crossing and driven back by a portion of Major General Wade Hampton's cavalry of nearly 5,000 men. Gibbon sent out a strong skirmish line which learned that the Confederate cavalry, strong in numbers on its own, had infantry behind it.

The day had begun early for Hampton's cavalrymen. They broke camp at 3:00 a.m. to move unseen to a position at Hancock's left, while the infantry left their camp a little later to engage the pickets at Malone's Crossing. (The skirmish which resulted was more or less a stalemate.) Hancock received another report which stated the enemy were seen moving to the north and west, apparently in an effort to cut off the route back to Globe Tavern. He called Gibbon's men back to the Station.

When the dawn came, bringing with it the promise of another long, hot summer day, Miles's troops relieved Gibbon's in the picket line and in the breastworks. They had been deployed in the right hand pits that ran from Jones Hole Swamp to the railroad, with the 140th Pennsylvanians on the right and the Eighty-first Pennsylvanians on the left, practically on the tracks themselves.

As soon as they took their places in the works, Miles had his pioneer corps slash more timber to strengthen the barrier in front of his men. He had another group cut roads in the woods at the rear. At 6:00 a.m., Hancock sent out cavalry to reconnoiter and ordered Smyth's brigade[10] to leave its position (connecting with the cavalry), assemble in a cornfield near the open (eastern) end of the works close to the church, and prepare to move against the enemy. The rest of the men were ordered to get into the entrenchments around the ruins of little Reams' Station.

Three hours later, Hancock ordered some of Smyth's men north along the Halifax Road to pick up some of the tools the tired soldiers had left behind the day before and to scout around to see if they could

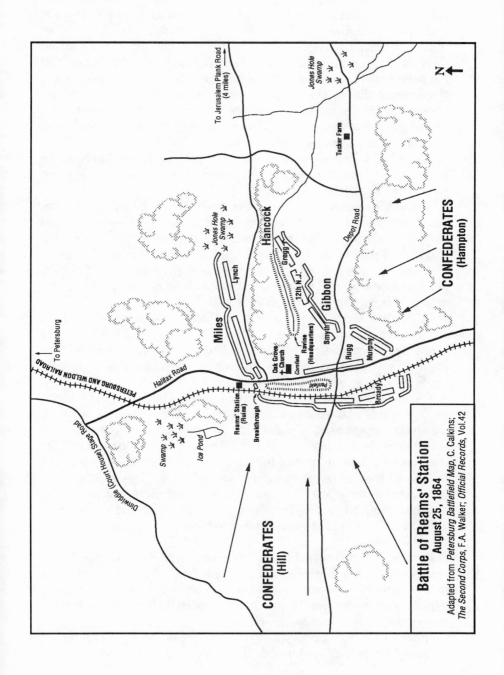

Battle of Reams' Station
August 25, 1864

Adapted from *Petersburg Battlefield Map*, C. Calkins;
The Second Corps, F.A. Walker; *Official Records*, Vol.42

find any men wearing gray. They did. About a mile up the road their skirmishers attracted fire from the pine woods. Chambliss's brigade of the Ninth Virginia Cavalry came upon the work party. They rushed the Union troops, who gave way instantly, abandoning their rifles and tools. As they proceeded up the Halifax Road, the Virginians and Pennsylvania cavalrymen spied each other. Before the Confederates could form a charge, the Union cavalry galloped off to Reams' Station. Meanwhile, Hill's and Major General Cadmus M. Wilcox's men were crossing Monk's Neck Bridge, planning to arrive at Reams' Station at 9:00 a.m. (They were late.) Miles's division now occupied the upper or north and west half of these earthworks; Gibbon's Second Division the lower, mostly southern half. Trees and brush obscured the eastern ends of the lines from each other.

"These entrenchments played a critical part in the ensuing battle. [They were] . . . hastily thrown up by troops sent to relieve General James H. Wilson during the skirmishing at Reams' Station on June 22nd when part of the tracks had been torn. The earthworks ran in two separate lines along the railroad for approximately 700 yards, north and south, then turned easterly for about 800 to a 1,000 yards at nearly right angles to the railroad.

". . . only a short base was presented to the enemy, and . . . both sides of the works, as drawn back on the right and on the left, were exposed to an enfilading fire. . . . The distance across, from one side to another, was so short that the enemy's artillery on either side could make the opposite lines untenable. . . ."[11]

The low parapet of earth that ran parallel to the railroad for about 20 or 30 yards and what few tree trunks and branches were left from the June engagement afforded dubious protection. By August the slashing in the abatis was well dried. The men had used most of it for their cooking fires or for starting the huge bonfires needed to heat the rails until they were hot enough to be bent. Some new slashing had been carried out by various regiments here and there, but not nearly enough. "Hancock allowed the night to pass as he and Gibbon had allowed the day to pass without effecting a single improvement in the breastworks. . . ."[12]

Beyond the earthworks the railroad ran through a cut, then up an embankment, roughly a rise of about four feet.[13] The terrain made it nearly impossible to bring up either ammunition or reserves without exposure to enemy fire. It also made it difficult, if not hazardous, to maneuver artillery pieces into place.

Gibbon sent both cavalry and infantry out to the right of the road at Stony Creek and a skirmish line developed at ten o'clock. More

Confederates appeared in support of their comrades and drove Miles's skirmishers from their rifle pits. At 11:00 a.m. troopers of Brigadier General John Dunovant's brigade of the Sixth South Carolina Cavalry charged the pickets of the Thirteenth Pennsylvania Cavalry. The Union troopers retreated to the swamp and ice pond northwest of the main breastworks. Pickets of Colonel Levin Crandell's Consolidated Infantry Brigade and the Fourth Pennsylvania Cavalry stemmed the advance and the Confederates withdrew. During this action Hancock moved his field hospital from the Emmons House, about a mile east of the railroad, down to the Church. At the same time Pennsylvania and North Carolina cavalry units were also fighting at the Tucker farm between the Halifax and Jerusalem Plank Roads. Engagements were breaking out in every direction.

By noon, a field telegraph was strung from Reams' Station to Headquarters about five miles north at Globe Tavern. General Hancock sent a dispatch at 11:45 a.m. advising Meade of the cavalry charge. Meade sent a reply at 1:00 p.m. by a staff officer who rode down the Halifax Road. (For some unexplained reason, although he knew it was working, Meade did not use the telegraph for any communications with Hancock until 7:30 p.m., causing his orders to be seriously delayed.) By 2:00 p.m. two Confederate assaults had been repulsed with considerable casualties; some Rebel soldiers fell as close as three yards to the Union works.

From the safety of the breastworks Colonel Smyth then sent out the First Delaware with the Twelfth New Jersey in support. Bullets flew from the Confederates in the woods; the First Delaware and Twelfth New Jersey replied. The Southerners withdrew deeper into the trees, then held; neither side had an advantage. Hearing the shots, Smyth sent the 108th New York up to secure the unprotected flank. The Confederates pulled back about a half mile to an open field beyond the woods where their reinforcements halted the Federals. Smyth ordered the rest of his brigade into action, commanding Lieutenant Colonel Thompson to "move the right wing of the Twelfth into a position outside the Confederate left—a task Thompson gave to Major Chew, at the head of Companies A, B, F, H and I."[14]

Chew and his men moved to the east side of the cornfield to fire into the Confederate left. They flattened themselves among the stalks to protect themselves from the horizontal rain of lead which, like knives, cut the plants down to the ground.[15] The Confederates withdrew to another field and joined more reinforcements, including cavalry and artillery. This was Lieutenant General A. P. Hill's 9,000 man corps, who had been in the area since June. They had been defeated in battle at the Weldon on August 21st and were angry and ready for revenge. The Confederates' movement brought them closer to Smyth's front and around to his right. Seeing the situation, Hancock recalled Smyth's men back to the Station and they obeyed with great enthusiasm. Hancock realized they had no other option. The Confederate forces consisted of three brigades of Major General Cadmus Wilcox's division, G. T. Anderson's brigade of Brigadier General Charles W. Field's division, and artillery. There were also two cavalry divisions, Wade Hampton's and Brigadier General M. C. Butler's. The Confederates threw reinforcements into the area all afternoon. General Heth arrived around three o'clock with two brigades from his own division and two of Mahone's not far behind. As ranking officer Heth assumed overall command when Hill's illness, either real or imagined, caused him to retire from field command.[16]

Many Union troops, sick and exhausted by the work of tearing up the tracks, hurriedly slashing underbrush, and building breastworks, functioned below capacity. In addition, some few had problems understanding their orders and some were so filled with dread of battle as to be nearly useless.

The Union forces went on the defensive. The five units in the cornfield, including the Twelfth in front, and with two regiments in support, could only fire and fall back. The rest of the men hid in the entrenchments as best they could. The Confederates now began an earnest assault. Hill's (Heth's) infantry, Wilcox's artillery, and Hampton's cavalry were more than enough to impress the bravest.

". . . the confidence of the troops in their leaders had been severely shaken . . . they almost ceased to expect victory when they went into battle. The lamentable story . . . cannot be understood without reference to facts like these."[17]

At about ten minutes to two there was a heavy attack on the First and Fourth brigades of the First Division, who were in front of the Oak Grove Church. After ten minutes the attack was repulsed. As the day wore on, the church, in the center of the action, was severely damaged and partially burned.[18] Shells fell into the breastworks from every direction except the east. The barrage lasted until about 3:00 p.m. when the Confederate infantry charged Miles's position.[19] The Union soldiers repulsed the first assault, then a second assault a half-hour later. After the second assault, Confederate artillery began shelling once more. The shells missed the men in the north trenches but fell inside the southern works, where Gibbon's men were. Dead and wounded lay all around; the men were demoralized. Union artillery

Reams' Station Battlefield as it Appeared in the 1930's.
The 12th New Jersey saw this View from their Entrenchments.
(*Courtesy of the Petersburg National Battlefield Archives*)

Reams' Station Battlefield as it Appears Today.
The Present Oak Grove Methodist Church is at the Far Left.
(*Photograph by Ralph G. Poriss*)

could not function as effectively as it might have since most of the horses used to pull the heavy guns had been killed by sharpshooters or in Wilcox's earlier charge. The guns could not be moved nor re-positioned as needed.

At 2:40 p.m. Meade had informed Hancock he was sending him Generals Gershom Mott's and Orlando B. Willcox's Divisions with about 1,000 fresh troops. They were ordered to march down the Jerusalem Plank Road to reinforce his position, but it was too late. Using this road instead of the Halifax Road took the fresh troops 12 miles out of their way. Hancock replied that the Confederates were too strong for them and it would be prudent to withdraw. However, he was unable to do so until the cover of darkness. Another assault on the entrenchments was mounted around 4:00 p.m. The Twelfth went forward to make a countercharge. Thompson made ready to lead his men through a field. Around 4:30, a shell "burst in the middle of the Twelfth, its fragments striking Lieutenant Colonel Thompson in the chest, leg and hand."[20]

The stricken Thompson was carried off the field on a piece of tent canvas while Major Chew managed to take command as a third wave of attackers roared out of the trees. Falling back before the gray wave, the Sixty-first New York recovered part of their line when Miles personally came up to try to rally them. But it was too much for the Federals; they fled, except for those regiments which surrendered.

Confederates poured through the hole these men left in the line. The Twelfth tried to hold. Company F's Lieutenant James D. Stratton was killed, and Company E's Lieutenant John R. Rich was mortally wounded. Captain Frank Riley was captured. In just over 30 minutes the Twelfth had lost three of its bravest leaders and its confidence. They joined the general retreat, heading for the protection of the dense woods. Miles called them all cowards. Stung by the accusation, Chew tried to hold a line among the trees with the few hundred who were left. With the gallantry the Twelfth had always possessed, they held from around five o'clock, when the final assault of artillery and infantry began, until dark. Hancock tried to rally them but his pleas seemed to fall on unhearing ears.[21]

At dark and in a pouring rain, they went back to Petersburg—defeated, dejected, and demoralized. The Second Corps was broken. Hancock rode along with his men, telling his aides he would rather have died than suffer this humiliation. Gibbon was dejected and Hancock was beside himself with rage, frustration, and humiliation. Hancock's aide blamed Meade. "If Meade did not intend to fight, Hancock should have been withdrawn. If he did intend to fight,

Hancock should have been powerfully re-enforced."[22] Meade "bore some of the responsibility for the disaster at Reams' Station in that he saw but disregarded the terrible condition of the First and Second Divisions of the Second Corps."[23]

The Twelfth lost 15 men.[24] The Union forces lost over 600 killed and wounded, and 2,000 as prisoners; the Confederates, about 720, killed and wounded. The Southerners had nine more field guns to work with than did the Federals but not more men, though that was claimed to be the case later.

In darkness, Hancock's defeated troops retreated to Shay's Tavern, where at 7:00 p.m. they met Brigadier General Orlando B. Willcox and his reinforcements. Instead of going into battle, they covered the retreat as rain came down dampening the bodies of the dispirited men. Two hours later Meade ordered more reinforcements and telegraphed Hancock at 11:00 that night. Hancock's men, camped now at the Williams House, sat as Willcox's division began its return to the Jerusalem Plank Road with the stragglers it picked up along the way. Gregg's cavalry was left guarding the Jerusalem Plank Road, the only Federals between there and Globe Tavern.[25]

The next morning, the Confederates buried the dead, collected abandoned equipment and tended the wounded. Probing eastward, a cavalry unit of the Seventh Virginia skirmished with Gregg's men and then withdrew. Despite the disgrace of the defeat, the Weldon Railroad was disrupted and lost to the Confederacy for good. This disruption worsened the already short supplies of meat and forage for the Army of Northern Virginia. The lack of adequate forage was especially telling in sustaining the cavalry upon which Lee depended so much.

As his comrades trudged morosely back to Petersburg, Thompson was on his way to medical help, his service as a line officer over. The next battle he would fight would be for his life.

Notes

[1] The Confederates could still bring supplies in from trains stopped at Stony Creek Depot. There, supplies would be loaded onto wagons that went to Dinwiddie Court House, then north along the Boydton Plank Road to Petersburg, roughly a 30 mile journey.

[2] For a detailed account of this expedition, see Robertson, W. G. (1987) *Back Door to Richmond*. Baton Rouge, LA, Pp. 56-59.

[3] Walker, F. A. (1891) *A History of the Second Corps in the Army of the Potomac*. New York.

140   WHILE MY COUNTRY IS IN DANGER

⁴ Nelson A. Miles (1839-1925) took over for Brigadier General Francis C. Barlow, who had been severely wounded at Gettysburg. Absent from duty for almost a year, Barlow had returned to duty, but on August 17th, his wounds forced him out once more. Miles was brevetted major general of volunteers for his service during the Battle of Reams' Station. See Warner, E. J. (1988) *Generals in Blue*. Baton Rouge, LA, Pp. 322-324.

⁵ On July 2, 1864, Elisha Hunt Rhodes wrote in his diary, "When we reached Reams' Station we found quite a village with a good depot, fair dwellings, work shops and well cultivated fields fenced in. When we left nothing remained but smoking ruins, trampled fields and a railroad useless for some days." Rhodes, R. H. (Ed.) (1985) *All for the Union: The Civil War Diary of Elisha Hunt Rhodes*. New York, p. 158.

⁶ Horn, J. (1991) *The Destruction of the Weldon Railroad.* . . . Lynchburg, VA, p. 114.

⁷ The rest of the division consisted of the Consolidated Brigade, formed by remnants of the Second and Third Brigades and the Fourth Brigade.

⁸ *Ibid.*, p. 117.

⁹ There was also a Malone's Road and a Malone's Bridge in the area.

¹⁰ Colonel Thomas Smyth's Third Brigade consisted of the Fourteenth Connecticut; First Delaware; Seventh West Virginia; Twelfth New Jersey; Tenth and 108th New York; Sixty-Ninth, Seventy-Second and 106th Pennsylvania; and Fourth Ohio, the only western troops in the brigade.

¹¹ Walker, *op. cit.*, Pp. 582-606.

¹² Horn, *op. cit.*, p. 119 and Pp. 122ff.

¹³ The battle area is located on Virginia State Route 604 between Interstate Routes 85 and 95. The Conservation Fund now owns 220 acres. Calkins, C. M. (1990) "Reams' Station" In Kennedy, F. H. (Ed.) *The Civil War Battlefield Guide*. Boston, p. 258.

¹⁴ Longacre, E. G. (1988) *To Gettysburg and Beyond.* . . . Hightstown, NJ, p. 245.

¹⁵ Haines, W. P. (1897) *History of the Men of Company F.* . . . Mickleton, NJ, Pp. 79-80.

¹⁶ Ambrose Powell Hill (1825-1865) was wounded at Chancellorsville. Whether this had a bearing on his future health or not, he was often ill for no apparent reason and often absent from duty. Today, it is thought that his

frequent illnesses were psychosomatic. He put himself on sick leave from May 8 to May 21, 1864, then resumed command but became ill again shortly afterward. Warner, E. J. (1988) *Generals in Gray*. Baton Rouge, LA, p. 135.

[17] Walker, *op. cit.,* Pp. 592-593.

[18] Built in 1820 and called "Hubbard's Meeting House," the church was remodeled and renamed Oak Grove prior to the Civil War. A separate building was built at the rear of the church and used for services for slaves from nearby farms. During the battle, situated as it was between the lines, the church suffered both from shell fire and its use as a Union hospital. Hit by shells several times, it became a Confederate hospital after the northern forces withdrew. The church suffered a great deal of damage. After the war, it was moved and converted into a grocery store; a second story was added. It is still standing but in ruined condition. The parish house, however, burned to the ground and was not replaced at its old location. Early in the twentieth century, a new church was built on the site of the old one with Federal funds obtained through the Southern Claims Commission. A vestry and belfry were added. Still in use today, the church houses a small museum of artifacts gleaned from the battle site; there is a cemetery in the churchyard.

[19] There were about 30 yards of slashing and old abatis in front of the Federal works; advancing Confederates crawled through this maze to the Federal lines, often taking as long as ten minutes. See Horn, *op. cit.*, p. 155.

[20] Longacre, *op. cit.*, Pp. 246-247.

[21] In his book, *A Stillness at Appomattox*, (p. 320), Catton quotes from p. 253 of *The History of the Tenth Massachusetts Battery of Light Artillery* that Hancock cried, "Come on! We can beat them yet! Don't leave me, for God's sake!"

[22] Walker, *op. cit.*, p. 585.

[23] Horn, *op. cit.*, p. 178.

[24] Killed: one officer (Stratton) and two enlisted men; wounded: two officers, Thompson and Lieutenant Rich, who died later, and four enlisted men; captured or missing: one officer (Riley) and five enlisted men. See Longacre, *op. cit.*, p. 249. A short report of the battle was printed in a local newspaper, *The Cape May Warrior*, for September 1, 1864:
"New Jerseys Troops in Thursday's Battle
"A correspondent of the *Philadelphia Inquirer* wrote the following mention of the gallantry of New Jersey troops in the fight at Reams' Station, on the Weldon Railroad, on Thursday last. The 12th New Jersey Regiment and portions of the Tenth New York and Fourteenth Connecticut, which voluntarily acted with Twelfth Artillery, are highly praised for their gallantry in

driving the enemy from a position near the center of our line, opposite the Station, where, after crossing our breastworks, they had established themselves behind an embankment on the railroad, which afforded them excellent protection, and to dislodge from which may be a task of no slight difficulty and danger.

"Lieutenant Colonel R. S. Thompson of the Twelfth New Jersey was severely wounded in making this charge.

"Captain Warren [Captain Christian Woerner] of the Third New Jersey Battery which was posted on General Gibson's [Gibbon's] line is worthy of particular mention for skill and efficiency with which he held his guns, firing sometimes to the west, sometimes to the south and almost every point of the compass, and always with telling effect upon the enemy.

"Lieutenant J. D. Stratton, of the Twelfth Regiment was killed during the engagement and buried on the field. Lieutenant Colonel Thompson is a native of Cape May County, and has won for himself an enviable name. He has on several occasions received the personal thanks of his division officer for good conduct and gallantry on the field.

"While leading the charge at Reams' Station on last Thursday, he was severely wounded by fragments of a shell, the same time losing the end of his right thumb."

25 Horn, *op. cit.*, Pp. 164ff.

Chapter Ten

A Greater Danger

. . . I was so unfortunate as to be struck by the fragment of a shell. . . .

RST to Hannah, August 26, 1864

For the survivors the fierce engagement at Reams' Station ended at nightfall. For Lieutenant Colonel Richard S. Thompson, it had ended at 4:30 in the afternoon. With the burst of an enemy shell,[1] his active military career came to an abrupt halt. Three of Thompson's men picked up their bleeding officer and carried him away from the fighting. Thompson was taken in an ambulance to a field hospital near the Williams house.[2] He describes the event in notes made after the war.

> Thursday, Aug. 25, 1864—Wounded at Ream's Station by shell while in command of my Regt. (12 N.J.V.) at 5:30 p.m. Thursday, Aug. 25, while making a charge through a sugarcane field, my right hand thumb was mashed to pieces against my sword hilt and I picked up my sword and continued on the charge, for about 30 yards, when a piece of shell struck me on my right side tearing my clothing and flesh and very badly bruising my body. I was carried on a half of an army tent by three men through the cane field[3] to our division at the edge of the timber. I was placed in an ambulance and rode eight miles to 2nd Div., 2nd Corps Hospital.[4]

The wartime ambulance was nothing more than a high-sided wagon with a canvas top and a layer of straw on its bed. The straw was used both as a cushion and to absorb the blood. An ambulance could carry

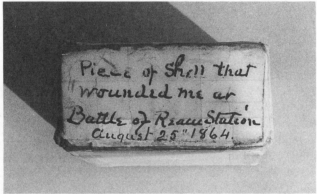

Confederate Shell Fragment that Struck RST during the
Battle of Reams' Station on August 25, 1864, and his
Notation on the Box in which it was kept.
(*Photograph by Ralph G. Poriss*)

two stretcher cases at a time or four to six men if they were able to sit up.

Thompson was now in more danger than when he faced the Confederate Army. Civil War era medicine was unimaginably inadequate, ". . . abdominal wounds were highly fatal . . . patients died so quickly. When the wound was in the large intestine, survival was 59%. . . with the patient facing almost certain peritonitis. . . . Medical treatment included . . . opium . . . coupled with absolute quiet and withdrawal of food. . . . The standard practice was to stuff the protruding intestines [back] into the cavity and sew [it up]."[5]

Thompson now faced several possibilities, any of which could result in death. He could die of shock, hemorrhage, peritonitis, bungling, or neglect. In addition, he risked contracting any number of diseases from the hospital area itself—typhoid, malaria, measles, pneumonia, dysentery or "hospital fever" (typhus).[6]

Thompson could be thankful that conditions prevailing early in the war had now improved. In April 1861, several women's relief societies in the New York City area joined to form The United States Sanitary Commission. These women considered existing government medical treatment inadequate for the men they sent to war. They raised money to provide extra food, clean clothing, blankets, soap, bandages, and simple medications to hospitals. They often delivered these items themselves and stayed to nurse the sick and wounded. Dorothea Dix developed a professional nursing service, hiring only "plain women" who would not distract the men. Clara Barton started the work that later would become the American Red Cross. There was also the United States Christian Commission formed by the cooperation of several religious groups to bring spiritual and moral assistance to the soldiers. In 1861 when it was founded, the Christian Commission brought Bibles and religious books to the men. By 1863, it was bringing food, writing material, clothing, and other supplies to the various field hospitals some of which the Commission helped to establish.

The practice of military medicine during the Civil War would be considered barbaric today, but it was vastly better than in previous years. If available, chloroform and ether, in use before the war, were used during amputations. Hemorrhaging was a serious danger. Primary hemorrhaging occurred if arteries and veins were severed. Secondary hemorrhaging, equally fatal, usually developed after surgery due to unsterile surgical conditions or surgical error.

Pain control during and after surgery was minimal. Doctors relied heavily on opium, laudanum (a solution of opium and alcohol) and/or morphine. Opium and morphine were given by mouth in water or applied in powder form directly to an open wound, the doctor using his wet and often dirty fingers. More than two million ounces of powdered opium were used during the war. More than 400,000 opium pills were dispensed.[7]

Thompson's future under these conditions looked dim. Notes written sometime after he recovered, state,

> Friday, Aug. 27 at 1 p.m. am taken in ambulance 12 miles to 2nd Div., 2nd Corps Hospital at City Point. [He confused the dates here; it was August 26.]

The wounded officer's trip to the hospital was probably a harrowing ride. City Point Depot Hospital, nine miles from Petersburg on the James River, was a merger of five corps hospitals. A primitive facility at first, it soon became the most outstanding field hospital of the war, covering 200 acres.[8] When he arrived at City Point, his wounds were given proper attention. As soon as he could, he made arrangements to notify Hannah of this sudden change in his military career. The following letter was written for him by Florence Blyler, a private from Company G, who attended him.

Field Hospital
2nd Div.
August 26, 1864

My dear Sister,

Yesterday afternoon during the very severe Battle of Reams' Station, I was so unfortunate as to be struck by the fragments of a shell which gave me a very serious wound in the groin. The wound proves very painful. I also lost the end of my right thumb. Will keep you informed of my whereabouts. I shall probably be sent away from here today or tomorrow, most likely shall be sent north.

Your brother,
Richard (By Florence Blyler)

Many of Thompson's fellow officers and friends spread the news. One such officer, who knew Thompson from their work together on the Judge Advocate staff, was Captain William Peters who took it upon himself to write Thompson's brother-in-law.

Headquarters
2nd Div., 2nd Army Corps
August 26, 1864

Major John Stevenson
3rd Pennsylvania Artillery

Dear Sir,

I regret to inform you that in the action of yesterday, 25th inst. at Reams' Station on the Weldon Road, Lieutenant Colonel R. S. Thompson was wounded. He was struck by a piece of shell in the right groin. It did not penetrate the bowels.[9] This, the surgeon, Dr. Satterthwait, informs me, will pass away in a few days. He also says that the wound will prove tedious as some inflammation is to be expected, but that no permanent danger will result from it. The Colonel is in good spirits and thinks a rest and a good nursing will bring him all right. He was sent to City Point today and will probably go north in a day or two.

I do not think that there is any need to be anxious concerning his wound. All it requires is rest and a little cooler climate. His Regiment behaved as it always does with great gallantry.

Give my regards to Mrs. Stevenson and believe me,

Very truly your friend,
Wm. E. Peters

Thompson's situation was more serious than Captain Peters indicated. He was now in more danger from his treatment than from the enemy. Surgeons' hands and instruments, especially in the field, were rarely sterile; often they were not even clean. Bandages and bedding also lacked sterility. "Hospital gangrene" killed more patients, especially amputees, than anything else. Surgeons sometimes tried to clean wounded areas with a swab of bromine or potassium permanganate and water, but often neglected this, unaware of the relationship between dirt and infection.[10]

Thompson remained at City Point Hospital only until August 27th when at two o'clock in the afternoon he was put on board one of the hospital steamers bound for Washington. His diary entry is terse.

Saturday, Aug. 27 at 2 p.m. Am placed on steamboat *State of Maine* and start for Washington at 3 p.m.

Sunday Aug. 28, arrive at Washington, D.C. Am then
taken in an ambulance to Emory Hospital 1 mile east
of Capitol where I am entered in Ward "C."[11]

Once Thompson was installed in Ward C, he had his orderly, George
W. Goodwin, a private in Company I, write to Hannah and tell her the
details (original spelling preserved).[12]

Emory Hospital
August 29, 1864

Dear Sister,

I am now situated in the above named Pleace, arrived here
yesterday. I shall be Transferred to a Philadelphia Hospital,
So Soon as my wound Shall allow me to be.

I was wounded at Reams' Stations on the Weldon road
dureing the Terible fight of Thursday August 25th. My wound
is by a Shell witch Struck on the lower Part of the Stonack and
the right groin and just above the right Hip. Fore investing so
largely they threw in a Small Peice of Shell witch carryed off
the end of my right thumb gratise.

I am a doing finely and will be ready to eat my share of
oysters when the month rolls round that has an *R*. There will
be no necesseity of my friends a comeing to Washington unless
I Should be delayed here longer than I expect to.

Will dispatch if anything like getting moved appears. RST

Thompson added this last line with his left hand as his right was
well-bandaged. The news rocked his family. As soon as she heard,
Hannah wrote the following letter, parts of which are quoted here.

[Cape May] Court House
August 31, 1864

My very dear Brother,

Thanks to the blessed Lord God for all his mercies to you.
O my dear brother, could you have seen the distress of your
four sisters and, in fact, the distress of the whole household
when we received that letter written from the Field Hospital,
you would ever believe you had those at home who love you
dearly.

Yes, I have suffered for you, I would not pass another such
sleepless night . . . as the one after we heard of your wounds.
O how I prayed that you might be spared . . . and that you
might come home to cheer our hearts once again.

[She then told him she wrote the news to the Scovels. She
also told him her husband would help him in any way he
could.]

Coly says he is *proud* of you; that compliment General
Hancock paid you has won *laurels* for you in his estimation.
Yes, we are all proud of you, and my fear was that you had so
much *love* bestowed upon you (and were almost your *sister's*
idol) to that extent that God, to punish me for my sins, might
in his wise judgment take you from me. But you are safe I
hope; now take every care of yourself, and if you can't be *calm,*
be as *quiet* as you can.

[I wonder] who wrote that letter I received today from
Washington; poor fellow, his early education has been sadly
neglected. Jo and Emma [her children] send their best and
purest love to you, and if all the tears they shed for their poor
wounded uncle could have been saved and measured, 'twould
have astonished both you and them.

[Next she spoke of the two older sisters, Mary and Isabella,
who would help him if they could.[13] She reminded him of the
care they gave him when they were all left motherless. She
told him that Mary's son "Buddie" was ill with "remittent
fever" (probably malaria, but it could also have been typhoid)
and could not visit the hospital to see him.]

[Hannah]

On September 4 Mary sent him a letter, hand-carried by Mr. R. R.
Thompson to Emory Hospital in Washington, sending her love and
encouragement for his recovery. Little Buddie, whose given name was
also Richard, died a short while later.

Sister Emma, highly emotional at best, became distraught. She
convinced herself that Richard would die. She wrote Hannah.

Fort Monroe, Va.
August 31, 1864

My ever dear Sister,

Alas! I have no words to tell my grief; I am wild with thoughts. John left yesterday for the front to see whether he could find out Brother's whereabouts. Should he be sent to this hospital, I will send you all passes and if taken to Washington, I shall go there immediately. If I only had someone to talk to, someone to be with me.

I enclose two letters, one from him which was written only a few hours before he was wounded and the other from Captain Potter. They came yesterday after the Major left. I should have sent them at once, but really I was not myself. I was not dressed the whole day. I am expecting a telegraphic dispatch any moment.

[Emma]

Dr. Fish, knowing how heavily time would weigh on the wounded man, began a series of almost daily letters. He gave Thompson a great deal of encouragement and influenced him to get out of the military hospital system as soon as he was able. Because he was not sure Thompson would get his letters, the worried doctor wrote three of them.

1607 Vine Street
Philadelphia
August 29, 1864

My Dear Richard,

You can well imagine with what a shuddering feeling I read the enclosed extract from this morning's *Inquirer*. You will notice the newspaper correspondent records you as severely wounded and gives no particulars. I tried to look on the bright side of this to me sadly-drawn picture and would gladly substitute the qualifying epithet *slightly* for *severely*, but then again I was forced to the conviction from my knowledge of your character and the accurate account of the severity of this action that the narrative *must* indeed be true. I thought of Belle Island, Libby Prison, Fort Thunder and other Rebel pest houses and the mere idea of you being severely wounded and

captured [and] I powerless to assist you filled my mind with
untold suffering on your part and dread on mine, apprehensive
it might prove true.

I immediately wrote a letter to your address also one to Dr.
Satterthwait or the surgeon in charge of the 12th Regiment,
whomever he may be, requesting a full and detailed account
of your injuries and your probable whereabouts and what
steps were to be taken to reach you. Before mailing my letters,
the postman left the letter signed Florence Blyler, whom I take
to be some kind good sister of mercy,[14] visiting our armies in
the field and performing various little offices of kindness so
satisfactory to the friends of the brave and unfortunate soldiers. You little know the satisfaction experienced by Mrs.
Fish and myself on perusal of this short note. We deeply
sympathize with you my dear friend in your affliction and
sincerely hope by the providence of God, you may soon be
returned to health. Shell wounds are always painful and the
slightest are severe in character and oftentimes long in duration; we hope you will experience no injury by transportation.

I now feel anxious to hear from you again and trust you will
keep me fully advised as to your exact condition. When you
are transported north, I hope as soon as you arrive in Washington you will either write me or telegraph that you are fit
for removal to our city. I will come on after you and bring you
to my house, where you shall have the best care and attention
that 1607 Vine St. affords. Now, dear Richard, have no hesi-
tation in risking any request of me. Your presence in my house,
even as my patient, will not in the least trouble my household
and I flatter myself I can contribute to your comfort far better
than the best-ordered military hospital. Write me again at
once. With much love and condolence from Mrs. Fish,

Your affectionate friend,
A. H. Fish

In a second almost duplicate letter Doctor Fish again offered his
home for Thompson's recuperation. He sent news that Thompson's
friends had learned of his misfortune.

August 30, 1865

Since I wrote you yesterday, Mr. Cortland Scovel I saw at
Asa's office and read Captain Potter's letter to him, by which

I am glad to learn that your wound, although of serious
character, is not of a dangerous nature, will disable you for
some little time but not permanently. I am anxious to hear
from you again. Should this letter reach you, write at once.
Mrs. Fish sends kind regards and much sympathy for your
affliction.

Your affectionate friend,
A. H. Fish

That same day, Asa Fish wrote Cortland Scovel, who then wrote
Kate. She had been visiting in Chicago when Thompson was wounded
and only learned the news on her return to Bloomington. By then
Thompson's recovery was more certain. A. H. Fish continued his daily
letters; a portion of one is included here.

1607 Vine Street
Philadelphia
August 31, 1864

My Dear Richard,
A highly satisfactory letter from Colonel Willets reached me
this morning stating that you were quartered at Emory Hospital, in good spirits and your wound doing well. I was gratified
to learn that you had been transported safely even as far north
as the national capital, was apprehensive from the nature and
character of your wound that ambulance conveyance would
not, to say the least, be at all beneficial.
... I then met Mr. Cortland Scovel and read Captain Potter's
letter, giving the opinion of Dr. Satterthwait as to the nature
of your injury, at which intelligence I was much pleased,
having indulged my fancy in many themes as to the severity
of your wound. I then wrote to you merely directing the letter
to Washington [and] placed the number of your regiment on
[the] envelope. Hence I infer it will reach the army before you
receive it. This letter you will doubtless receive long before the
others. In relation to your injury as to the best military
hospital for officers in this city, I must confess profound
ignorance. The best civil hospital with which I am acquainted
is at 1607 Vine Street; the surgeon in charge I know inti-
mately; he will give you every attention. The sisters of charity
attached to this institution are kind and faithful, indeed
companionable. You know cheerful society contributes largely

to establish convalescence in any sickness, more especially wounded patients.

I deeply sympathize with you, my dear friend, in your affliction, hope by proper care and attention you will soon be in fit condition for removal, when I propose to come after you and bring you to the hospital of which I speak so flatteringly. As soon as you are enabled to write, give me the full particulars of the manner in which you received your injury. If disabled from writing, get Colonel Willets or some other kind friend to keep me well advised as to your condition. This is written in great haste as I am unusually busy today. If your surgeon has time, I should like to receive a letter from him describing your case.

Your affectionate friend,
A. H. Fish

Like so many other soldiers, Thompson had often complained to his family and friends that they did not write him often enough. After he was wounded, they all mobilized to keep letters flowing to his bedside. Coleman Leaming wrote as soon as he could.

Cape May Court House
August 31, 1864

Dear Richard,

Well, you are in Washington and doing well with your wounds! Hannah today received your letter telling the above. When the first few lines came from the Camp Hospital vaguely describing your condition, it frightened us all greatly. At Hannah's suggestion I went to the city next morning to see the Fishs, get further information, and if deemed advisable, go to Washington and hunt you up. Asa posted me fully in your situation and told me you had written to Doctor Fish that you had every attention and that you were uncertain to what hospital you would be sent and that with the certainty that he would visit you at a moments notice, you did not think it necessary nor advisable.

Asa promised to express to me any information requiring the immediate attention of your sisters or myself and was very decided in his counsel that your sisters should remain at home unless they could be of service to you; so I returned home last evening much comforted and today we received your cheerful letter from Washington threatening destruction to the oyster in a few weeks. Bell and children have been spending some time with Hannah. Jo and Emma are in the middle of their vacation. The mosquitoes are thicker than ever before within Uncle Norton's memory.

The season at Cape Island is nearly over and we are soon to have fall and winter upon us. You will no doubt come on to Philadelphia as soon as you are able and thence home, when we will expect full particulars of your wounds and your other experiences at the front.

Asa told me your right leg was paralyzed at the time the shell struck you. You do not say anything about it; when you write again, get your surgeon's opinion in regard to the probable soundness of your body and limbs and the time when you can omit doctor stuff. As long as you need surgical aid, you no doubt have the best the country affords in the hospital and you would be unwise to leave. But as soon as you can dispense with plasters, splints, bandages, powders, field lotions, and doctor's stuff generally, take up your line of march for Court House and try the virtues of spring chicken and oysters.

Hannah will or has promised to write you this afternoon but I thought I would take a sheet to myself. Let us hear from you often and have full particulars.

Your brother,
Coleman

If I could be of any use or comfort to you by coming to Washington let me know and I will come at once.

C. L.

Thompson was made fairly comfortable at Emory Hospital and was able to write his family a long letter detailing his injuries.

Emory Hospital
Washington, D.C.
September 2, 1864

My dear good Brother and Sister,

If you will excuse my southpaw handwriting, remembering I am on my back, I will try to thank you for your goodness in writing me such good and kind letters as I have just received.

I did not think you could assist me any and therefore did not write for you to come down. From your letters I judge you did not see the mention of my being wounded in the *Inquirer* of the 29th August in the first article.

My wounds are doing better than well, in fact my rapid recovery is a matter of surprise and wonder to surgeons, nurses, and myself. When first struck, I was thought to be past recovery and the next day was paralyzed in the lower part of body and both legs. From the center of my stomach wound my right side to back bone I was belted with black and blue or rather black eight inches wide, besides the cut in lower part of stomach. Now only a small patch of the black remains and only my right leg and right groin are paralyzed. I think, and the surgeon assures me, there will be no permanent injury and I thank God for his great mercy.

I know a hospital is the best place for me until I am better and can aid myself a little. I am still unable to sit up. I shall be transferred to Philadelphia sometime [the] first part [of] next week [where I am] going in hospital and then, of course, shall be where you can see me. I shall go to hospital in Philadelphia, and, of course, will not need either or any of my sisters to stay with me, but would be glad to see them by way of attention and kindness . . . and I have sent my servant that I brought from the regiment with me.

I should like to get home before Jo and Emma leave. When do they go? If I were there now, I would be just baby enough to claim all their time and attention. There is nothing I want that I cannot procure here except ice cream and gooseberries. For these two things especially the latter, I have longed ever since I was wounded.

My spirits are good and my appetite begins to return. For four days no mortal can ever know what I suffered. My flesh of beggarly amount at the best of times is gone excepting my face which is but little changed, and visitors mostly think my thumb is the extent of my wound from the fresh and hearty look of my face.

Now there is all about myself excepting that I love you all the same as ever and trust we may soon meet. A kiss to Jo and Emma from their Uncle Richard.

                                                              [Richard]

Asa Fish wrote Dr. Leaming on September 2nd, giving more details of Thompson's situation. Meanwhile, Emma traveled up from her and

Major Stevenson's quarters at Fort Monroe to Washington with George Goodwin as her protector. She attended her brother faithfully and sent George out to do errands. She wrote a rambling letter to Hannah, quoted in part.

Emory Hospital
Washington, D.C.
September 6, 1864

My dear Sister,

I am scribbling by the side of our wounded brother; he looks . . . well but his wounds are pretty bad. I came from Fort Monroe yesterday, arrived here this morning. I wish you were . . . here . . . and could help to cheer him up. His appetite has returned somewhat, but there is nothing in the hospital for him to eat . . . pudding and potatoes served in the same plate, bread pudding at that, and the potatoes no more than half done. . . . He says deliver him from his diet. He is very [weak] and unable to sit up, but if well enough we shall leave for Philadelphia next Thursday.

. . . I go on with him as he wishes me (I will leave the next day Friday for Fort Monroe), maybe not.

From Em

Thompson seriously considered Dr. Fish's suggestion that he enter a private hospital. In such an institution he could have his own private room and his personal orderly. Private hospitals often catered to wounded officers, some charging as much as $100 a day, an exorbitant fee for those days. Board for an orderly was an additional ten cents daily; the officer would be required to purchase his own food. In order to avail himself of the facilities of private hospitalization, Thompson had to obtain a leave of absence from the service. He applied for such leave and it was granted on September 6th. Dr. Fish made all the arrangements for the transfer to St. Joseph's Hospital in Philadelphia.

Dr. Fish's home seemed to be a gathering place for Thompson's friends where they exchanged all the news regarding his progress that they could. Coleman Leaming came up from Cape May; James and Cortland Scovel came as often as their duties permitted. James Scovel wrote Thompson on September 7th, just before he left the military hospital. Scovel offered the use of his home, horse, and wagon for Thompson's benefit during his convalescence and mentioned that his own military duties ended August 14th. (In Scovel's letter, the sentence, "We all admire your *pluck* in going to a hospital," is enigmatic. Obviously, he did not trust hospitals, but it is uncertain whether he was frightened of military or civilian hospitals, or both.)

On September 8th, Thompson, Emma, and George Goodwin were taken in an ambulance at ten in the morning to the Baltimore depot. Inside, the Sanitary Commission provided a room for the wounded and their families to wait in private for a train that would take them to Philadelphia. He languished in this room until eight o'clock that evening. From the station in Washington to the Broad Street Station in Philadelphia was a journey of seven hours. He must have endured intense suffering during these moves. At 3:00 a.m. on September 9th, he left the train for a hospital opposite the station. A waiting ambulance took the party to St. Joseph's Hospital on the corner of 17th Street and Girard Avenue. This would be his "home" for the next month.

After seeing her brother safely installed in this new hospital, Emma returned to Fort Monroe. Had she stayed, she would have seen her brother endure one of the most painful experiences of his life. When they examined him on the 10th of September, the doctors realized the infection in his right thumb required radical measures. They amputated. After the surgery, and with him fully conscious, they dressed his wound with what he described as a "liquid caustic." In his notes, he uses the words, "fearfully painful."[15]

In his letter of September 12th, brother-in-law Stevenson sent his support and the love of Emma and their daughter Bess, who often "talks of poor Uncle Richard who was shot by the Rebs." Stevenson went on to say that he was unhappy with the army and not in his commanding officers' good graces, so he expected to be kept from promotion. He then mentioned he thought he might resign from the army as he had lost interest in doing any more military duty.

During his hospital stay Thompson received many letters bringing him news of the war's progress. This letter from Potter is one of the most descriptive, telling him what happened after he left the field.

Headquarters
2nd Div., 2nd [Corps]
September 11, 1864

Dear Thompson,

I should have written you before this but we have been shifting almost constantly since you left. Our Corps (1st and

2nd Divisions) has built a line of works extending from beyond the Williams House (which you remember, is near the field hospital where you lay the morning after you were hurt) to the left, across the Norfolk Road nearly to the point where our Brigade was thrown out immediately after you joined us in June. The object of this work is to protect the left flank of the Army from any attack from the direction of Reams' Station. A railroad is now completed from City Point to General Warren's position on the Weldon Railroad. As I write, I hear the shrill whistle of a Whitworth bolt, which the enemy has sent at a passing train.

General Warren is almost impregnably fortified on the Weldon Railroad. He had already completed several large forts, one of which with four bastions has a face of five hundred feet [Fort Wadsworth]. His lines are elliptical in form with a double row of abatis around their entire length.

In our vicinity nothing new is occurring except occasional clashes on the enemy's picket line. In one of these two nights since, Mott drove their line capturing about 100 prisoners. Our Division is lying just now in front of the "Deserted House" which you remember was Headquarters for the Corps when we lay at the "Southwell House."

Your leave after much inquiry, I found, had been pigeon-holed through some misunderstanding in the office of the Surgeon-in-Chief. I at once had it disinterred and forwarded to Corps Headquarters. Captain Chew informs me that the leave has been received at the Regiment and forwarded to you in care of A. I. Fish, Esq. I regretted very much to learn that Lieutenant Rich died from his wound though it seemed to be a fatal hurt from the first. He was a gallant and noble boy, worth a score of those who are shirking in ease and comfort at home. You will be pleased to learn [Captain Frank] Riley's friends have been heard from alive. He writes from Libby Prison August 28th saying that he is there unhurt and as comfortable as can be expected. Lieutenant [Edward M.] DuBois tells me that he received a line from Mr. Scovel saying that he is sitting by your bed and that your right leg is still paralyzed. I had hoped you would have recovered its use before this. Latest theories and others say, however, that it is only a question of time and that you will not be permanently disabled.

I think there is great reason to rejoice that you escaped a more serious hurt. Shells are unpleasant customers when they hit, which, thank God, is very seldom. A piece of the same shell which wounded you came as near me as I care to have them.[16] I hope you will let me hear from you personally soon, giving particulars as to your health, locality, etc.

I have written to my brother David to present my claims to Governor Parker for a commission as field officer in one of the new regiments raising in New Jersey, basing my application on the fact that I have seen more than two years service in the field and most of the time being in the face of the enemy. I can furnish, as you know, vouchers for uniform fidelity to duty and good conduct from general officers and others with whom I have served.

If his Excellency, Governor Joel Parker, chooses to promote me for service in the field and familiarity with the military service, I shall be glad to have a commission as field officer. If, however, it requires not evidence of such service but political influence to obtain promotion, I do not wish it, for in the first place, I have no such influence; in the second place, I believe that I have been too long a soldier to employ it even if I had it to use.

Give my regards to Mr. Fish and other of my friends whom you may see. Let me hear from you soon. I trust in the meantime that you may speedily recover your accustomed health and vigor. Wishing you much happiness in your stay among your friends. I remain as ever your friend,

Wm. E. Potter

Thompson's fellow officers visited him when they could and wrote him when they could not. With his sudden evacuation from the field, his horse, boots, and other personal possessions were left behind. He wrote to the Quartermaster for help in the disposition of these items. Lieutenant Dubois answered.

Quartermaster's Office
12th N.J. Regt.
September 11, 1864

Dear Colonel,
Your letter received this morning and as the Sabbath before all other days is peculiarly adapted to letter writing, I will

commence. There is nothing new in the Army. Our Division, after building rifle pits and forts from Fort Warren [later called Fort Davis] on the Jerusalem Pike around in the rear of the Army beyond the Prince George C. H. Road, are enjoying a short rest on the field near the deserted house where Corps Headquarters were over a month ago. The new railroad from City Point to the Weldon Road is completed and runs immediately in front of our camp. The Johnnies shell every train that passes, and the shells and Whitworth bolts fall very close to our Regiment. Yesterday one exploded not ten feet from Chew's horse which is fastened just in rear of his (Chew's) tent. You remember the pickets that were so close to our line near the fort we visited that Sunday? Night before last our boys relieved them, capturing in all over 100. This has led to picket firing on that part of the line, but our picket line is where theirs was and theirs at a respectable distance off. I issue[d] all the clothing the boys could ask for yesterday and for once have pants and every other article left—except tents. And the Regiment looks well. Yes, Colonel, I noticed the death of the noble [Lieutenant John R.] Rich in the Washington paper. No braver man ever lived and his loss will be and is deeply felt in the Regiment.

Colonel, who would you recommend as lieutenant for K? Certainly, we can or ought to find someone in our own Company. Captain Chew is anxious to promote to the position Sergeant Stratton of Company F; he may be a good man, but he is not as intelligent nor any more of a soldier or gentleman than Henry Gaskill. Gaskill is loved by every man in the Company, keeps his papers all correct and would make as good an officer as there is in the Regiment.

Captain Doten offered me $125 in cash for your horse yesterday. If he is still of the same opinion, I shall take it tomorrow and I think Lieutenant Colonel Moore will take the boots. I looked over your haversack this morning and confiscated for my own use a towel and pair [of] gloves and four paper collars. The gloves and towel you can purchase new when you are able to come back, and I will buy these of you, being in need of both articles and they being of a better quality than sutlers keep.

If I sell your horse for $125, I would ask the loan of the $25 providing you have no immediate use of the money. Paying Dr. Gilman $180 has nearly drained me of small bills and the commissary don't trust, and I will remit to you the $100 now and $25 payday, unless you could get your friend Scovel of Camden to collect from Wm. Calhoun $25 I loaned McComb; said Calhoun is settling McComb's business. I have nothing to show, however, that he owes me the money, he being nearly [dead] at the time. Your ordnance returns are all right and will be ready to send to the department tomorrow. Let me hear from you often and I will keep you posted in all affairs of importance.

Very respectfully, your obedient servant,
Edwin Dubois

Considering the nature of his wounds, Thompson was as comfortable as possible. He made steady progress although he had to remain flat on his back. He passed the long dreary hours by writing and reading letters and making notes from his diary entries that he probably intended to put into his memoirs. On September 12th and 14th both Major and Emma Stevenson sent him letters from Old Point Comfort. Hannah visited as often as possible and soon he was feeling strong enough to send George Goodwin back to the army.

As the area of the amputation began to heal, he practiced learning to write all over again. He tried using his left hand for awhile, then practiced placing the pen between the first and second fingers of his right hand, managing to produce a scrawl. He eventually retrained his hand.[17] About two weeks after he lost his thumb, he was able to send Hannah some good news.

Saint Joseph's Hospital
September 23, 1864

My Dear Sister,

When you come to the city, bring the crutches and my cap that is at Mary's. Should the cap want a strap and buttons, you can supply the want from some of my old caps at home. If there are any slippers at home, bring me a pair.

My wounds are doing well and I am gaining strength everyday. Dr. Page[18] thinks I will be able to stand on my feet in two weeks. My love to all from your affectionate brother,
Richard (by J. A. Mathis)

Certainly time weighed heavily on him. He made a diary notation, complaining slightly.

Sept 29. 5 weeks since wounded and I had not been off
my back, not even to lie on my side.

However, by October 3rd he was able to sit up in bed for the first
time. By then he had received the following letter from George Goodwin (original spelling preserved).

Camp Near Petersburg, Va.
September 25, 1864

Dear Conolel

I take my pen to hand to write you a few lines. I am well at
present and I hope these few lines may find you improving. I
got back to the regiment to day. The Devision they relieved
the 10 corps. they lay up in the works they have in here there
tents Steaded and dirt trench up to keep the Bullet from
striking them. there was nothing much for me to do up to the
regiment. So I came down to the train and I am going to take
care of your horse and saddle. I will take good care of them till
you come Back. little Buck Tail is as fat as a pig and he is onary
as he can bee. Conelel, i Shall never forget you for Bringing
me on home with you and if you ever want any thing done that
I can do I am ready to do it for you. Captain Strattan and father
is down to the regiment trying to get Lieutenant [James
Stratton's] Body. The reason I came to the train, quartermaster said He could not take care of all of the horses and So he
said I had better come and Captain Chew was willing. Good
by. I remain your obediant Servant,

G. Goodwin

One week after he first sat up, Thompson took his first steps on
crutches. This memorable day was October 10th.[19] After having been
bedridden for so long, he found the autumn air rather chilly. He wrote
a short note to Hannah calling for warm underwear and slippers.

St. Joseph's Hospital, Philadelphia
October 11, 1864

My dear Sister,
Please send by first opportunity my red flannel drawers.
You will find them in my trunk that I left at home when
returning to the Army last spring.

I am still improving and can now stand alone and walk a few steps with the aid of the crutches. I long to recover enough to travel to Cape May and shall not feel contented until I get there. Don't forget about the drawers and also slippers. Write me at once and tell me whether there is a pair at home fit to send here.

With much love I remain as ever your affectionate brother,
Richard

October 18th was the day for which Thompson had waited nearly two months; he left St. Joseph's Hospital. He moved to Dr. Fish's home where he remained until the middle of November enjoying the fond ministrations of both the doctor and his family. By the second week he tried walking out-of-doors on his crutches. He walked two blocks on October 29th, no small triumph for the wounded man who would be using crutches or a cane for the next four months. He tired easily but was able to remain out of bed for about six hours daily, during which time he continued to write letters to his loved ones.

Philadelphia
November 7, 1864

My dear Sister,

As Dr. Fish thinks I would still be endangering myself by attempting to go home on Wednesday, I have concluded to remain here until Saturday next, November the 12th, when I will be ready to go home.

With much love to all and the hope of soon enjoying you[r] society at the dear old homestead,

I remain your brother,
Richard

Have not heard from Em since Friday.

R.S.T.

Because his wounds took so long to heal and the paralysis he experienced was reluctant to leave, he had to apply for an extension of his leave of absence. After he became proficient enough on his crutches or cane, the army officially posted him to Philadelphia where he remained until November 10th. From the 10th to the 28th he enjoyed time at home. Then, in obedience to army orders, he left Cape May and returned to Philadelphia to report to the Adjutant General.[20] On December 19th, he was detailed as president of a General Court Martial for officers held at 917 Locust Street in Philadelphia. He served in this capacity until February 1865, when he requested to resign from the Army of the Potomac.

When Colonel Willets resigned in December, Thompson and Major Chew were both eligible for his position. Thompson was the likely choice but he was on convalescent duty. Since he was unfit for active duty and there were men in the field taking his place who deserved to be promoted, he felt it was unfair to remain as their Lieutenant Colonel in name only.[21]

Court Martial Chambers
917 Locust Street, Philadelphia
February 1, 1865

To Adjutant General
U.S. Army War Dept.
Washington, D.C.

I have the honor to make this, my application for discharge, upon the following reasons:

On account of a serious wound in the abdomen, received at Reams' Station, Va., on the 25th day of August 1864, I have been absent from my regiment since that time.

I am still suffering from my wound; am unable to walk without the aid of a cane, and shall not be fit for field service for some time as per enclosed Surgeons Certificate. I am now on Court Martial duty by virtue of Special Order No. 303 from Headquarters, Dept. of Pennsylvania, Dated Philadelphia, Pa., Dec. 19, 1864.

In justice to the officers of my regiment now doing my duty in the field, I desire my discharge so that they may receive commissions in time to be mustered for the unexpired term of the regiment. To accomplish this they will have to receive their musters previous to March 4th, 1865. I am, Sir Your Obedient Servant,

Richard S. Thompson
Lieut. Col. 12th Regt. N.J. Vols.

His request was granted. On February 7, 1865, he was honorably discharged from his beloved Second Corps and the Twelfth New Jersey

Regiment. Proud of his military career, he retained his military title and was known as Colonel Thompson for the rest of his life. A few days after receiving his discharge papers, he wrote to Hannah.

Camden, N.J.
February 21, 1865

My dear Sister Hannah,

Please send me by express the sword and scabbard I sent home from Ellicott's Mills, the one standing in the trunk room by the hat rack. Do this at once. Direct it to me to be called for at the Express office. Send it [by] the first train after receiving this. I will explain another time.

I am now a civilian having had my resignation accepted, and received an honorable discharge from the service. I will be down to Cape May next week.

With much love, I remain your affectionate brother,
Richard

Thompson was once more a civilian. He was free to continue his private life, marry the girl he loved, and serve his country in ways far less hazardous than his military duty of the previous two and one half years.

After Thompson left the field and the Union forces withdrew from Reams' Station, his regiment went into winter quarters near Petersburg. General Hancock's old wound forced him out of action. General Andrew A. Humphreys replaced him. After Thompson received his discharge, Chew was made Lieutenant Colonel. The colonelcy went to an English-born officer, Colonel John Willian. He was an able commander, but the men would have preferred Thompson.[22]

After the spring thaw the Twelfth New Jersey returned to a war that would soon be over. Lee abandoned Petersburg on the night of April 2nd. When the Twelfth was at Appomattox, Colonel William Potter had the honor to be one of the men who took the captured Confederate standards to Secretary of State Seward in Washington.

On May 23rd and 24th the Twelfth took part in the Grand Review[23] and paraded past President Andrew Johnson in Washington. They returned to New Jersey to be mustered out on June 17th. After many days of delay the gallant survivors finally signed the muster-out rolls and picked up their final pay and discharge papers. The town of

Bridgeton gave the men of Company K a welcome-home party on June 19th. Of the original 100 men who left there in 1862, 35 came home.[24]

Notes

[1] Through the courtesy of Mr. Chris Calkins, the authors were able to photograph the piece of the Confederate shell that struck Thompson. Since Colonel Thompson made no mention of it in his letters, how he got possession of the fragment is unknown.

[2] There were field hospitals in the area near the Emmons House, the Williams House, and the Oak Grove Methodist Church. Most of the first casualties were put into the church which was on the battlefield.

[3] There is a disagreement here. Thompson thought he was in a sugarcane field. Sugarcane does not grow in Virginia. On maps and in official reports, as well as newspapers, it is called a cornfield. General Wade Hampton, cavalry commander and plantation owner from South Carolina, called it a sorghum field. Union soldiers were not likely to recognize sorghum and probably had never heard of it. In its early growing stages it looks very much like corn.

[4] Coco, G. A. (1988) *A Vast Sea of Misery*. Gettysburg, PA, p. xiv, ". . . by 1863, the U.S. Army realized that one surgeon [for] each regiment was not the best method for the application of medical science. These . . . surgeons . . . more like our modern day military 'medics' or corpsmen, generally administered only first aid techniques at 'dressing stations' near the firing line, prior to sending the patient to the rear. . . ." Each division had its own field hospital, located in safe areas, where the more skilled physicians performed "more serious pursuits such as applying anesthetics, performing amputations, probing and extracting bullets and shell fragments, tying of ligatures, and fighting fevers and infections."

[5] Adams, G. W. (1985) *Doctors in Blue*. Dayton, OH, p. 135.

[6] "Hospital fever" or typhus is an infection carried by lice living on the bodies of rats and mice. Men living in trenches were often "lousy" and when brought into hospitals, their clothing and bodies were infested. Typhus was not confined to soldiers; even in peacetime there were several cases a year reported in American medical records. Medical personnel often confused typhus and typhoid fever, so what records are available are not considered accurate. The authors are indebted to Dr. "H" for his help. See also *Ibid.*, Pp. 215-216.

[7] *Ibid.*, Pp. 116, 119. It is not known how many men became addicted as a result of the generous use of this substance.

[8] At City Point Depot Hospital, loss of life from the unsanitary conditions and exposure to cold weather prompted the authorities to build a series of log houses, called "pavilions," which measured 50 x 20 feet. At its peak there were 90 similar buildings and an additional 324 hospital tents to house the enormous number of wounded. There was a water system, graded streets and sidewalks. Except for latrine facilities, it was the best run of all field hospitals. Hospital railroad cars with their straw-covered floors were cold in winter and hot and stuffy in summer, with extremely limited sanitary facilities. These trains caused such a great deal of suffering that men were fortunate to survive the trip to the hospital. *Ibid.*, Pp. 153ff.

[9] The shell fragment which struck Thompson was from a hollow three-inch projectile which may have weighed from eight to ten pounds when intact. The fragment that Thompson saved showed lathe markings along one side. He was fortunate the piece of iron did not penetrate his intestines; however, it injured him sufficiently to render him immobile. The force of the shell that hit Thompson may have produced the acute paralysis he describes in his later letter of September 2, 1864. Although Longacre states Thompson was wounded in the leg, none of his notes or letters mention this.

[10] American medical schools often graduated doctors after 8 to 14 weeks of training, although some schools required five or six months. Anesthesia had been discovered in 1831 but was not widely used. Nitrous Oxide (laughing gas), ether, and chloroform were used when available. Antisepsis and the theory of bacteria causing infection and disease were just coming on the horizon. Modern sterilization methods were unknown but some enlightened doctors made an effort at cleanliness. Baron Joseph Lister (1827-1912) began his work in 1865. Also in that year the sterilization of bandages became a more common practice. However well-meaning, doctors found field conditions so overwhelming that common cleanliness was difficult and sterilization impossible. See Damman, G. E. (1983) *A Pictorial Encyclopedia of Civil War Medical Instruments and Equipment, Vol. I.* Missoula, MT, p. 5.

[11] The steamer he mentioned was one of several used by the hospitals. Often in poor condition, they were slow. Sanitary conditions were next to non-existent. After so many men died on board, the steamers were put under the operation of a medical Director General of Transportation. He eventually upgraded the craft and the situation eased. From his Philadelphia office the Director routed ships along the eastern seaboard, sending them to whichever hospitals in six major coastal cities had beds available. Philadelphia boasted 27 hospitals in and near the city; these had the reputation of being the best. Many of the doctors were Quakers, known for their compassion and efficiency. Philadelphia hospitals also provided above average food and good plumbing; both items rated high on the wounded soldiers' lists. See Adams, *op. cit.*, p. 105.

[12] George Goodwin had acted as Thompson's servant/orderly from the early days in the Army of the Potomac. Apparently he was from the Bridgeton area. In 1906 Goodwin sent a letter to Thompson's summer cottage on Columbia Avenue in Cape May. After all the years, he once more expressed his gratitiude to Thompson for taking him away from the fighting. The letter was forwarded to Thompson's home in Chicago. On the front of the envelope, Thompson pencilled, "the boy I brought with me on my way to hospital in Phil. Sept. 25, 1864."

[13] Isabella's life was in turmoil. Her husband had died October 7, 1861, and their four-year-old son Joseph would die while Richard was at St. Joseph's Hospital in Philadelphia. Apparently she was a victim of breast cancer; she lived only until October of 1866. She was buried in the same grave as her son.

[14] Dr. Fish thought Florence Blyler to be female, an understandable mistake.

[15] Physicians often operated in street clothes, wearing an apron to protect their suits. When cauterization after amputation was necessary, any of the following chemical styptics were available: silver nitrate, sulphate of copper, alum, tannic acid, tincture of ferric chloride, potassium iodide, mercuric sulphide, or just plain potash and lime. Some of these chemicals caused pain so severe to the patient as to cause shock. *Ibid.*, p. 123 and Dr. "H."

[16.] Captain Potter was close by Thompson during the charge and the shell missed him by a hair's breadth.

[17] The letters he wrote from the hospital show a marked change in penmanship. The authors consulted with their medical advisor for the method of retraining a hand that had lost a thumb.

[18] Lieutenant Colonel Charles Page, a native of Virginia, served at various United States army hospitals. He was with the Army of the Potomac in 1864-65. See *Records of Living Officers of the U.S.* Philadephia, 1883, p. 43.

[19] From a diary notation.

[20] On December 16th, the Thompson family physician, Dr. John Wiley, signed an affidavit that Thompson, unable to walk without crutches, was still unfit for field duty.

[21] Sometime in December, former Governor Charles Olden wrote a letter to President Lincoln, recommending Thompson for the full colonelcy. A number of Thompson's friends and supporters included statements on his behalf. As part of his papers Thompson saved a copy of an extract of Hancock's letter, "Col. Thompson is well known to me as a good officer. I had occasion to learn that fact at Deep Bottom, when he had command of the pickets. . . . It

will always afford me pleasure to do Col. Thompson a service and it would gratify me to have him in my command."

Included in the letter to Lincoln were recommendations by Brigadier General Alexander Hays, Brigadier General Thomas A. Smyth, former Governor Olden and Governor Williams A. Newell. Lincoln replied on January 3, 1865, using the reverse side of Olden's letter to write his answer, "The within are good testimonies, but unless it be a colored regiment, I know not how the appointment can be made. I submit the case to the Secretary of War, asking his favorable consideration." A. Lincoln.

Nothing came of the recommendation. It may be that for Thompson, it was serve with the Twelfth or nothing at all. Thompson preserved a copy of Lincoln's letter in his files.

22 Longacre, *To Gettysburg and Beyond.* . . . Hightstown, NJ, Pp. 259-260.

23 The Grand Review was the last parade of the combined volunteer Federal Armies. There were about 150,000 men in the ranks who marched before the President and the Commanding Generals. Afterward, the volunteer armies were disbanded and the men proceeded to their homes.

24 Additional background material for this chapter came from Lyons, A. S., Petrucilli, R. J., II , et al. (1987) *Medicine, an Illustrated History.* New York.

Chapter Eleven

A Citizen of Chicago

Cape May County . . . may well be proud of her illustrious son . . . .
Cape May County Gazette, Aug. 12, 1904

After Thompson's honorable discharge from the Army of the Potomac on February 2, 1865, he turned his energies to the resumption of his personal life. In May he was pronounced completely recovered from his wounds. He then took the first step toward establishing his future; he and Kate Scovel married. The ceremony was performed at 8:00 in the evening of June 7th at St. Matthew's Episcopal Church in Bloomington, Illinois, with the Reverend Alden Scovel, Kate's father, presiding. Richard was 28; Kate 24. The second step in his new life was the resumption of his career. Jeremiah Leaming ("Uncle Jerry"), who had practiced law in Bloomington during the war, had now moved to Chicago, and he invited Thompson to join him. With Col. Thompson's excellent scholastic record, sterling war reputation, and acknowledged gift for oratory, Leaming would have a bright and distinguished young man as his partner. Thompson's newly issued certificate from the Illinois Bar Association, entitling him to practice law in that state,[1] was signed and sealed November 2, 1865.

Once in Chicago, he and Kate purchased property in an area of sturdy trees known as the village of Hyde Park. They were among the early "pioneers" to settle there, wishing to avoid the pressures of urban living. When their home was finished in 1868, there were few streets in the area; it was quiet and had the special air that often pervades an affluent community. Eventually, the city would reach out and annex this suburb, which grew to be one of the wealthiest in the city on the shores of Lake Michigan.

Architecturally, their house could be called country Victorian; it also had Italianate features. It was a tall two and one-half story home of frame construction, faced with clapboarding. The curved-top windows sported shutters. A partially above-ground basement story was shielded on the street side by a lattice. A picket fence surrounded the property, which was situated on a lot 50' by 158' on the west side of the street. A plank sidewalk brought visitors to the flight of steps which ended on a covered and pillared front porch, from which they had a lovely view of the lake.[2]

The same year, 1868, also marked the birth of the Thompson's first child, a dark-haired daughter, on September 25th. Baptized Louise, she was usually called "Bonnie." Then, old friend and wartime comrade William Potter came to Chicago as a delegate to the Republican National Convention; the two friends spent a most enjoyable time reminiscing. In that same year Hannah's youngest child, 11 year-old Edwin (Ned) died. Blonde daughter Mary Thompson was born in 1874. There is no record of other children.

Kate, Richard, and the two girls enjoyed a busy social life in the family home. Kate, an attractive woman, was likely a poised and accomplished hostess. Talented in music, she played piano well. In her youth she had met the attorneys and Congressmen who visited in her parents' parlor. Now as the wife of an attorney and rising politician, she called upon what she had learned to entertain the wives of her husband's influential friends. Like other mothers of her time and social class her duties included the oversight of her daughters' education and social development so that they would be prepared for their station in life. After the girls married, the elder Thompsons lived alone in the house until the Colonel died in 1914.

When the Great Fire destroyed Chicago in 1871, the Thompson home was not endangered. However, the firm of Leaming and Thompson lost most of their office records. Also gone were Thompson's pension records. He had to reapply and the pension was renewed.

From his early manhood Thompson was interested in railroads, so much so that even during the war he used some of his military pay to invest in railroad bonds. His friends and family members also bought railroad bonds, which soon proved to be excellent investments in a growing industry. However, he came to have a certain bitterness against the railroads in general, possibly stemming from the fact that certain family woodlands were burned down owing to negligence on the part of the Cape May Railroad when it was under construction.[3]

Thompson's law career, social stature, and influence grew with the city. Several corporations retained his services but most of his cases

Home of Richard and Catherine Thompson in the Village of Hyde Park, Chicago c1890
(*Courtesy of John W. Kuhl*)

Catherine Scovel Thompson c1890
(Courtesy of John W. Kuhl)

Richard Swain Thompson c1890
(From the Authors' Collection)

concerned the railroads. On several occasions, he represented private citizens in claims cases against the railroads. Thompson also entered local politics. On November 5, 1872, he was elected a member of the 28th General Assembly from the Second Senatorial District. He ran on the Republican ticket, serving a single four year term in the Illinois Senate, during which time he developed a reputation as an accomplished parliamentarian.

Seven years after the end of the War, on May 31, 1873, Chicago proclaimed "Decoration Day." Various organizations and private individuals went to Chicago's cemeteries to pay tribute to the War dead. Colonel Thompson delivered an oration to those assembled at Oakwoods Cemetery to honor the fallen buried there. The printed copy of his address ran to four pages of the souvenir booklet published for the event and was printed in full by the *Chicago Daily News*. He was understandably proud of his part in the War. He kept in touch with many of his old comrades and attended Grand Army of the Republic (GAR)[4] reunions whenever possible.[5] He preserved a star cut from the field of a U.S. flag carried during the War and a fragment of one of the Twelfth's regimental flags.[6] He received these mementos through the mail from the Trenton GAR office in September of 1877, the letter being addressed only, "The Hon. Richard S. Thompson, Chicago, Illinois." In a city the size of Chicago such a sparse address was testimony to his prominence.

In the years from 1869 to 1875 he served as corporation counsel for Hyde Park village and for the following five years was counsel for the South Park Commission.[7] He served as legal counsel for both bodies for many years.

Mr. and Mrs. Thompson were invited to meet President and Mrs. Grover Cleveland when they visited Chicago. At a theater reception the Thompsons mingled in the company of such famous Chicagoans as John B. Carson, George Pullman, and Marshall Field.

Each year brought some new challenge or honor. In September of 1878, Thompson argued a case before the Illinois Supreme Court, details of which were printed in the *Chicago Tribune*. He represented the South Park Commission and won the case.

In 1879, the GAR held their 14th reunion at the elegant Palmer House Hotel in downtown Chicago. Thompson socialized with such notables as former President U. S. Grant, Generals Sherman and Sheridan, Mark Twain, and Chicago Mayor Carter H. Harrison. On December 6th, Grant planted an elm tree in South Park (now Washington Park). James Morgan,[8] then president of the South Park Commission, spoke first, then Grant. Thompson, as attorney for the

South Park Commission, was the third speaker. A full account of the ceremony was published in the *Tribune* on the 7th.

Through the years, Colonel Thompson's personal fortune and prestige grew. In photographs it can be seen that his once thin frame was now portly. He was comfortable financially, but he kept an eye on his veteran's benefits, especially when the payments either failed to arrive or were incorrect.

> *Headquarters*
> *2nd Corps Club*
> *Army of the Potomac*
> *Washington, D.C.*
> *February 6, 1886*

My dear Colonel,

Yours received. If my letter to you was like suddenly meeting an old friend, what must have been my feelings when your claim was placed on my desk for adjustment of muster? You can readily imagine that it became at once a "special" and I will state that it appears to me to be a perfectly clear case, and it now only awaits a report from the Paymaster General as to your first payment as Captain to be concluded, which I firmly expect will be early the coming week. Of course, if you were paid as Captain to include August 14, 1862, your case in that particular falls, but I do not anticipate that for if you were so paid the paymaster was derelict under then existing regulations. Rest assured, *mon Colonel,* I will rush it through as rapidly as official service will allow. As to papers or blanks required when application is made in 2nd Auditor's office, there are some, but to prevent waste of time all you need do is to draw up a "general" affidavit stating succinctly what you claim under your amended record, giving dates, and close with the statement that you have had no other military service, provided that is the fact; if you have served in any other regiment, state that service. That is all that is required, I will state *par parenthèses,* that Gitt is considered a good attorney.

The requisites to membership in the 2nd Corps Club are faithful service in the field in that Corps (or the 3rd) and an honorable discharge therefrom "all of which you *are.*" Its objects are to keep alive the friendships born of such service, subserve to the proper delineation of history, and etc. and etc.—about the same as the Grand Army only closer companionship if such could be. We meet annually at place and date of meeting of Society of Army of the Potomac. We will meet on August 3rd in San Francisco, where the West will greet the Trefoil in a way to make your head swim. Doubtless, the fares will be greatly reduced allowing us all to get there with comparatively small expense. I will keep you advised. The initiation fee is $1—dues $1 annually—with the extra dollar for certificate of membership, total $3; the enjoyment—"camaraderie" [of] 3 million. Hancock was here last week and tells me he anticipates immense enjoyment in August. He attends all the meetings and he is *just one of the boys* with us. You must join.

I inquired particularly for you on the 4th of last September in Bridgeton when the old 12th had a reunion and regretted you were not there. When I say that we met in Bridgeton you know that we had a huge time; it reminded us of the 4th September, 1862. One hundred twenty-three boys responded to their names but as they grow older, they are becoming more disloyal; they have doffed the blue and are rapidly donning the gray, but the same bright eyes peer through the wrinkles. The same loyal and true hearts beat under the rapidly weakening frames. Our enjoyment was intense but with all our jollity and abandon there was an undercurrent of sadness. We are rapidly passing away and were there another call for troops to support the dignity of the government, we would be rejected—too old for service; yet, as you say, the scenes of the war are to us but as yesterday, but the truth is another generation has come on the stage. Those have grown up "who knew not Pharaoh," and what to us are living realities to them are as a "tale that is told," [9] worthless and of no interest.

I had the honor to be elected President of the 12th New Jersey Association and the still further honor of presiding over our reunion in Bridgeton. Frank Riley was elected as my successor; Potter and Ned Dubois are getting "pursy," fearfully stout. Upon what meat doth these our comrades of Company K feed that makes them all so great (a neat paraphrase of Shakespeare). [10] Harry Chew is getting bald and white. [Captain Newton M.] Brooks' hair is thinning and his countenance getting stern. Adjutant Paxson was at the reunion and no one knew him, old, decrepit, stout, and gray. I have in my possession a copy (and the only copy) of a speech on the campaign of Gettysburg I delivered before the association of the 12th in Salem. If you desire to read it and will immediately return it, I will send it to you. Write soon,[11]

Your comrade,
Charles E. Troutman

Headquarters
2nd Corps Club
Army of the Potomac
Washington, D.C.
March 2, 1886

My Dear Colonel,

It affords me pleasure to state that you have been recognized as Captain, Company K, 12th New Jersey Volunteers, from August 14 to September 4, 1862, which gives you about $80. Your claim as Major was rejected on the ground that regiment was below minimum and had sufficient Field Officers until May 12th, 1864, when [Lieutenant Colonel Thomas H.] Davis was killed, on which date you were mustered in as Major.

You were mustered in as Lieutenant Colonel from July 2, 1864, date of your commission to July 18, 1864, which gives you about $10, in all $90. You will in the course of a day or two receive official communication of the above facts. Had I known that your claim was on file, this consummation would have been reached long ere this. As it is, I rushed it through immediately upon my reaching it. Now go in and get your funds, and God Bless you.

Yours fraternally,
Charles E. Troutman

The death of Catherine's father, the Reverend Alden Scovel, occurred in 1889 when he was 88. One year later daughter Louise married Samuel A. Whitney of Boston. The young couple set up their home in Boston (where the Whitney Glass Works was located), and eventually had two children.[12] Also in 1890, Elizabeth Whitney[13] wrote her uncle the following letter from the Gettysburg battlefield.

Glassboro, N.J.
November 30, 1890

My dear Uncle Richard,

John and I have just returned from a visit to Gettysburg, and I have been so haunted by your presence and thrilled by your courage that I must give vent to my pride in you. I honor the same traits in the adversary, but again, the more daring the foe, the greater the victory, so it really redounds to our glory.

The field is so marked by monuments that the tide of battle seems almost flowing today and the eddies where the greatest surges rolled are so filled with lifelike groups, figures, and records of noble deeds that all the martial blood in my veins responded. One of the most gratifying to my eyes was a plain slab of granite, situated about halfway between the combatants, denoting a spot where valor reached a standard hardly excelled on this field of unsurpassed exhibitions of bravery.[14] I think you told me when we visited the panorama of Gettysburg together that you commanded the charge on the Bliss barn. Really, that view was very good but how much more interesting would it have been if you could have been our guide over the real site. I procured two photographs of the monuments commemorating the 12th New Jersey's exploits. They are graven on lasting granite, and though of the 315 erected they are among the plainest, still the part you take in their history will, I know, commend them to you as it did to me. John [her husband] procured a stick cut from "Devil's Den" which I suppose will reach you in due season.

All this family join me in love to all and hoping the pictures reach you safely.

Believe me your affectionate niece,
E. T. Whitney

Leaming and Thompson specialized in condemnation suits and suits involving damages to property made during the construction of railroads, underpasses, and the like. One such case went to court in the fall of 1891. On November 6th Thompson's client won a judgment against the Chicago South Side Rapid Transit Company for $132,340. It was the largest sum so far awarded against that company.

After Jeremiah Leaming retired, Thompson carried on by himself, using an office at 63 Clark Street. The law firm of Leaming and Thompson had been well-known and respected; Thompson continued the tradition. Chicago's newspapers often carried his name, either on a professional or social level. Later in his career he opened an office at 612 Chamber of Commerce Building, 138 Washington Street.

During the summers when the near-suffocating heat and humidity of the city became too much, the Thompsons returned to the Cape May area. For a few weeks they either rented a hotel suite or a cottage. They visited sisters Hannah and Mary, who had married R. S. Magonagle following Reverend Tindall's death, and their old friends. The local newspapers wrote up their visits with flattering articles that glorified Thompson's exploits as "a local boy who made good."[15]

In 1896, four years after the death of Kate's mother, Eliza, Thompson went to Chattanooga, Tennessee, to settle what appeared to be a case of fraud involving Kate's and Cort's inheritance. The mayor of Chicago, George B. Swift, wrote a letter of introduction to G. W. Ochs, mayor of Chattanooga, who would be Thompson's host and guide in that city.[16]

While Thompson was on a sightseeing trip to Lookout Mountain, Daniel J. Duffy, who was involved in the case, entered Thompson's hotel armed with a double-barreled shotgun. In the lobby he announced that his integrity had been challenged and he intended to shoot Thompson on sight. Frightened, the hotel authorities called the police and Mr. Duffy left quietly. (Onlookers later stated Duffy had apparently imbibed a considerable amount of alcohol.) The next day, a sober Duffy reappeared and the matter was settled peacefully.[17]

Thompson's oratorical gifts, powerful even in his youth, developed as he matured. In his middle and later years he was often asked to speak to civic groups both in and around Chicago. On February 11, 1897, Thompson delivered his master work in oratory. Entitled *A Scrap of Gettysburg*, he delivered this moving oration before the Illinois Commandery of the Military Order of the Loyal Legion (MOLLUS),[18] an organization to which he had been elected on January 14, 1895. The speech was printed in pamphlet form and distributed to members of the organization and his many friends.[19] It was so well received that he was asked to repeat it to the MOLLUS chapter in Milwaukee, Wisconsin, in 1908.

In September of 1905, Dr. Charles A. Wiedemann, former hospital steward with the Twelfth New Jersey and one of the first medical personnel to treat Thompson when he was wounded,[20] wrote Thompson and asked him to deliver the address at the Twelfth's

Reunion dinner for that year. As Thompson was unable to attend, he sent portions of his diary relating to the Battle of Chancellorsville to be read.

The Thompsons continued to be prominent in Chicago society. On October 9, 1899, they attended a banquet honoring President McKinley, who had come to Chicago to lay the cornerstone of a new government building. Later that year they attended a ball in honor of a visit of Admiral and Mrs. George Dewey.

Daughter Mary Thompson became Mrs. G. Kenneth Sage in January of 1903.[21] Her son, G. Kenneth, Jr. was born in 1909, but died at the age of six. Thompson's beloved sister Hannah died in 1910.

Thompson himself became ill early in 1911. There is no record of what the illness was but his handwriting shows he shook considerably and holding the pen was difficult. His daughter Louise (Bonnie) wrote him a letter gently taking him to task for succumbing to an illness.[22] He recovered enough so that in September of that year, he bought a new car, a two-passenger electric coupe with a total horsepower of three. He was so proud of this vehicle that he preserved all the documents relating to the transaction.

In 1912, in his 75th year, Thompson retired from the practice of law. His life ended on June 3, 1914. He was buried in the family plot in Oakwoods Cemetery where once he eulogized other Civil War heroes. Kate, Mary, her husband and baby son are also interred there.[23]

Kate lived on in the family home until her death on April 20, 1926. Her funeral was conducted from the parlor according to the rites of the Episcopal Church, the family having been longtime members of St. Paul's.[24] The Thompson daughters probably inherited the property jointly. The historic house was razed in 1930.

Throughout Thompson's career, many honors and awards were bestowed on him. In addition to membership in The Chicago Bar Association, he belonged to the prestigious Union League[25] and the Kenwood Club of Chicago, which he served as President for 1891-92.[26] He also belonged to MOLLUS, the Western Society of The Army of the Potomac, and the Twelfth New Jersey Volunteer Association. In addition, he had membership in the Dearborn Rifle Club for a time. Both he and Kate were members and patrons of the Art Institute of Chicago.

Among the many eulogies given after his death are the following words, "Colonel Richard S. Thompson . . . eminent attorney, distinguished statesman, honored veteran of the Civil War, and man of unswerving honesty of purpose and unblemished moral character, ranked among the leading men of Chicago."[27]

So ended the life of Colonel Richard Swain Thompson. He served his country well for more than two years as an officer in the United States Volunteer Army. He loved and served, with equal devotion, his family, fellow man, community, and state during the 49 years he lived after the Civil War.

On September 6, 1932, the final reunion of the Twelfth New Jersey Volunteers took place, nearly seventy years to the day they had first mustered in. Fifteen men were known to be still living but only three came. For 57 years formal reunions had been held; there would be no more.

Notes

[1] Thompson had already been admitted to the Bar in Philadelphia. He had a certificate dated August 21, 1865, which stated that he had been admitted to the practice of law on March 8, 1862, in the Court of Common Pleas of the city and county of Philadelphia. (attested by Asa I. Fish) He also had a certificate dated March 8, 1862, that he was duly sworn and admitted to the Bar for the District Court of The City and County of Philadelphia by the motion of A. I. Fish, but by 1910 the original license had been lost. Thompson applied for a duplicate, but the Court declined to issue one. Instead, they offered him a certificate attesting to his date of admission and good standing as a member of the Bar. The issuance fee was $2, which Thompson paid.

[2] When a street system was laid out in Hyde Park, the location of the house was at Chestnut and Park Avenues (Park Avenue was also called Park Street). Later Chestnut was changed to 54th Street and Park Avenue became East Avenue, the mailing address being 5406 East End Avenue. Still later, East End Avenue became Hyde Park Boulevard. The community of Hyde Park was annexed to Chicago on July 15, 1889. For more information on this historic old village, see Chamberlin, E. (1974) *Chicago and its Suburbs*. New York, Pp. 352-354. Thompson is listed among the prominent citizens of Hyde Park. Also see Drury, J. (1976) *Old Chicago Houses*. Chicago, IL, p. 245ff. Information on the street names and the lot size and orientation courtesy of the Hyde Park Historical Society.

[3] While Thompson was serving in the army, sparks from one of the first trains to run through the Cape May area set fire to part of the wooded property he and his sisters owned. Quite a bit of valuable timber was lost. No record has been found of any suit but letters did mention a settlement was reached.

[4] The Grand Army of the Republic was a voluntary organization of veterans of the Union Army or Navy who served in the Civil War. Its purpose was to preserve the history of the war, perpetuate the memory of the dead, assist families of deceased members as needed, and promote fellowship among the

members. The veterans of the Confederate army called their organization the United Confederate Veterans (UCV).

[5] In 1875, Frank M. Riley of Bridgeton, representing the Committee of Ten (one from each company) of the Twelfth New Jersey Volunteers Association, wrote him requesting he write his wartime experiences for publication in a regimental history. He also received a letter from Henry F. Chew dated September 7, 1906, noting that many of their old comrades were passing away.

[6] These items are in the collection of John W. Kuhl.

[7] The South Park Commission, organized by pioneer Chicago attorney Paul Cornell, founder of the village of Hyde Park, was the forerunner of the Chicago Park System. *Ibid.*, p. 247.

[8] Morgan, a kinsman of Thomas Morgan whose land eventually became Morgan Park, a subdivision of Chicago, was a successful lumberman who settled in Hyde Park in 1873. *Ibid.*, Pp. 247 & 393.

[9] He is quoting from Psalm 90, verse 9, "For all our days are passed away in thy wrath: we spend our years as a tale that is told." (King James translation).

[10] Troutman's reference is to *Julius Caesar*, Act I, Scene 2, "Upon what meat doth this our Caesar feed, That he is grown so great?"

[11] Charles Troutman had been the Second Lieutenant of Company G, Twelfth New Jersey Volunteers.

[12] The two children of Louise and Samuel Whitney were Catherine and Richard Thompson. Catherine Whitney married a Mr. Maxwell. Richard Thompson Whitney married Miss Ruth Potter. They had two children: Barbara and Jeannette Richard. See Appendix A.

[13] Elizabeth T. (Thompson?) Whitney was the daughter of Emma and John Stevenson. She married John Perkins Whitney and had a daughter Josephine. It is not known if John P. Whitney was related to Louise's husband, Samuel.

[14] She refers to the site of the Bliss farm.

[15] While in Cape May, they stayed in a cottage at 729 Columbia Avenue. It is still there, named "Tysmyin." The *Ocean Wave* of August 5, 1891, and the *Cape May County Gazette* of August 12, 1904, both printed articles announcing their presence in the area. The articles, which may have been saved by Kate, were found among Thompson's papers. The *Cape May County Gazette* article read,

"Col. Richard S. Thompson and family, of Chicago, have just arrived in this city and are now stopping at the Chalfonte, where they will remain the balance of the season. Col. Thompson is a native of Cape May County, and received his academic and classical education at the Bordentown High School, N.J., under Rev. Alden Scovel, now deceased. He subsequently studied law with Asa Fish, Esq., of Philadelphia, since deceased, and was admitted as a member of the Philadelphia Bar. He afterwards enlisted as Captain of Company K, in The Twelfth New Jersey Regiment and became Lieutenant Colonel of the same, and served until the end of the war. He was severely wounded at the battle of Reams' Station in 1864, by the bursting of a shell from the enemy's camp, during the siege of Petersburg, the key to Richmond.

"At the Battle of Gettysburg he made with his regiment, one of the most desperate charges in that engagement, by which he captured the Bliss Barn filled with rebel sharp shooters, who were picking off our officers. Since the war Col. Thompson has been practicing law in the City of Chicago and has been and is now one of the most prominent and successful lawyers there. Railroads and corporations are mostly his clients. At one time he represented the richest and most populous section of Chicago in the Illinois State Senate, where he became the Republican leader. He owns and occupies a palatial residence bordering on Lake Michigan.

"The Colonel is also an interesting and eloquent speaker, and at the time General Grant planted the oak tree in one of the parks in Chicago, he was selected as the orator of the day. Cape May County therefore may well be proud of her illustrious son, and he should have the freedom of the city while here.

"Colonel Thompson is a brother of Mrs. Coleman F. Leaming, of Cape May Court House, and was born here."

[16] The letter, dated January 31, 1896, said in part, "Colonel Thompson is one of our leading citizens, an attorney of repute, and I bespeak for him your kindest consideration." Born in Tennessee, George Washington Ochs (also called Oakes) (1861-1931) was a brother of Adolf S. Ochs, publisher of the *New York Times*. Also prominent in journalism, G. W. Ochs was editor of the *Chattanooga Daily Times*. See Malone D. (Ed.) (1934) *Dictionary of American Biography*. Vol. 8. New York, Pp. 600-602.

[17] Information courtesy of John W. Kuhl.

[18] MOLLUS was created on April 15th, 1865, when Lieutenant Colonel Thomas E. Zell and others formed an honor guard for President Lincoln. They continued to meet as a society in commemoration of the events and principles of the Civil War. The Commandery of the state of Pennsylvania, in which the first chapter of MOLLUS was formed, officially organized on November 4, 1865. Averaging six meetings a year, every meeting included the reading of an historic paper. Thompson joined the organization as a "Companion of the

First Class." MOLLUS has a permanent home in Philadelphia. Taylor, F. H. (1913) *Philadelphia in the Civil War 1861-1865.* Philadelphia, Pp. 322-324.

[19] Thompson, R. S. (1899) *A Scrap of Gettysburg,* "Military Essays and Recollections: Papers Read Before the Commandery of the State of Illinois, Military Order of the Loyal Legion of the United States," Pamphlet printed from Volume III, Chicago, Pp. 97-99. See Appendix H.

[20] Charles A. Wiedemann had replaced Dr. Satterthwait's brother, John, as a hospital steward. Thompson never forgot Wiedemann's ministrations and corresponded with him long after the war ended.

[21] In 1902, a large two and one-half story red brick home was built at 5450 Hyde Park Boulevard. Records give the owner as a "R. S. Thompson." It well may be that this home was a wedding gift to daughter Mary. Hyde Park Historical Society Archives.

[22] March 26, 1911; collection of John W. Kuhl.

[23] With her son-in-law's help Catherine Thompson applied for a widow's pension in late June of 1914. Thompson's original pension was $22.50 a month; at the time of his death he was receiving $90.00 dollars a month.

[24] St. Paul's Episcopal Church was the first of that denomination to be established on the south side of Chicago (Hyde Park). The church was organized in a private home (later purchased by James Morgan) and a building built at 50th Street and Dorchester Avenue, not too far from the Thompson residence. Drury, *op. cit.,* p. 246.

[25] On June 25, 1862, Republicans in Pekin, Illinois, met to organize a patriotic society called a "Union League," to counteract the effects of the Copperheads and other pro-Southern groups, uphold the Federal government, and bolster the strength of the Republican Party. By September the movement had spread to many other cities including Chicago. In November a Union Club of Philadelphia was formed which became, on December 22, 1862, the Union League. The society soon spread to cities in the north, midwest, and far west. Unquestioned loyalty to the Union was the basic requirement for membership. While he was in the army, Thompson probably read some League-sponsored books and pamphlets. See Whiteman, M. (1975) *Gentlemen in Crisis: The Union League of Philadelphia.* Philadelphia; and Silvestro, C. M. (1961) *None but Patriots: The Union League in Civil War and Reconstruction.* Ann Arbor, MI.

[26] The Kenwood Club was a social club founded in 1884 by the residents of Hyde Park, Kenwood being an affluent community within the Hyde Park area. Thompson became a member the year it was founded, served as one of the eight Directors from 1885 to 1887, and as president in 1891-92. The object of

the club was to promote "social intercourse between its members and their families," according to a club publication. Information courtesy the Chicago Historical Society.

[27] Excerpt from the collection of John W. Kuhl.

Appendix A

The Thompson Family Tree

The Thompson family of Cape May descended from Benajah Thomson (Thompson's great-grandfather), who married Toudl-Hkiligo (Snowflower), sister of King Nummis or Nummy, chief of the Kechemeche tribe of the Lenni Lenape Indians, a class of the Algonquin group. She was baptized and given the name, Prudence Eldridge. Benajah Thomson was a captain in a New Jersey militia unit in 1776. He died in 1780; Prudence died in 1778. They had eight children: James, Nehemiah (1766-1796), Richard (12/Feb/1768-12/Dec/1824), Constant (1770-1793), Anson (d. 1817), Christiana, Manley (1775-1848), and Warren (1778-1853).

Benajah's son Richard changed the spelling of the name to Thompson. He was a captain in the Fishing Creek, New Jersey, artillery in 1814 and a first lieutenant in the First Regiment of Cape May. He married three times. His first wife, Judith Swain, was a descendant of Richard Swain, who was one of the first seven white owners of Nantucket Island, Massachusetts. The Swains were a whaling family, whose roots went back to Ireland. Her grandfather was Ebenezer; her father, Silas Swain. Richard and Judith had four children: James H.(1789-1870), who moved to Illinois in 1836; Richard (b. 3/Dec/1795 at Fishing Creek, Cape May County, and d. 27/Sep/1857); and two daughters, Judith and Sarah, who died in infancy. Judith Swain Thompson died April 16, 1802.

Richard next married Charlotte Leaming of Dennisville (b. 1765, d. 2/Dec/1812). The widow of Parsons Leaming, whom she married in 1781 at the age of sixteen, she was known for her beautiful face and figure. Leaming died in 1807, aged 51. Her children from this marriage opposed her union to Thompson as they did not want a stepfather. This marriage produced no children.

After Charlotte died, Richard married his third wife, Sarah Price. They had one child, Sarah Ann, who married Nathaniel Holmes and had five children. After Richard's death, she married James Conrad of Cape May.

The Thompson brothers, James and Richard, inherited a farm at Green Creek. Richard was interested in commerce, owned several ships, and had other shipping interests. He had a half-interest in a freight schooner called the *Isabella Thompson*. Politically active, he became the first postmaster of Goshen, New Jersey, in 1818; clerk of the County of Cape May from 1824 to 1829, county sheriff from 1830 to 1833, and a member of the state legislature from 1834 to 1838. In addition, he served in the Assembly and the Council of New Jersey, as well as being secretary of the state senate.

Richard married Mary Pisant (b. 1793, d. 24/July/1821) on February 14, 1819; they had one child, John P. (b. 1819, d. 1821). Richard's second wife was Elizabeth Holmes (b. 18/Feb/1800, d. 12/Jan/1844), youngest of the six children of Nathaniel and Hannah Hand Holmes. They were married on February 15, 1823, and had five children:

1. Mary Elizabeth (b. 14/May/1824, d. 1/Apr/1895). She married the Reverend Napoleon Bonaparte Tindall, first pastor of the First Baptist Church of Cape May. They had five children: Elizabeth, Virginia, Mary, Eva, and Richard T.(Buddie) who died in 1865. After the Reverend Tindall died, Mary married R. S. Magonagle (or Magonigle).

2. Isabella (b. 1826, d. 21/Oct/1866). She married Joseph Falkenberg Leaming in 1855. They had three children: Isabella, Joseph, and a baby who died in infancy. Son Joseph (b. 2/Dec/1860, d. 14/Sep/1864) and Isabella are buried in the same grave. Her husband preceded her in death.

3. Hannah (b. 1829, d. 1910). She married Dr. Coleman Forman Leaming. They had three children: Josephine, Emma (b. 1853), and Edwin (Ned) Thompson (1857-1868).

4. Emma H. (d. 6/Aug/1899), who married John S. Stevenson, had a daughter Elizabeth who married John Perkins Whitney. Their daughter Josephine married Boyd Nixon.

5. Richard Swain (b. 27/Dec/1837, d. 3/June/1914). He married Catherine Scovel. They had two daughters: Louise (b. 25/Sep/1868) and Mary (b. 26/July/1874). Louise married Samuel A. Whitney, January 1, 1893. They had two children: Catherine (b. 18/May/1894) who married a Mr. Maxwell, and Richard Thompson Whitney (b. 22/June/1895), who married a Miss Ruth Potter. They had two children: Barbara and Jeannette Richard. Richard's and Catherine's daughter Mary married George Kenneth Sage (b. 11/Dec/1869) on January 1, 1903. They had one son, George Kenneth, Jr. (b. November 16, 1909, d. 1915). Mary was still living in 1940.

Through marriage, the family was related to the early pioneer families of Massachusetts and New Jersey: Swains, Leamings, Hands, and Holmeses. Two of Richard Swain Thompson's sisters married members of the Leaming family, which traced back to colonial and Pilgrim ancestors.

Scovel Family

Reverend Alden C. Scovel was born April 4, 1809, in Peru, Berkshire County, Massachusetts. He married Elizabeth (Eliza) R. Barker (Hutchinson), born June 6, 1808, in New Jersey on September 27, 1827. They had two children: son Cortland and daughter Catherine C. who was born May 9, 1890, at Stockport, New York. Reverend Scovel died July 16, 1889, in Chicago; Mrs. Scovel died November 5, 1892, in Chicago.

Leaming Family

Jeremiah and Abigail Falkenberg Leaming had two sons: Joseph Falkenberg and Jeremiah (b. 20/Jan/1831). Joseph Falkenberg Leaming married Isabella Thompson in 1855; their daughter Isabella married Dr. Lewis Leaming Forman. Jeremiah Leaming married Harriet Scoville or Scovel. Colonel Richard S. Thompson called Jeremiah Leaming "Uncle Jeremiah," as he was an uncle of Thompson's wife Catherine, but he was also a brother to Thompson's brother-in-law, Joseph.

Appendix B

Orders and Reports, November 12, 1862-December 31, 1862 Camp at Falmouth, Virginia

Orders

Headquarters, 8th Army Corps
Baltimore, Md., Nov. 12, 1862

Captain R. S. Thompson, Provost Marshal at Ellicott's Mills will not send to this place any political prisoners without examination, and if no charges are sent in conformity with General Orders No. 22 & 27, dated 10th and 25th August 1862, they will either be sent back or discharged.

John E. Wool, Major Genl.

Headquarters, 8th Army Corps,
Baltimore, Md., Nov. 12, 1862

Captain R. S. Thompson
Provost Marshal at Ellicott's Mills, Md.

Captain,

You will send to these Headquarters on the day after tomorrow the witnesses and the charges of desertion against James Chase and John Hayworth, now confined in the Police-Station House. And also written and sworn charges against three political prisoners, named John L. Butler, Moses Paulett and Francis Shipley.

By command of Maj. Genl. Wool
T. Christensen, Major USA & ADC

Headquarters, 8th Army Corps
Baltimore, Md., Nov. 12, 1862

Captain R. S. Thompson,
Provost Marshal at Ellicott's Mills

Will proceed to Laurel Station to obtain the charges and evidence against the guilt of John Bartles and Moses Paulett.

When this business is accomplished he will return to the city of Baltimore, as a witness in the case of James Chase and John Hayworth, two deserters, and bring with him the other witnesses in these two last named cases.

By command of Maj. Genl. Wool
T. Christensen, Major USA & ADC

Quarterly Report, 1862

[This Quarterly Return notes a change in armament for the Twelfth New Jersey. Thompson's notation on the face of the document reads, "This shows the change from Austrian Rifles to Smoothbore Muskets—Buck & Ball, Dec. 12, 1862." The Return was sent to the Chief of Ordnance, Washington, D.C., on June 13, 1863, and signed by Richard S. Thompson, Capt. Co. K, 12th N.J. Vols., Commanding. On the reverse face of the document Captain Thompson states that the Return shows a correct statement of the public property in his charge during the 4th quarter ending December 1862, while in camp near Falmouth, Virginia, January 23, 1863.]

Quarterly Return of Ordnance and Ordnance Stores, 4th Quarter, 1862

October 1, On Hand from Last Return:

90 Austrian rifles, calibre .58
90 Bayonet scabbards
90 Cap punches and cone picks
90 Cartridge boxes, .58 calibre
90 Cartridge box plates
90 Cartridge box belts
90 Cartridge box belt plates
90 Gun slings
90 Waist belts, privates
5 Ball screws
8 Worms [double screw on the end of a rammer used for extracting a wad or cartridge from a muzzle loader]
22 Screwdrivers and cone wrenches
90 Wipers
5,000 Elongated ball, calibre .57

October 13, Received from Col. of 12th N.J. Vols.

5,000 Elongated ball, calibre .57

December 12, Received from Arsenal at Washington, D.C., from Col. R. C. Johnson, 12th N.J. Vols.

82 Smoothbore Harpers Ferry Springfield muskets, calibre .69
9 Ball screws
88 Screwdrivers and cone wrenches
9 Spring vises
88 Spare cones
88 Tompions [plug for the muzzle of a gun when not in use]
88 Wipers
8,800 Ball carts. for smoothbore, calibre .69

October 27, Received from Col. 12th N.J. Vols.

5,000 Percussion caps

October 27, Received from Col. 12th N.J. Vols.

3,500 Buck & Ball, calibre .69

December 12, Turned in at the Arsenal at Washington, D.C., by order of Col. R. C. Johnson, 12th N.J. Vols.

90 Austrian rifles, calibre .58
5 Ball screws
22 Screwdrivers and cone wrenches
90 Wipers
4,800 Elongated ball, calibre .57
Expended as per abstract in action & practice
5,200 Elongated ball, calibre .57

December 12

4,800 Ball carts. for smoothbore, calibre .69
5,000 Percussion caps

December 13, Lost or destroyed per certificate

3 Bayonet scabbards
3 Cap pouches and cone picks
3 Cartridge boxes, calibre .58
3 Cartridge box plates
3 Cartridge box belts
3 Cartridge box belt plates
3 Gun slings
3 Waist belts, privates
3 Waist belt plates
3 Screwdrivers and cone wrenches
3 Spare cones
3 Tompions
3 Wipers

Appendix C

The Battle of Gettysburg: Two Official Reports

[Excerpt from the] *Report of Major John T. Hill, Twelfth New Jersey Volunteers*. [From the *OR*, Series I, Vol. 27, Part 1, Chapter 39, Pp. 470-471.]

Headquarters
12th Regiment, New Jersey Volunteers
July 16, 1863

Sir:

At 5 p.m. on the 2d instant, four companies, (B, H, E, and G) were detailed to take a large barn on our picket line, taken from us and held by the enemy. Under command of Captain Jobes, Company G, they charged gallantly upon the building, surrounding it, and capturing 92 prisoners, including 7 commissioned officers; losing in the attack 2 officers and 40 men killed and wounded.

At 6 p.m. the same day the balance of my command moved to the front line, taking position behind a stone fence to the left of Kirby's battery, remaining in this position until the afternoon of the 5th instant.

At 7:30 a.m. of the 3d instant, five companies (D, C, K, F and A), under command of Captain Thompson, Company K, again drove the enemy from the shelter of the barn, capturing a major and 1 man, relieving our lines from an annoying fire from the enemy's sharpshooters posted therein.

At 4 p.m. of the 3d instant, the whole line became engaged in repulsing an attack in force made by the enemy, completely routing them, capturing prisoners estimated to number 500 men, and 2 colors.

We collected and turned in 751 small-arms, picked up in our immediate front.

Officers and men behaved with the greatest gallantry. I take pleasure in calling your attention to meritorious conduct of Captains Thompson, Jobes, and Chew; Adjutant Franklin; Lieutenants

McComb, Trimble, Acton, Phipps, Williams, Eastwick, and Dare; Sergeant-Major DuBois, and Color Sergeants Cheeseman and Griffin.

I am, Colonel, very respectfully, your obedient servant,
John T. Hill, Major,
Commanding Twelfth New Jersey Volunteers

Colonel Morris
Comdg. Second Brig., Third Div., Second Army Corps
[Thompson, in his dairy and his letters to his sisters, states they captured a major and four privates, while Major Hill makes note of only one private in his report.]

[Excerpt from] *Report No. 123 of Colonel Thomas M. Smyth, First Delaware Infantry, Commanding Second Brigade.* [From the *OR,* Series I, Vol. 27, Part 1, Chapter 39, Pp. 464-465.]

Headquarters
Second Brig., Third Div., Second Corps
July 17, 1863

Sir:

Four companies of the Twelfth New Jersey Volunteers were sent to retake the barn and to dislodge the enemy's sharpshooters, which they succeeded in doing, capturing 93 prisoners, including 7 commissioned officers. The enemy advanced in turn, and recaptured the barn.

The First Delaware Volunteers and four more companies of the Twelfth New Jersey Volunteers, under command of Captain Thompson, Twelfth New Jersey, were subsequently sent to again take possession of the barn, which they did, having taken 10 prisoners, one of whom was a major. Observing that the enemy was moving in force along a ravine toward the barn, Captain Thompson thought it proper to retire.

Very respectfully, your obedient servant
Thos. A. Smyth
Colonel, First Delaware Volunteers, Comdg. Brigade

Capt. George P. Corts, Assistant Adjutant General

Appendix D

Report of the Battle at Bristoe Station

Report No. 54 of Lieutenant Colonel Thomas H. Davis, Twelfth New Jersey Volunteers. [From the *OR*, Series I, Vol. 29, Part 1, Chapter 41, Pp. 297-298.]

Headquarters
Twelfth New Jersey Volunteers
October 17, 1863

Sir:

I have the honor to report the part taken by the Twelfth New Jersey Volunteers in the action of October 14, as follows: While moving by the flank at route step, the enemy opened a brisk fire on us from the left bank of the railroad. We were then ordered by Colonel Smyth, commanding brigade, to move by the left flank and charge across the field at double-quick, which was done under a heavy fire, to the railroad. Driving the enemy from the railroad, formed line and advanced across the road through the wood; then halted until ordered to fall back to railroad, which was done in good order. After recrossing the railroad was then ordered by Colonel Smyth to support Ames' battery, which order was executed, and remained in support until the battery was withdrawn, and we were then ordered to join the brigade.

Casualties were as follows: 1 commissioned officer severely wounded; 1 enlisted man killed, and 5 enlisted men wounded.

I will add that while on the march, a short time previous to the engagement, a number of stragglers, belonging to the Third Corps, who were arrested by the provost guard, were placed in the ranks of this regiment. The number that followed the regiment to the fight behaved nobly, 5 being wounded. Owing to the short space of time and continual marching, we were unable to learn their names, regiment, or company.

The following officers were in the engagement, and conducted themselves in the best manner: Major John T. Hill, and Adjt. Josiah

P. Franklin; Capt. Sylvester S. Chase, Company A; Lieuts. Benjamin
F. Lee and Richard C. Wilson, Company B; Lieut. Newton M. Brooks,
Company C; Capt. James McComb and Lieut. James L. McIlhenny,
Company D; Capt. Daniel Dare, and Lieuts. Philip M. Armington and
Stephen G. Eastwick, Company E; Lieut. James S. Stratton, Company
F; Lieut. James T. Lowe, Company G; Lieut. Samuel Williams, Com-
pany H; Capt. Henry F. Chew, Company I; Capt. Richard S.
Thompson, Company K; Sergt. Maj. Charles D. Lippincott; Color-
Sergts. Charles E. Cheeseman and William H. Griffin.

Very respectfully,
Thos. H. Davis
Lieutenant-Colonel, Commanding

Capt. William P. Seville
Acting Assistant Adjutant General

Appendix E

Orders and More Orders: April 1864 through June 1864

Headquarters, Vol. R. Service, N.J.
Trenton, N.J., April 5, 1864

Special Orders No. 93

Pursuant to instructions received from the War Department Adjt.
Genl's Office dated March 31st, 1854, Capt. Richard S. Thompson,
12th N.J. Vols. will take post at Camden, N.J., for the purpose of
recruiting for the Regiment [to] which he belongs.

Capt. Hufty at that Post will furnish transportation and subsistence
for all recruits enlisted by Capt. Thompson.

By order of the Superintendent

Headquarters, Vol. R. Service, N.J.
Trenton, N.J., June 2, 1864

Special Orders No. 149

Capt. Richard S. Thompson, 12th N.J. Vols. will on Monday, June 6th, 1864, close his Recruiting Office at Camden, N.J., and proceed to rejoin his Regiment in the field, reporting at Trenton, N.J., *en route.*

By order of the Superintendent

Washington, D.C., June 8, 1864

Col. J. C. Kelton, Asst. Adj. Gen.

I hereby make application to remain in Washington, D.C., until the 9th inst. for the purpose of completing my outfit for the Army.

Respectfully from your Obedient Servant,
Richard S. Thompson
Capt., 12 N.J. Vols.

Approved by order
Maj. Genl. Halleck

Headquarters, Rendezvous Distribution, Va.
June 10, 1864

Special Orders No. 118

1. Major R. S. Thompson 12th N.J. Vols. will at once take command of a detachment of men for the Army of the Potomac, to be turned over to him by Capt. Thos. H. Marston, Commdg 1st Division of camp.

2. Major R. S. Thompson will have his command ready and will move at 9 o'clock a.m. tomorrow June 11, 1864, fully armed and equipped, with shelter tents; 100 rounds of ammunition and five day's rations each. He will report with his battalion, to Brig. Genl. Briggs at Alexandria, Va. for transportation and for further orders.

3. The following named commissioned Officers will at once report to Major R. S. Thompson, 12th N.J. Vols., for duty. [Ten names and units have been omitted here.]

Saml. M. Kelsey
Lt. Col. Commdg.

Headquarters Rendezvous, Drafted Men Vols.
Alexandria, Va.
June 11, 1864

[Extract of] Special Orders No. 96

4. A provisional battalion of troops for the Army of the Potomac under command of Major R. S. Thompson, 12th N.J. Vols., will proceed this day per steamer *Cossack* to White House, Va., *en route* to that Army. Upon arrival at that point the commanding officer will report for instructions to the commanding officer at that post. The following troops will compose the battalion. 627 men from rendezvous distribution recruits from this rendezvous.

[Fifteen names and units have been omitted here.]

Headquarters, U. S. Forces, Point of Rocks, Va.
June 13, 1864

Special Orders No. 14

Maj. John McClure will turn over to Maj. R. S. Thompson, 12th N.J. Vols., all enlisted men in his charge belonging to or for the 126th Ohio Vols. now in the Army of the Potomac together with their descriptive lists and all other papers and property pertaining to them. Maj. Thompson or the officer to whom the men may be assigned will receipt to Maj. McClure for all property in his charge, pertaining to the command. Maj. John McClure, 57th Ohio Vols.; Lieut. Wm. Hannor, 124th Ohio Vols.; and Lieut. A. B. France, 116th Ohio Vols. are relieved from duty in charge of the above named men as soon as they are transferred to Maj. Thompson.

By order of Brig. Genl. J. W. Turner
P. A. Davis, Capt. & ADG

By Telegraph from Genl. Butler's Headquarters
June 18, 1864

To Maj. Thompson, 12th N.J.

You will proceed up Appomattox to Point [of] Rocks, disembark and report to Genl. Turner near that point.

J. W. Shaffer
Col. & Chief of Staff

Headquarters, U.S. Forces
Point of Rocks, Va.
June 20, 1864, 10:40 p.m.

Maj. Thompson, Comdg. Distribution Camp

You will immediately report with the troops in your camp to Col. Pond, Comdg. Brigade for duty on the line tonight. The troops will take their blankets with them.

By order Brig. Gen. Turner
Israel Sealy
Capt. 4th N.Y. Vols. AAAG

Headquarters, Pond's Brigade
Near Point of Rocks, Va.
June 21, 1864

Maj. Thompson, Sir,

By direction from Div. Headquarters you will take your command back to camp.

By order of Col. F. B. Pond, Comdg. Brigade
Hatch, 1st Lt. & Act. Adj. Genl.

Headquarters, U.S. Forces
Point of Rocks, Va.
June 21, 1864

Maj. Thompson, Comdg. Distribution Camp

The Brig. Gen. Comdg. directs that you return with your command to camp, if you have not already done so.

Very respectfully, Yr. ob. svt.,
Israel Sealy
Capt 4th N.Y.V. AAAG

Headquarters, U.S. Forces
Point of Rocks, Va.
June 21, 1864

Maj. Thompson, Comdg. Dis. Camp

By direction of the Brig. Genl. Comdg. you will hold your command in readiness for duty on the line this evening. A staff officer will be sent to you with further orders.

Very Res., Yr. ob. svt.
Israel Sealy
Com 4th N.Y. Vols., AAAG

Headquarters, Army of the Potomac
June 21, 1864

Major R. S. Thompson
12th N.J. Vols.

Sir:

The Comdg. Genl. having learned that near seven hundred men, that left recently Camp Distribution under your command for this Army, are at the Point of Rocks, directs me to inquire whether you have received any instructions authorizing you to delay reporting here and if no such orders have been given you to ask why you have not reported.

I am Very Respectfully, Your obt. servant
[?] Williams
Asst. Adj. Genl.

Headquarters, Camp Distribution
At Point of Rocks
June 22, 1864

Assistant Adjutant Gen., Army of the Potomac

In compliance to your communication of the 21st inst. I have the honor to report: By order of Brig. Genl. Briggs commanding the rendezvous of drafted men and volunteers Alexandria, Va., I reported with my command at Bermuda Hundred to Maj. Genl. B. F. Butler from whom I received an order to report to Brig. Genl. Turner at Point of Rocks. Genl. Turner ordered me to establish camp at this point. My command is now on duty in the entrenchments near this point.

Respectfully, Your Obt. Servt.
Richard S. Thompson
Maj. 12 N.J. Vols., Comdg. Camp Distribution

Appendix F

An Eyewitness Account of the Mine Explosion at Petersburg

[Excerpts from a letter written by Sergeant William Taylor, 100th Pennsylvania Infantry, July 31, 1864 (His Letter #125) to his wife. From the Taylor correspondence in the Manuscripts Collection of Earl Gregg Swem Library, College of William and Mary; used with permission.]

. . . I felt [the ground] heave and roll beneath me and jumped up. A terrible explosion followed and the rebel fort that had annoyed us so much . . . was blown up high into the air—men, guns, and everything it contained. . . . Our batteries commenced firing. Our division led the charge and went in and took the first line of Rebel works. . . . We went out to the gap in the earthwork that led to the blown-up fort. Out there somewhere . . . our regiment was, but no one could tell me. . . . The regiment . . . was scattered and mixed up with others so it was impossible to tell where it was . . . everyone was on his own hook. . . . Just then our Negro troops started through the gap on a charge. . . . There were 200 yards of ground to pass over, raked by the heaviest fire of grape, canister, shell and minies ever I heard. . . . In about ten minutes I was astonished to see a number of officers rushing up to the gap, and others coming through and drawing their swords and pistols. Presently, the wave came. Back came the Negroes bearing everything with them. They were in a drove . . . they tramped right over me. . . . [He got to safety in a shallow pit.] With a great deal of exertion and after killing some of them, the Negroes were driven back, but the day was lost by that time. Not only had the Negroes run, but a great part of the white troops, and the Rebels improving the chance charged and retook the line of rifle pits and charged back to the fort. What troops remained repulsed them after a very hard struggle. Their loss was very heavy. We killed one whole regiment except 40 men who surrendered. In the charge our best troops suffered most. The worst ran with the Negroes. . . . When the stampede commenced, I thought my chances for Richmond [prison] were very good. . . . A second stampede now took place, but not so bad as the first one. Orders were given to abandon the fort. But it had now become more dangerous to leave it than to go to it a few hours before. [Taylor goes into more detail about killed, wounded, etc. and his own condition.]

We gained no ground that we did not have to give up and the day closed on the 9th Corps considerably demoralized. The old soldiers are ashamed of it. They are not numerous [enough] to redeem the vast amount of poor material that has been put in it. As to the Negroes, I think they did tolerable well. None but veterans could have been held in the place they were put and it was wrong to put them for the first time in such a bad fix. As to running off, the first two men who ran were two generals. Why blame the niggers for doing so too? Some of them only fell back as far as the destroyed fort and were there still fighting when the last man got in that we saw. A rumor came (I know not how) that on finally giving up the ground at the fort, the Rebels rushed in and bayoneted everyone there, even the wounded, both black and white. I don't state this as a fact, only a rumor.

Appendix G

A History of the Twelfth New Jersey Volunteers

by Colonel William E. Potter

[Excerpts from a speech delivered at the first reunion of The Twelfth New Jersey Volunteers on February 22, 1875, at Woodbury, New Jersey, as reported in the Bridgeton Chronicle, February 26, 1875.]

The 12th Regiment New Jersey Volunteers was organized under the provision of an act of Congress approved July 22, 1861, and under a call issued by the President of the United States, dated July 7, 1862, for 300,000 additional volunteers, to serve for three years, or during the war. This Regiment was one of five required from this State under the call named. The organization of the Regiment was begun in July . . . fully completed . . . officered and equipped by the 4th day of September 1862, at which time it was mustered into the service of the United States. . . . The several companies of the Regiment were raised in the following named counties, respectively: Co. A in the County of Salem; Co. B in the Counties of Burlington and Camden; Co. C in the County of Camden; Co. D at large; but chiefly, I think, in Camden; Co. E in the County of Camden; Co. F in the County of Gloucester; Co. G in the Counties of Camden and Cumberland; Co. H in the County of Salem; Co. I in the County of Salem; Co. K in the County of Cumberland.

The Regiment left Woodbury, where it had been encamped, and the state, September 7, 1862, under orders for Washington; but on its arrival at Baltimore was diverted from its route by General Wool, and ordered to Ellicott's Mills, on the line of the Baltimore and Ohio Railroad, then threatened by the advance of the Rebel Army into Maryland. The strength of the Regiment when it left the state was: officers, 39; non-commissioned officers and privates, 953; total 992. As a proof of the severity of its service it may be mentioned that its strength present for duty at Cold Harbor, Va., June 4, 1864, less than two years afterwards, was: officers, 3; non-commissioned officers and privates, 90; total, 93. The Regiment joined the Army of the Potomac and was put in position on the Rappahannock, about three miles above the towns of Falmouth and Fredericksburg, on the 19th of December, 1862, and from that time until the close of the war, wherever and whenever hard service was done by that army, our Regiment had its full share.

I . . . [could] tell how it held its ground at Chancellorsville until its right was turned by Jackson's corps, and its colonel and 178 of its officers and men were stricken down—how sternly at Gettysburg it stood upon the right of the left centre of the army, the key of its position, and with the rolling fire of its smoothbore muskets smote as with the blast of death Pettigrew's brigade of North Carolina troops, which formed the left of Longstreet's charging column; of its suffering in the severe winter campaign of Mine Run; of how it plunged through the icy waters of the Rapidan at Morton's Ford; of the wonderful campaign of the Wilderness, where in a short space of 30 days our devoted Regiment lost more than 300 killed and wounded, out of a total of 425 muskets; of its service, its losses, its sufferings by night and by day during the summer of 1864, and until the Rebel Army surrendered, and war was ended–but to you it is a familiar story. . . .

During the period of its service the Regiment was present and under fire in more than 30 general engagements, besides a large number of combats and skirmishes, *viz*:

Chancellorsville, Va., May 3 and 4, 1863.
Gettysburg, Pa., July 2 and 3, 1863.
Falling Waters, Md., July 13, 1863.
Auburn Mills, Va., October 14, 1863.
Bristoe Station, Va., October 14, 1863.
Blackburn's Ford, Va., October 16, 1863.
Robinson's Tavern, Va., November 27, 1863.
Mine Run, Va., November 28, 29, 30, 1863.
Morton's Ford, Va., February 6, 1864.
Wilderness, Va., May 5 and 7, 1864.
Spotsylvania, Va., May 8 to 11, 1864.
Spotsylvania C.H., Va., May 12 to 18, 1864.
North and South Anna River, Va., May 24 to 26, 1864.
Totopotomy, Va., May 30 and 31, 1864.
Cold Harbor, Va., June 2 to 12, 1864.
Before Petersburg, Va., June 16 to 23, 1864.
Deep Bottom, Va., July 25 to 29, 1864.
Mine Explosion, Va., July 30, 1864.
North Bank of James River, Va., August 14 to 18, 1864.
Reams' Station, Va., August 25, 1864.
Fort Sedgwick, Va., September 10, 1864.
Hatcher's Run, Va., October 27, 1864.
Boydton Plank Road, October 27, 1864.
Hatcher's Run, Va., February 6 to 8, 1864.
Dabney's Mill, Va., March 25, 1865.
Boydton Plank Road, Va., April 1, 1865.
Capture of Petersburg, Va., April 2, 1865.
Sailor's Creek, Va., April 6, 1865.
High Bridge, Va., April 7, 1865.
Farmville, Va., April 7, 1865.
Lee's Surrender, Appomattox C.H., April 9, 1865.

There died in the service, of its officers, 9; of its non-commissioned officers and men, 252; making its total loss by deaths, 261; being a loss by death of little more than one-fourth of the original number of its rank and file, and its officers exclusive of the medical staff and the quartermaster. Its other losses were: officers discharged, 12; resigned, 14; total 26; of enlisted men discharged, 159; total resigned and discharged, 185; add losses by death, 261; total losses from all causes, 446; being almost one-half of its original number. Resignations and discharges were chiefly on account of disability caused by wounds or disease contracted in the service.

Of the field and staff, Lt. Col. Thomas H. Davis was killed. Of the total number of officers originally commissioned in the Regiment, and exclusive of the Medical Staff and Quartermaster, and of those who were killed, or died of their wounds, 12 were wounded in action with greater or less severity, 17 were mustered out before the expiration of their term of service, and but three who served the full term escaped unhurt; and of the enlisted men a very large number who were mustered out of the Regiment bear the scars of honorable wounds. The official register in the Adjutant General's office shows that no regiment of this state, up to and including the Fourteenth, suffered as heavy a loss in deaths as the Twelfth, except the Eighth and Tenth. ..

The Regiment was first attached to the 2nd Brig., 3rd Div., 2nd Army Corps, then to the 3rd Brig., 2nd Div., 2nd Army Corps, and at the close of the war was attached to a Provisional Corps—all in the Army of the Potomac. A part of the Regiment was mustered out at camp near Munson's Hill, Va., June 4, 1865, the remainder . . . near Washington, on July 15, 1865. The names of the officers who were killed or died of wounds received in action are: Lieut. Col. Thomas H. Davis, killed in action at Spotsylvania C.H., May 12, 1864; Capt. Charles K. Horsfall, Company E, killed in action at Gettysburg, Pa., July 2, 1863; Capt. James McComb, Co. E, died July 2, 1864, of wounds received at Cold Harbor, Va., June 3, 1864; First Lieut. John M. Fogg, Co. H, killed in action at the Wilderness, May 5, 1864; First Lieut. John R. Rich, Co. E, died Sept. 2, 1864, of wounds received at Reams' Station, Va., Aug. 25, 1864; First Lieut. John R. Lowe, died Oct. 20, 1863, of wounds received at Bristoe Station, Va., Oct. 14, 1863; First Lieut. James S. Stratton, Company K, killed in action at Reams' Station, Va., Aug. 25, 1864; First Lieut. Joseph Pierson, Co. F, killed in action at Chancellorsville, Va., May 3, 1863; Second Lieut. Richard H. Townsend killed in action at Gettysburg, Pa., July 3, 1863.

Such, Comrades, is in brief the history of our regiment.

Appendix H

A Scrap of Gettysburg

by Colonel Richard S. Thompson

[Excerpts from a speech delivered to the Military Order of the Loyal Legion in Chicago on February 11, 1897.]

Prior to ten o'clock on the morning of July 3rd, the artillery firing had ceased; the firing on the skirmish line had quieted down, and a stillness that seemed oppressive had settled over the Battlefield of Gettysburg. It was like the hush in nature's elements which so often precedes the bursting into fury of the storm. Like the ominous gathering clouds, the enemy were moving great masses of troops and artillery. We waited. An hour passed and still we waited. Another hour passed into history and yet we waited. Even the occasional report of a rifle on the skirmish line seemed rather to emphasize than break the stillness. Eleven o'clock—twelve o'clock—one o'clock; then away to the enemy's right a single gun was fired, the shell from which struck the ground in rear of Hays's division. It did not burst; it lay there, a tongueless messenger of evil. Soon a second gun was fired from the enemy's extreme left, and struck the ground not far from where the first shell landed. A minute or so passed and then a gun in the enemy's centre fired and with it their entire line, from right to left, occupying a concave front of three miles in length, burst into flame. The command, "Down, Down," was heard everywhere. Our men rushed to their places in the line and threw themselves upon the ground, and none too soon. In an instant there fell upon the position occupied by the divisions of Hays and Gibbon of the Second Corps an avalanche of bursting shells.

It is impossible to give an adequate description of the unparalleled cannonade. Our colors had to be rolled and laid on the ground to keep them from being torn to pieces. The heat of the July sun, the effect of the smoke from the bursting shells and from our own artillery upon the eyes and lungs, even to those who escaped the greater ills of wounds, was an experience which no one who was in that line will ever forget.

Few who read the story appreciate the magnitude of that cannonade. Consider for a moment the conditions. The fire was concentrated upon a position occupied by part of two small divisions. One hundred and forty guns (a conservative estimate), each firing twice per minute, would make 280 projectiles per minute, or 42,000 in two and a half hours.

After the continuance of this artillery fire until it seemed as though Old Time had at last halted in his unchangeable march and turned over his scythe to the Angel of Death, a soldier in the line cried out, "Thank God! There comes the infantry!" He voiced the feeling of his comrades. Anything that promised action was better than inaction under the horrors of that cannonade.

From their cover on the wooded slope of Seminary Ridge emerged the assaulting column of the enemy. It advanced in double line of battle with a strong force of skirmishers in front. The right of their line consisted of three brigades of Pickett's division, with Wilcox's brigade in support of their right flank; the left of their column consisted of the four brigades of Heth's division, then under command of General Pettigrew, closely supported by the brigades of Scales and Lane of Pender's division, under the command of General Trimble. Two batteries of artillery also advanced in support of the assaulting column. On they came, a column 17,000 strong, with flags flying, bands playing, and arms at right shoulder shift. All in open sight of friend and foe, over the green valley they marched in battle's magnificent stern array.

Commencing at the right of Hays's division, which rested on Ziegler's Grove, the front line was occupied as follows: 39th New York; 126th New York, of Willard's brigade; then followed the Twelfth New Jersey, First Delaware, and Fourteenth Connecticut, of Smyth's brigade, in the order named. In rear of the right regiment at Ziegler's Grove was stationed Woodruff's Battery I, First U.S. Artillery, supported by the 108th New York of Smyth's brigade. While in rear of the Twelfth New Jersey and the First Delaware were the 111th New York and 125th New York, of Willard's brigade.

At the left of Hays's division the low wall, made of loose stones and fence rails, turned at a right angle to the front for about 50 feet and then at a right angle resumed the general southerly direction toward Round Top. On the left of Smyth's brigade of Hays's division, and with their right resting in the advance angle of this wall, were the brigades of Webb, Hall, and Harrow, of Gibbon's division, in the order named, with Stannard's brigade of the Third division of the First Corps thrown in front on the left. Gibbon's division, in order from right to left in the front line was as follows: Seventy-first Pennsylvania; Sixty-ninth Pennsylvania, of Webb's brigade; Fifty-ninth New York; Seventh Michigan; Twentieth Massachusetts, of Hall's brigade; Nineteenth Maine; Fifteenth Massachusetts; First Minnesota; and Eighty-second New York, of Harrow's brigade. In rear of Webb's brigade was Cushing's Battery A, Fourth U.S. Artillery, supported by the Seventy-second Pennsylvania, of Webb's brigade. In rear of Hall's front were Brown's Battery B, First Rhode Island Artillery, and Rorty's Battery B, First New York Artillery, supported by the Forty-second New York and the Nineteenth Massachusetts, of Hall's brigade, while Arnold's Battery A, First Rhode Island Artillery, was stationed in rear of the junction of these two divisions.

The distance between the lines of the two armies at the point in question was between 1,300 and 1,400 yards. The charging column advanced for some time without interruption, the enemy's artillery continuing its fire upon the divisions of Hays and Gibbon. When about a third of the distance had been covered by the advancing column, the Union artillery stationed on the left, toward Round Top, opened fire. The bands of the enemy then retired. As the assaulting column neared our line, the artillery of the enemy ceased its fire on the divisions of Hays and Gibbon and turned its attention to the batteries in the other portions of the line.

Relieved from the cannonade, we immediately unfurled and raised our colors. The batteries in the divisions of Hays and Gibbon had nothing but canister left. As the enemy came within canister range, these batteries opened. Hundreds fell, but from the fact that their lines were somewhat converging, the tendency was to thicken, rather than leave the gaps open.

Our infantry held their fire until the enemy were within about 250 yards, when a sheet of flame flashed along our front and the rifle regiments were in action. For a moment the enemy hesitated, in the next they returned the fire, which they continued as the advance progressed.

The Twelfth New Jersey regiment had about 400 men in line. They were armed, as already stated, with smoothbore Springfield muskets. The regulation cartridge contained a ball and three buckshot; but the men always provided themselves with extra buckshot, and on occasions like this, when close work was to be done, added a generous supply of buckshot to the regulation charge. General Hays ordered that this regiment be kept down until the enemy were within 40 yards.

Hence, on its immediate front seemed the safest road to our line. As the alignment of the advance became more and more broken, there was a very decided thickening and doubling up in the position of apparent least resistance. It was with the greatest difficulty that the men were kept down, and when the mass in that front was less than 50 yards, and the men could be restrained no longer, the caution was given, "Aim low." The order that followed was neither needed nor heard; it was drowned in the roar of musketry, and the position of least resistance was to be looked for somewhere else.

The front of the column opposite Smyth's brigade went down. The brigades of Scales and Lane of Pender's division, being immediately in rear of Heth's right, were staggered for a moment, but, recovering, advanced over the fallen double line of Heth's division in the face of a fire that had settled into that continuous character where firing is at will instead of by volley. Soon all semblance of the enemy's line of battle was abandoned; yet still they advanced until the foremost reached a position about 12 to 15 yards from our line, where the entire force in front of Hays's division gave way, not in sullen retreat, but in disordered flight. Many threw themselves upon the ground to escape the deadly fire. Large numbers of Hays's division rushed to the front to capture battle-flags and secure prisoners.

As the firing on Hays's front ceased, we discovered the enemy's flags flying in the angle to the front on our left, where Pickett's division had broken through the line held by Webb's brigade of Gibbon's division. Instantly Smyth's brigade opened an oblique fire on the left of this mass of Pickett's division occupying the angle. Stannard's brigade was pouring upon them a destructive fire from their right rear, while Gibbon's division, on their front and right, was bravely closing in on them. It was a slaughter-pen. Pickett's temporary success was soon over and the remnant of his division in flight. The memorable charge of Gettysburg had ended. It was a gallant charge, heroically met!

Appendix I

Obituary Notice of Richard S. Thompson

[From a newspaper clipping in the collection of John. W. Kuhl.]

Pioneer Lawyer and Veteran of Civil War Succumbs

Colonel Richard S. Thompson, a resident of Chicago for nearly 50 years and prominent in legal circles, died yesterday at his home, 5406 East End Avenue. He was born in Cape May Court House, N.J., Dec. 27, 1837, and was graduated from Harvard in 1861.

Mr. Thompson was admitted to the bar in Philadelphia in 1862 and the same year organized a company which was mustered to service in the Civil War as Company K, Twelfth New Jersey Volunteers. He was severely wounded at the battle of Reams' Station, Va. In October 1865, Colonel Thompson came to Chicago and established a law practice in partnership with Jeremiah Leaming.

He is survived by a widow, Mrs. Catherine S. Thompson, and two daughters, Mrs. S. A. Whitney of Boston and Mrs. G. Kenneth Sage of Chicago.

Funeral services will be held tomorrow afternoon at 3:30 o'clock from the residence. The services will be private. Burial will be in Oakwoods Cemetery.

Bibliography

Primary Materials

Taylor, Sergeant William. Unpublished letters to his wife. Rare Books Department, Earl Gregg Swemm Library, College of William and Mary, Williamsburg, VA.

Thompson, Richard Swain. Unpublished diary excerpts. John W. Kuhl collection. Pittstown, NJ.

Thompson, Richard Swain. Unpublished diary additions, notations, and letters. Ralph G. and Gerry Harder Poriss collection, Williamsburg, VA.

Documents

U.S. War Department (1880-1901) *The War of the Rebellion: A Compilation of the Official Records of the Union and Confederate Armies*. 128 Vols. Washington, DC: U.S. Government Printing Office.

Newspapers

Bridgeton Chronicle. Bridgeton, NJ. Saturday, August 10, 1862 & Friday, February 26, 1875.

Cape May County Gazette. Cape May Court House, NJ. Friday, August 12, 1904.

Cape May Ocean Wave. Cape May, NJ. August 5, 1891.

The Cape May Warrior. Capt May, NJ. September 1, 1864.

Chicago Daily Tribune. Chicago, IL. Undated clipping.

The National Tribune. Washington, DC. Thursday, December 15, 1910 & Thursday, December 22, 1910.

The Woodbury Constitution. Woodbury, NJ. September 12, 1862.

Magazines and Pamphlets

Fleming, G. T. (1913) *General Alexander Hays at the Battle of Gettysburg: Extracts from "Life and Letters of Alexander Hays" and Gilbert A. Hays, "Under the Red Patch."* Pittsburgh. Signed by G.A. Hays, found among RST's papers.

Horn, J. (1991) Charge of the Tarheel Brigade, *Civil War Times Illustrated.* January-February, Pp. 45-51.

Thompson, R. S. (1899) *A Scrap of Gettysburg.* Chicago: The Dial Press.

Warriner, N. E. (1984) *Register of Military Events in Virginia, 1861-1865.* Falls Church, VA: Confederate Printers Edition reprint of Virginia Civil War Commission 1959 edition.

Wool, A. E. (1989) A Tour of Cape May County. *Cape May County Magazine of History and Genealogy.* Vol. 14, No. 3., Pp. 185-210.

Atlases and Maps

Battlefields of the Civil War, with descriptive notes. (April, 1961) National Geographic Magazine Atlas, Plate 14. Baltimore, MD: A. Hoen & Co.

Griess, T. E. (Ed.)(1986) *Atlas for the American Civil War.* West Point Military History Series. Wayne, NJ: Avery Publishing Group.

National Park Service, United States Department of the Interior, Petersburg National Battlefield, VA.

Thompson, R. S. Hand drawn map of Battle of Gettysburg.

Thompson, R. S. Hand drawn sketch of Battle of Reams' Station.

Youseloff, T. (1958) *The Official Atlas of the Civil War.* New York: Thomas Youseloff. Reprint of the Government Printing Office 1891 edition.

Books

Adams, G. W. (1985) *Doctors in Blue.* Dayton, OH: Morningside.

Bache, R. M. (1897) *Life of General George Gordon Meade, Commander of the Army of the Potomac.* Philadelphia, PA: Henry T. Coates & Co.

Boatner, M. M. III, (1959) *The Civil War Dictionary.* New York: David McKay Co.

Bowman, J. S. (Ed.) (1983) *The Civil War Almanac.* New York: Gallery Books, W. H. Smith Pub.

Boyer, G. F. & Cunningham, J. P. (1985) *Cape May County Story.* Avalon, NJ: Avalon Publishing Co.

Calkins, C. M. (1990) Reams' Station. In Kennedy, F. H. (Ed.) *The Civil War Battlefield Guide.* Boston, MA: Hougton Mifflin.

Catton, B. (1952) *Glory Road.* Garden City, NY: Doubleday.

Catton, B. (1953) *A Stillness at Appomattox.* Garden City, NY: Doubleday.

Chamberlin, E. (1974) *Chicago and its Suburbs*. Metropolitan America Series. Chicago: Arno Press. Reprint of T. A. Hungerford's 1874 edition.

Chandler, D. G. (1979) *The Dictionary of Napoleonic Wars*. New York: Macmillan.

Christ, E. W. (1993) *The Struggle for the Bliss Farm at Gettysburg*. Baltimore: Butternut & Blue.

Coco, G. A. (1987) *On the Bloodstained Field*. Gettysburg, PA: Thomas Pub.

Coco, G. A. (1988) *A Vast Sea of Misery*. Gettysburg, PA: Thomas Pub.

Coco, G. A. (1989) *On the Bloodstained Field II*. Gettysburg, PA: Thomas Pub.

Coddington, E. B. (1979) *Gettysburg Campaign: A Study in Command*. Dayton, OH: Morningside. Reprint of C. Scribner's 1968 edition.

Cullen, J. P. (1968) *The Battle of Chancellorsville*. Yorktown, VA: Eastern National Park & Monument Association Eastern Acorn Press.

Damman, G. E. (1983, 1988) *A Pictorial Encyclopedia of Civil War Medical Instruments*. Vols. 1 & 2. Missoula, MT: Pictorial Histories Pub. Co.

Davis, B. (1982) *The Civil War: Strange and Interesting Facts*. Avenel, NJ: Wings Books. Reprint of Holt, Reinhart & Winston's 1960 *Our Incredible Civil War*.

Davis, W. C.(1986) *Gettysburg: The Story Behind the Scenery*. Las Vegas, NV: K.C. Publications.

Drury, J. (1975) *Old Chicago Houses*. Chicago: U. of Chicago Press.

Encyclopedia Britannica. Eleventh Edition, Vol. 4. (1910) New York: Encyclopedia Britannica Co.

Expilly, J. J. d' (1978) *Dictionnaire Geographique Historique et Politique des Gaules et de la France*. Vol. 5. Amsterdam, Netherlands: Kraus-Thomson Reprint of 1767 Nedeln/Liechtenstein edition.

Foster, J. Y. (1868) *New Jersey and the Rebellion: A History of the Services of the Troops and People of New Jersey in Aid of the Union Cause*. Newark, NJ: Martin R. Dennis & Co.

Garrison, W. (1992) *Civil War Trivia and Fact Book*. Nashville, TN: Rutledge Hill Press.

Glass, P. & Singer, L. C. (1968) *Singing Soldiers: A History of the Civil War in Song*. New York: Da Capo Press.

Haines, W. P. (1897) *History of the Men of Co. F with Description of the Marches and Battles of the 12th New Jersey Volunteers*. Mickelton, NJ: privately issued.

Harvard Alumni Association. (1913) *Harvard University Directory*. Cambridge, MA: Cambridge U. Press.

Harvard University Archives. (1859) *A Catalog of the Officers and Students of Harvard University for the Academic Year 1859-60*. Cambridge, MA: Sever & Francis.

Hawthorne, F. W. (1988) *Gettysburg: Stories of Men and Monuments*. Hanover, PA: The Association of Battlefield Guides & The Sheridan Press.

Henderson, W. D. (1987) *The Road to Bristoe Station: Campaigning with Lee and Meade, August 1-October 20, 1863*. Lynchburg, VA: H. E. Howard, Inc.

Horn, J. (1991) *The Destruction of the Weldon Railroad, Deep Bottom, Globe Tavern, and Reams' Station August 14-25, 1864*. Lynchburg, VA: H. E. Howard, Inc.

Jago, F. W. (1967) *12th New Jersey Volunteers, 1862-65*. Gloucester City, NJ: The Gloucester County Historical Society, privately issued.

Johnson, R. C. (September 11, 1862) Letter to Major E. A. Acton. *Lewis Leigh collection*. Book 8. Carlisle Barracks, PA: United States Army Military History Institute.

Jones, A. (1992) Military Means, Political Ends. In Boritt, G. S. (Ed.) *Why the Confederacy Lost*. New York: Oxford U. Press. Pp. 53-56.

Linderman, G. F. (1987) *Embattled Courage*. New York: The Free Press.

Long, E. B. (with Barbara Long) (1971) *The Civil War Day by Day: An Almanac, 1861-65*. New York: Da Capo Press.

Longacre, E. G. (1988) *To Gettysburg and Beyond: The Twelfth New Jersey Volunteer Infantry, II Corps, Army of the Potomac, 1862-1865*. Hightstown, NJ: Longstreet House.

Lyons, A. S., Petrucelli, R. J. II., *et al*. (1987) *Medicine: An Illustrated History*. New York: Abradale Press.

Malone, D. (Ed.) (1934) *Dictionary of American Biography*. Vol. 8. NY: Scribner's.

Millar, J. F., (1990) *Country Dances of Colonial America*. Williamsburg, VA: Thirteen Colonies Press.

Pleasants, H. Jr. & Straley, G. H. (1961) *Inferno at Petersburg*. Philadelphia: Chilton Co.

Price, W. H. (1961) *Civil War Handbook*. A Civil War Research Association Series. Fairfax, VA: L. B. Prince Co.

Records of Living Officers of the United States Army. Philadelphia: L. A. Hamersly, (1883).

Rhodes, R. H. (Ed.) (1992) *All for the Union: The Civil War Diary and Letters of Elisha Hunt Rhodes*. New York: Vintage Books.

Robertson, W. G. (1987) *Back Door to Richmond*. Baton Rouge, LA: L. S. U. Press.

Schiller, H. M. (1988) *The Bermuda Hundred Campaign*. Dayton, OH: Morningside.

Siebold, D. J. & Adams, C. J. III. (1987) *Shipwrecks and Legends 'Round Cape May*. Barnegat Light, NJ: Exeter House Books.

Sifakis, S. (1988) *Who Was Who in the Civil War*. New York: Facts on File Pub.

Silvestro, C. M. (1961) *None but Patriots: The Union League in the Civil War and Reconstruction*. Ann Arbor, MI: University Microfilms International.

Smith, A. W. (1911) *Reminiscences of an Army Nurse during the Civil War*. New York: Greaves Publishing House.

Stewart, G. R. (1980) *Pickett's Charge*. Dayton, OH: Morningside. Reprint of Houghton Mifflin's 1959 edition.

Swinton, W. (1882) *Campaigns of the Army of the Potomac: A Critical History of Operations in Virginia, Maryland, and Pennsylvania, from the Commencement to the Close of the War 1861-1865*. New York: Scribner's.

Taylor, F. H. (1913) *Philadelphia in the Civil War 1861-1865*. Philadelphia: Dunlap Printing Co.

Toombs, S. (1888) *New Jersey Troops in the Gettysburg Campaign* Orange, NJ: The Evening Mail Publishing House.

Trudeau, N. A. (1989) *Bloody Road South: The Wilderness to Cold Harbor, May-June 1864*. Boston, MA: Little, Brown & Co.

Tucker, G. (1980) *Hancock the Superb*. Dayton, OH: Morningside. Reprint of Bobbs-Merrill 1960 edition.

Tucker, G. (1983) *High Tide at Gettysburg: The Campaign in Pennsylvania*. Dayton, OH: Morningside. Reprint of Bobbs-Merrill 1958 edition.

Walker, F. A. (1887) *History of the Second Army Corps in the Army of the Potomac*. New York: Scribner's.

Warner, E. J. (1988) *Generals in Blue*. Baton Rouge, LA: L. S. U. Press.

Warner, E. J. (1988) *Generals in Gray*, Baton Rouge, LA: L. S. U. Press.

Whiteman, M. (1975) *Gentlemen in Crisis: The Union League of Philadelphia*. Philadelphia: The Winchell Co.

Youseloff, T. (1963) *Campaigns of the Civil War*, Vols. 6 & 12, New York: Thomas Youseloff.

Index

Gerry Harder Poriss and Ralph G. Poriss share interests in collecting rare stamps and covers and Civil War manuscripts and letters in their retirement, she from teaching elementary school and art, he from the real estate business. Both have published philatelic articles in such magazines as *Linn's Stamp News, Gibbon's Stamp Monthly, the Phoenix Philatelist*, and *The Confederate Philatelist*. Mr. Poriss, who attended the University of Virginia, has also written for *Manuscripts*, the publication of the Manuscript Society, in connection with their Civil War materials. Mrs. Poriss, who has an undergraduate degree in history and art from Rosary College in River Forest, IL, and a Master's degree in elementary education from Arizona State University, wrote a column titled "The Collector is a Lady" in *Linn's Weekly*. After a period of dealing in antiques in Maine, the Porisses now reside in Williamsburg, VA.

*The text of this book is set in 10 point
New Century Schoolbook type face; the title page,
cover, and dust jacket are in Goudy.
A Glatfelter neutral pH paper has been used to assure
the future permanence of the book; the binding is a vermin proof,
moisture resistant, impregnated Arrestox B cloth
made by Industrial Coatings Group, Inc. of Tennessee.
The printing and binding was done by McNaughton & Gunn, Inc.
Composition and design are by Edmonston Publishing, Inc.
Jacket design is by Ellen Walker.*

Also of Interest from Edmonston Publishing.

No Middle Ground: Thomas Ward Osborn's Letters from the Field (1862-1864) edited by H. S. Crumb & K. Dhalle

The Eleventh Corps Artillery at Gettysburg: The Papers of Major Thomas Ward Osborn edited by H. S. Crumb

History of the 16th North Carolina Regiment in the Civil War by George A. Mills

The Merrimac by Alan B. Flanders

Unfurl the Flags edited by W. E. Edmonston